VIRTUAL MUSIC

VIRTUAL MUSIC

How the Web Got Wired for Sound

William Duckworth

Routledge
Taylor & Francis Group

NEW YORK AND LONDON

Published in 2005 by
Routledge
Taylor & Francis Group
270 Madison Avenue
New York, NY 10016

Published in Great Britain by
Routledge
Taylor & Francis Group
2 Park Square
Milton Park, Abingdon
Oxon OX14 4RN

Printed in the United States of America on acid-free paper
10 9 8 7 6 5 4 3 2 1

International Standard Book Number-10: 0-415-96674-4 (Hardcover) 0-415-96675-2 (Softcover)
International Standard Book Number-13: 978-0-415-96674-0 (Hardcover) 978-0-415-96675-7 (Softcover)
Library of Congress Card Number 2005005960

Library of Congress Cataloging-in-Publication Data

Duckworth, William.
    Virtual music : how the web got wired for sound / William Duckworth.--1st ed.
        p. cm.
    Includes bibliographical references (p.) and index.
    ISBN 0-415-96674-4 (hardback : alk. paper) -- ISBN 0-415-96675-2 (pbk.)
    1. Music--Computer network resources. 2. Interactive multimedia. 3. Internet. I. Title.

ML74.7.D83 2005
781.3'4--dc22

2005005960

Taylor & Francis Group
is the Academic Division of T&F Informa plc.

Visit the Taylor & Francis Web site at
http://www.taylorandfrancis.com

and the Routledge Web site at
http://www.routledge-ny.com

For Nora
Whose help and love are endless

Contents

CONTENTS IX

Introduction:
Making Music in Thin Air

Is it a fact . . . that, by means of electricity, the world of matter has become a great nerve, vibrating thousands of miles in a breathless point of time?—Nathaniel Hawthorne, *The House of the Seven Gables*, 1851

It hasn't been that long, if you stop to think about it, that people thought electricity was a new delight, much in the same way that we think about computers and the Internet today: high-tech toys, tools, and now personal companions that will change forever the way we live. And for those of us interested in the combining of technical and artistic progress on a grand scale, this is certainly the time to be alive; the "electricity" in the air surrounding online music is reminiscent of the energy of the 1960s avantgarde: the feeling that something new and important was happening all the time. So when the opportunity to write a book about virtual music arose—to describe its beginnings and weigh its potential, even as it is unfolding before us—I immediately jumped at the chance. I had, after all, been actively involved with Web music almost since the beginning, which at this point is a grand total of some five or six years.

The encouragement to write a book about music on the Web came initially from two phone calls, both at the end of 2001: one from Richard Carlin, my editor at Routledge in New York, asking if I had thought about writing a book about *Cathedral,* the Web work Nora Farrell and I had created; the other, a few weeks later, from Diego Minciacchi, a composer and neuroscientist in Florence, Italy, asking if I would come to Venice to speak about virtual music (as online interactive music is now generally called) to an international conference of neurobiologists in October 2002. As it happened, this Venice talk fell between two other invitations to speak about music on the Web, one in Brisbane at the Mini[ ]Max Festival in August 2002, the other at TAMA Art University in Tokyo in May 2003. And even before the phone conversation with Diego had concluded, I was beginning to realize that these three talks could be the basis for a book.

But between that initial impulse and the time I began to write some months later, the ground had shifted—or, to be more precise, the interesting topics had changed. And although the talks had been given, and the papers filed for publication—the one from Venice now in the 2003 *Annals of the New York Academy of Sciences*—it still didn't feel quite as if I was discussing the right material.[1] Parts of my work seemed to go out of date almost as quickly as I wrote them, as the technology and software evolved and Web sites disappeared. The problem, I finally realized, was that when events are moving at Internet speed it's hard to pin anything down; it all transforms too quickly. The technology, and what artists do with this new set of tools, moves forward in all directions at once, with both technical and artistic innovations occurring so rapidly on the Web that ideas that seemed revolutionary and cutting edge a few years ago, or even a mere few months past, today already feel commonplace, or have disappeared altogether.

But then, that's the nature of the Internet; it changes. And it changes the things it comes into contact with; and, today, that is almost everything: people, software, *and* machines. The world is fundamentally different now because of what this new global connectivity not only allows but also encourages and demands. So why shouldn't we expect art to make significant changes as well? And why shouldn't new forms of music emerge from these new materials, complete, as the technology is, with a new worldwide means of distribution, and more importantly, the potential for continuous artistic interaction on a global scale?

I read recently that the Computer History Museum has opened its new headquarters in Silicon Valley. The museum, it seems, has been collecting things since 1979, first in Boston where it was founded, and now in California, where most of the collection has been in storage for over a decade. Apparently, the museum already has something in the neighborhood of five thousand computers, or "computer artifacts" as the *New York Times* called them, plus some ten thousand images and more than four thousand linear feet of computer documentation.[2] Quite a collection for a "thinking machine" many of us still regard as a recent invention. The personal computer (PC) dates back to the MITS Altair 8800 of 1975. Laptops came along six years later, beginning with the Epson HX-20 of 1981, which weighed three pounds, nine ounces, and came complete with a full-size keyboard, built-in display and printer, and a battery with fifty hours of life. By comparison, the computer some consider the first portable computer, the Osborne 1 (also from 1981), weighed twenty-four pounds and drained the battery after a mere four hours.[3]

The idea of a museum dedicated to computers should give us all a moment's pause, not only to reflect on just how long computers have really been a part of our lives but also to consider how much faster, thanks largely to computers, the events of our daily lives now unfold. And this zero-to-sixty environment in which we all find ourselves today is particularly relevant for artists on the Web, all of whom seem to move at warp speed. Because, even though computers have been around since the thirty-ton, room-sized Eniac was delivered to the U.S. Army in 1946, the Internet didn't really become a reality for most of us until America Online (AOL) went online in 1985—or, more likely, it was with the appearance of the Netscape Navigator browser in 1994, and the ease with which it allowed us to begin to explore the Web. Interactive art on the Internet, by contrast—art that allows the user to become actively involved in the process of creation—got its start later still, victim, as it was, of the slow processing speeds and even slower baud rates of those early years. Bauds, incidentally, are those really slow transmission speeds in use before the much faster 14.4 kilobits per second (kbps) rate became the norm—which itself is considered hopelessly slow today, when 56 kbps is considered normal in most places of the world, whereas the cable modems and broadband of the Western industrialized nations are faster still.

Today, those of us who are actively involved with art on the Internet are witness to the first artistic movement capable of developing and transforming itself at net speed. John Naughton, in *A Brief History of the Future: From Radio Days to Internet Years in a Lifetime,* points out that while it took radio thirty-seven years to build a listening audience of fifty million, it only took television fifteen years to attract that same number of viewers, and the World Wide Web reached that level of participation in "just over three years."[4] By 1994, the first year of Netscape Navigator's availability, it was estimated that the Internet was growing at a rate of two million new users a month.[5] And, in case anyone is still unconvinced about how rapidly events have and are unfolding online, there are already museums located throughout the world dedicated to cataloging and preserving this new form of net art before it, too, disappears, as some of it, most certainly, already has. But that speed, that instantaneous dissemination of information, image, and sound, in and of itself, can create its own problems, as anyone knows who is trying to keep up with the continuously emerging technology, the latest software, or the most recent online gadget or game.

My working title for the book was *Making Music in Thin Air*, because that was the closest I could come to describing what creating Internet music felt like in the late 1990s and first few years of the new century. It was as if music was suddenly appearing everywhere, out of nowhere, all at once—music on the Internet that could be heard on your computer at home. And by the turn of the century, I thought I had had some degree of experience working with music in cyberspace (a term invented in the early 1980s by the science fiction writer William Gibson).[6] After all, media artist and programmer Nora Farrell and I had been collaborating on an interactive Web piece called *Cathedral* since 1997, and by late 2001 we had successfully created an ongoing Web site, a group of new virtual instruments, an Internet band, and a forty-eight-hour webcast, streaming thirty-four concerts live from five continents—still the largest festival of Internet music held to date.

So, when I began to consider the possibility of writing a book about music on the Web, I thought I had a pretty good idea of its scope and the range of topics it ought to cover. But as I wrote, the topics, as I said, kept changing, and I kept deleting and rewriting as the first draft turned into a second and then a third. This transformation came about, I eventually came to realize, because, at first, I was putting too much emphasis on the technology, and as it changed, so did the book. Eventually, I came to see that it is the *people* with the ideas who make the story interesting, and as I began to think and write more about them, the book began to take on its present shape.

And, over time, my plan for this book became to chronicle not only how we got to where we are today but also to explore what may be possible, if not necessary, for music on the Web tomorrow. My intention is not only to provide a basic insight into what online artists working in some of the newer fields of musical experimentation are interested in today but also to offer some thoughts about newly emerging concepts of musical creativity, and what this may someday mean for all of us. Furthermore, as a composer, I want to speculate about the future, and what it might be like musically. I also want to raise the possibility that some forms of music on the World Wide Web will be continuous, regenerative, and constantly in a state of global interaction and flux. And I want to offer the potential for community music being created and recreated online by people like you and me, acting together, and working in creative partnerships, some in ways never before considered or thought possible.

In short, the Web is changing music, not only by offering a new set of tools and a new means of distribution but also by shifting the focus of what it means to be musical. As a result of this shift, a new global artistic consciousness is emerging with its own unique set of characteristics. And just as surely as listeners in the nineteenth century heard their music live, and twentieth-century audiences experienced the majority of their music in broadcast or recorded form, listeners of the twenty-first century will obtain their music primarily from cyberspace. Even now, many people can see the promise and the potential for a universal jukebox with immediate Internet access to any music ever recorded, and some of us can envision more interactive experiences and the possibility of a worldwide "cyberband" connecting a global artistic community online.

Certainly, as a composer, I know that my own work during the past decade has undergone a profound change. And my concepts of who my listeners are, what they hear, and what the circumstances are in which they hear it have all undergone major transformations. Until the mid-1990s, for example, most of my music was written for traditional forces. Nora Farrell and I didn't begin to envision, much less develop, a work for the Web until 1996. So it is important to keep in mind that what I am now going to describe as fact in the pages of this book was almost unimaginable, and certainly physically impossible, a mere decade ago. In 1992, for example, there were an estimated fifty active (as opposed to some one million registered) sites on the World Wide Web. So it is equally important to keep in mind both how recently this paradigm shift began taking place, and how far and how fast this new world of the Web has propelled the new art form of virtual music.

How this new paradigm may affect how people listen to music, or what they might hear, or the philosophical questions this new art form may someday raise is, at this point, anybody's guess. But what I can describe is where we as Web artists are now, and how we got here, and what the next step is, at least for Nora and me. Along the way, I also want to characterize and define this new art form as best I can through a series of case studies: the first on music in motion as seen in Phil Kline's *Unsilent Night;* the second, on music in interactive space as it occurs in Tod Machover's *Brain Opera:* the third, on Internet time as experienced in *Cathedral;* and the fourth on the importance of critical mass in cyberspace and the issues surrounding *The Grey Album* and the Grey Tuesday protest in February 2004. First, however, I want to begin by considering the concept and practice of interactive music over the past century, from Erik Satie to Moby; identify how music first became established on the Web; introduce some of the new tools now at our disposal, and discuss the change in artistic focus they are helping to bring about; as well as describe more recent art made with telephones and satellites. I also want to take the opportunity to think ahead a bit, and identify some of the artistic and ethical issues facing the future of online music, while, in the final chapter, I want to connect virtual music to its artistic past, define its basic characteristics, and speculate on what it may become.

There are, of course, innumerable people to thank for their advice and council in the preparation of *Virtual Music.* First and foremost is Nora Farrell, whose expertise in all matters digital is matched by an active and creative artistic imagination, and whose help and advice in both art and life cannot be overstated. I also would like to thank Richard Carlin, my editor at Routledge, for his encouragement, patience, and understanding. Good editors are not that easy to locate these days; first-class ones, like Richard, are even harder to find. Beyond that, well-deserved thanks also should go to a group of friends and colleagues for everything from facts and information, to reading and commenting on parts of the manuscript. These include John Bischoff, Phil Burk, Warren Burt, Marek Choloniewski, Nicolas Collins, Colette Domingues, Richard Fleming, Kyle Gann, John Maxwell Hobbs, Ryan Ingebritsen, Sergi Jordà, Ben Johnston, Mary Judge and the

Foundation for Contemporary Performance Arts, Michael Kauffman, Søren Karstensen, Phil Kline, Jaron Lanier, Craig Latta, Golan Levin, Tod Machover, Diego Minciacci, Frank Oteri and The American Music Center, Michael Payne, Vincent Plush, Robin Rimbaud, Neil Rolnick, David Rosenboom, Arthur Sabatini, Dante Tanzi, Ken Thomson at Cantaloupe Records, and "Blue" Gene Tyranny. Your help and encouragement was more valuable than I will ever be able to tell you.

1
A BRIEF HISTORY OF INTERACTIVE MUSIC

Interactive music—that is, music that in some way involves the audience in the process of its own creation—did not begin with the Internet, and Web composers are not the first group of artists to want to share the creative process (whether by method, whim, or chance) with their audience. Even Mozart got involved, writing snippets of music, but allowing others to throw the dice to determine which measures they would go in, thus allowing us to co-compose with him, as it were. Once you leave the West, of course, there are entire cultures that actively seek to involve the whole community in music making, such as the gamelan traditions of Java and Bali, or some of the African drumming traditions. But even within Western concert music—a passive-listening, sitting-in-rows type of activity, for the most part—attempts at real composer/audience interaction have a legitimate history going back more than a hundred years.

Erik Satie and the Art of Boredom

During all of the nineteenth and most of the twentieth centuries, the composer/performer/listener model, in which everyone was expected to play their role to perfection, was so ingrained in Western concert music that it was difficult for most people to envision attending musical performances created in any other format. Anything else wasn't a concert. Concert music required not only your full attention, but also your complete cooperation as well, as, for example, with the applause that was (and still is) expected and accepted only at preapproved points in the program.

Beginning as early as the 1890s, however, and picking up considerable steam from the experimental composers in the avant-garde of the 1960s, there were some musicians who seriously questioned this arrangement. One of the first to do so was Erik Satie (1866–1925),[1] a *fin de siècle* French composer best known, perhaps, for his short, often mystical piano pieces, who became a guiding light for experimental musicians from the late nineteenth century to the present—even though he always maintained that he had never founded a "School of Satie" and didn't want one, either. Satie also was one of the first composers to play *with*, as opposed *to*, his audience, creating, for example, furniture music for the intermission of a concert that he instructed the audience to ignore. Known as something of an eccentric, Satie had, by the age of twenty-seven, even founded his own church, The Metropolitan Church of Art of Jesus the Leader, of which he was the only member. If nothing else, it gave him the opportunity to excommunicate a few music critics with whom he disagreed. And although the degree of seriousness of this sudden conversion is certainly open to doubt, his deeper motivations—one of which, perhaps, being to anger the Rosicrucians with whom he had recently split—remains unclear. With Satie, even now, one can never be entirely sure what his true intentions really were.

Satie was also given to making cryptic and enigmatic pronouncements, such as "Before writing a work I walk around it several times accompanied by myself." Or, "I have never written a note I didn't mean."[2] He also had the annoying habit of giving his music odd, unconventional titles, such as *Dessicated Embryos, Veritable Flabby Preludes (For a Dog),* and *Three Pieces in the Form of a Pear*—this last, a work for piano four hands, written because his friend, Claude Debussy, the most revered of the French Impressionist composers, had told him that he thought his music lacked shape and that he, Satie, had a rather simplistic understanding of the subtleties of modern musical form. Today, if you wish, you can still see Satie, portraying himself, dapper-dressed in his trademark gray velvet suit and bowler hat, cavorting on the rooftops of Paris in *Entr'acte,* an early Dadaist (*faux* surrealist) film made by a young René Clair, for which Satie composed the score.

But Erik Satie also was musically deeper and more artistically mysterious than any of this surface charm of funny titles, eccentric behavior, and convoluted utterances would make it appear. Satie was not only friends with Debussy but also a friend and collaborator of Pablo Picasso and Jean Cocteau. Cocteau, a leading French literary light and man of the arts, was the central figure around whom the younger French composers—disaffected with the status quo, and rebelling against Richard Wagner's continuing influence on French music more than thirty years after his death in 1883—had begun to congregate. From this entourage would emerge *Les Six*, as they were dubbed by the press, a group of composers with Satie as their father figure, with the ephemeral goal of creating "a French music for France." But before any of this occurred, Picasso, Cocteau, and Satie, working together, set the standard by creating *Parade* in 1917.

Parade was premiered in Paris by Sergei Diaghilev's Ballets Russes in 1917, the same troupe who, costumed as American Indians, had danced Igor Stravinsky's *La Sacre du printemps* in that same city five years earlier, and then watched as a riot had ensued. *Parade*, with its noisy cacophony of sirens, car horns, musical instruments, typewriters, and shots from a gun, created a similar scandal, with fights in the gallery, and a riot on the streets all its own. Always a loud and vigorous defender of his art, as well as of himself—he generally carried a small silver hammer for protection—Satie was not only arrested and sentenced to jail for eight days for promoting cultural anarchy but also was sued for defamation of character by a critic. Satie, now fifty-one years old, became an overnight cause célèbre.

A noisy and meaningless demonstration to some, *Parade* was, to others, an ultramodern form of expression combining all the arts. With its use of sounds from the music hall, early ragtime, the circus, and "the paraphernalia of modern life," *Parade*, as the historian Roger Shattuck declares, "set the tone for the postwar years."[3] But if *Parade* was the barometer, it set a tone, not of realism but of the absurd—an affirmation and celebration of the perceived absence of values in the world—yielding a staged spectacle where everything seemed recognizable and commonplace, yet nothing was exactly as it seemed. It was all absurd: the premise, the plot, the décor, the music, and the dance. It was all a celebration of the value of having no values.

The Aesthetic of Boredom

In the end, though, it was Satie's unorthodox musical ideas, and not his eccentricities, that forever altered and reattuned twentieth-century ears, and established Satie as one of the founders of the new aesthetic of boredom. Satie not only welcomed boredom in his music, he made an art out of using it. He had, after all, created a masterpiece of boredom in 1893 with *Vexations,* the short, but static and disconcerting piano piece, composed of a slow bass line alternating with slow three-part dissonant harmony—about eighty seconds of music in all—that Satie instructs the performer to repeat 840 times in a row. When American composer John Cage gave the first complete performance of *Vexations* in New York in 1963, he used a team of ten pianists working in shifts, and the performance lasted eighteen hours and forty minutes. The *New York Times* entered into the spirit of the performance by sending a relay of reporters to review it in two-hour segments.[4]

Now at first glance, *Vexations* may seem to be the *ne plus ultra* of boredom. But anyone who has ever taken part in a performance, including the listeners who have stayed for extended periods of time, will tell you otherwise. *Vexations* is a transforming experience for everyone who comes into contact with it. Stephen Whittington, an Australian pianist and expert on Satie says that, "The act of performing or listening to a complete performance of *Vexations* cannot be compared to any other musical experience."[5] And Cage explained that there came a point during his 1963 performance when "something was put into motion that changed me. I wasn't the same after that performance as I was before." He characterized the change as "a moment of enlightenment."[6]

Satie's willingness to incorporate boredom into his definition of art meant that his music was founded on aesthetic principles fundamentally unlike those embraced by any other Western composer, even his friend Debussy, whose own music—with its seeming lack of melody and quicksilver harmony that never "progressed"—sounded, as some suggested at the time, like breaking from the mooring and drifting at sea—a backhanded reference to the lack of "proper melodies" and cadences in Debussy's monumental Impressionistic tone poem *La Mer.* Shattuck, in describing the origins of the avant-garde in France, says that while Satie's music did, indeed, abandon dry land, it did not do so in the same way that Debussy's did. For Shattuck, who characterizes Satie's descriptive piano pieces as being "as much studies in immobility and secret movement as is still-life painting,"[7] Satie's abandonment of nineteenth-century tradition resulted in his devoting his life to "watching the waves breaking on a tiny section of shore, fascinated by both the monotony and the variety of their fall." Shattuck concludes that for Satie, form is neither about setting a course nor about drifting at sea. Instead, "it is a fascination with a series of points which turn out to be one point. His music progresses by standing still."[8] Satie himself explained that "The listener is defenseless against boredom. Boredom subdues him"; another time he wrote, "The public venerates boredom. For boredom is mysterious and profound."[9]

Furniture Music (1920)

The first performance of a piece of furniture music—that is, music that was intentionally written to be ignored—took place on March 8, 1920, at the Galerie Barbazange, a small art gallery in Paris. The program, which included music by members of *Les Six,* as well as a few songs by Stravinsky, centered around a three-act play, *Always the Ruffian; Never a Bum,* by Max Jacob. It was during the two intermissions between the three acts of the play that Satie, assisted by Darius Milhaud, one of the composers of *Les Six,* created the performance. For the occasion, they assembled a small orchestra of three clarinets, a trombone, and a piano; gave them fragments of themes from a variety of well-known pieces to repeat as many times as they wished; and stationed them in various places around the hall, exhorting the audience to talk and move about as if nothing was going on.

Alan M. Gillmor, in his book *Erik Satie,* says that Satie got the idea for furniture music when in a café with his friend, the painter Fernand Léger. Unable to sustain a coherent conversation because of the loud playing by the orchestra, Satie reportedly said to Léger: "You know, there's a need to create furniture music, that is to say, music that would be a part of the surrounding noises and that would take them into account. I see it as melodious, as masking the clatter of knives and forks without drowning it completely, without imposing itself. It would fill up the awkward silences that occasionally descend on guests. It would spare them the usual banalities. Moreover, it would neutralize the street noises that indiscreetly force themselves into the picture."[10] Later, in explaining the idea of furniture music to Cocteau in a letter, Satie wrote, "We want to establish a music designed to satisfy 'useful' needs. Art has no part in such needs. Furniture music creates a vibration; it has no other goal; it fills the same role as light and heat—as comfort in every form."[11]

Sadly, Satie's blueprint for the first furniture music performance did not create quite the experience he had planned. The audience, once they heard the music begin, sat back down, refused to leave, and listened in silence throughout both intermissions, forcing Satie to rush about encouraging everyone to "Talk, keep on talking. And move around. Whatever you do, don't listen!"[12] This occurred despite the program notes that Satie had written, which explicitly stated: "We urgently beg you not to attach any importance to it and to act during the intermission as if the music did not exist. Specially written for Max Jacob's play, ... it hopes to contribute to life the way a casual conversation does, or a picture in the gallery, or a chair in which one is or is not seated."[13]

Technically speaking, of course, Satie's concept of furniture music comes uncomfortably close to what we think of as Muzak today—usable, if nondescript, music that fills in the silences and masks out the unwanted sounds. Muzak is a good or bad thing, depending on your point of view. But either way, Satie gets the credit for thinking of it first. Today, Muzak has grown so pervasive that we must often search out public spaces in which to escape its reach. Shattuck points out that, "Since that day [in 1920] jukeboxes, radios, television, music while you work, canned music, audiotheraphy—a whole race of creatures—have sprung into existence to fill the aural background of our lives the way interior decoration fills the visual background."[14] Only Satie, of course, could tell us how close this comes to his original plan. Whittington, however, preferring to focus on the artistic and aesthetic significance of furniture music, calls it Satie's "most sacrilegious discovery," and "the ultimate blasphemy against the religion of Art." He also refers to furniture music as "*Vexations* industrialized," meaning that Satie had moved directly from trying to emulate the musical purity of the Middle Ages into emulating the current lesspersonal era of mass production, "ignoring all of musical history from the Renaissance on."[15]

Relâche *(1924)*

The crowning achievement of Satie's fascination with boredom and his *pièce de resistance* of furniture music was created in 1924 when Francis Picabia invited Satie to compose the music for a ballet he was creating with Jean Börlin, the principal male dancer and choreographer of the Swedish Ballet. Picabia, "a gregarious Cuban-French poet, painter, and unrepentant prankster," according to Gillmor, had already named the ballet *Relâche,* meaning "no performance," or "theater closed," to signal "a complete break with convention, a resolute slamming of the door on tradition."[16] Picabia also had the grand idea to include a film within the ballet, the first time such a thing had been tried, and he engaged René Clair, then twenty-six years old, to make it. Satie provided the music for Clair's film (at first titled *Cinéma,* but now more commonly known as *Entr'acte*), as well as for *Relâche,* the ballet. During the performance, a short segment of the twenty-four-minute film was screened immediately after the overture, and the remainder was shown at the intermission between the two acts.

From its inception, *Relâche* was unlike anything ever presented in the guise of French classical music and dance. Labeling it an "instantaneous ballet," Picabia said that *Relâche* amounted "to a lot of kicks in a lot of rears, sacred and otherwise."[17] To begin with, the audience that arrived at the theater on opening night, a highly advertised premiere, found no one there and the theater closed and dark; the actual opening didn't take place until three days later. We'll never know for sure whether this was the ultimate Dadaist joke, or a legitimate result of Börlin's sudden illness, as the creators claimed. But when opening night finally did occur, at the very end of November 1924, a stranger cast of characters had seldom, if ever, been assembled on a European dance stage before. Two of the main protagonists of the ballet were a woman in an evening dress, who in the second act stripped down to flesh-colored tights, and a fireman who mostly wandered about the stage pouring water from one pail to another. He also smoked cigarettes incessantly, as did most of the dancers. And eight of the male dancers, including Börlin, costumed in full evening dress, took off their clothes and then redressed right on stage. As for the formal dance numbers, if that is what they should be called, they centered around a wheelbarrow, a crown, and a revolving door. Picabia said none of it had any meaning at all.

Darius Milhaud, who attended the premiere, described Satie's music for *Relâche* as ranging from truculent marches to dances of exquisite tenderness.[18] Others, less inclined to be kind, had a different response. Written mostly in simple rhythms and eight-measure phrases, Satie's music drew on popular, mostly bawdy, if not downright lewd, songs, familiar to any Frenchman with anything beyond a passing experience with soldiers in their barracks or drunks in a singing mood. Satie, it seems, had not only appropriated all of the tunes for his ballet, he had chosen tunes that were *déclassé*, even for the Dada-inspired Paris of 1924. And as if that were not insult enough to the audience, Satie then recycled most of this music from the first act into the second, reclothing it in different harmonies and timbres, but with little attempt to hide the now twice reused material. The audience was suitably incensed; some felt in the presence of true genius, others that they were being had.

But it was René Clair's film, and Satie's music for it, that attracted the most admiration, then as well as now. A plotless romp through a random sequence of events, *Entr'acte* includes everything from a bearded ballet dancer (shot from beneath a glass floor), to a cannon shot at the audience (by Satie), to a mock funeral procession around the Eiffel Tower with a runaway hearse drawn by a camel (some of it shot in slow motion), to a corpse who returns from the dead at the end of the film and makes everyone, including himself, disappear. And to the delight of the onlookers, *Entr'acte* also included images of Man Ray and Marcel Duchamp playing chess, as well as both Satie and Picabia, playing themselves.

But if Satie's music for *Relâche* was written in broad, bawdy strokes, his music for *Entr'acte* was the ultimate in furniture music for film, the epitome of what we today have come to expect of a film score. It was as if Satie knew instinctively that the music for *Entr'acte* must be of a different character from that for the theater. Certainly, the furniture music that he wrote appears designed less to draw attention to itself than to support the events happening on the screen. Alone, Satie's music for *Entr'acte* sounds unmemorable, if not unintelligible. But heard in combination with René Clair's film, the music comes alive and sports a different character, one not only supporting the visual action, but also helping to draw us in and make us a part of some secret Dadaist conspiracy, all the while hovering in the background, filling in, unconcerned about developing a statement of its own.

Today, of course, *Entr'acte* is considered a classic of early experimental film, and the music Satie wrote for it has been widely praised. Gillmor, for instance, writes that not only did Satie anticipate Dada by a decade in his earlier works, but that, with *Relâche,* he also "provided the [Dadaist] movement with one of its most glorious spasms."[19] Darius Milhaud, characterizing the millieu of the Parisian twenties as one of "anything goes," said that the audience for *Relâche* was not at all surprised at the end of the performance "to see Satie arrive on stage, to the acclaim of his cheering friends, in a little 5 horsepower Citroën car driven by Picabia."[20] This image, of Satie and Picabia driving around the stage at the end of *Relâche*—a symbolic journey from the nineteenth century to the twentieth—also can represent, in some Dada-like way, Satie's arrival on the world stage, a stage now prepared and ready, thanks in large part to him, for both the new century and the new aesthetic to begin. Shattuck suggests that *Relâche,* this combination of "the braggadocio of *Parade* with the unobtrusiveness of furniture music, provided the properly scandalous finale for Satie's career."[21] Perhaps so, but from today's perspective, Satie no longer appears quite so scandalous, or as much of an anomaly in the history of Western art music as he did a hundred years ago. Instead, Erik Satie has become one of its stalwarts, a composer who, almost single-handedly, altered the stream of art for everyone yet to come.

John Cage and the Charms of Chance

Although only five years old when *Parade* was premiered, and twelve when Satie and Picabia drove a car across the stage in *Relâche,* John Cage (1912–1992),[22] throughout all of his professional life, shared a kindred spirit with Erik Satie. Many people, in fact, would label him Satie's successor, for all the right, as well as the wrong, reasons. Because Cage—the son of an inventor who often spoke of watching his father creating new things everyday at home—came to believe that his proper role as an artist was to seek out and bring into being new ways in which to create, experiment with, and experience sound. He came to believe early in his own career that if he had anything to offer music, it would be, like his father, in the area of invention.

Cage also claimed that he didn't have an ear for music, and couldn't sing or even remember very many tunes all the way through. Although this comment infuriated some, others came to see it as an overstatement that was often misunderstood. But even if it wasn't overstated and Cage really *didn't* have an ear for music, what he did have was an inventor's mentality, driven by a fertile imagination, under the control of a first-class mind. And this combination of attitudes and talents, put at the service of experimental art for over fifty years, created some of the most beautiful, controversial, and talked about music of the twentieth century.

Furthermore, because Cage's life spanned most of the century, he gained access to an emerging plethora of technology (musical and otherwise), an experimenter's luxury never afforded Satie. For Satie, the "new" technology in his life included the telephone (1876), the phonograph (1878), and the movies (1895), still silent in 1925, when Picabia incorporated *Entr'acte* into *Relâche*. Cage, by contrast, lived not only to see but also to make artistic use of such technological innovations as the radio, first employed by him in *Credo in US* in 1942; magnetic recording tape, first used in *Imaginary Landscape No. 5* and *Williams Mix*, both in 1952; television as an instrument, in *Sounds of Venice*, created for an Italian TV station in 1959; and computers, in the evening-length, multimedia work *HPSCHD* (for seven harpsichords and fifty-eight channels of sound), which was cowritten with Lejaren Hiller at the University of Illinois between 1967 and 1969. And as is obvious from the continued use Cage made of everything from radios to computers, not only did he embrace these new technologies as they arose, he tried, whenever possible, to subvert their uses to the purposes of art, which included for him finding new sounds, creating new musical environments in which these sounds could coexist independently, and placing his audiences into new situations where they would experience these sounds differently. Cage believed that these new sounds would, perhaps, help people attain a more thoughtful and intense awareness of their own daily lives.

But Cage's search for new sounds didn't stop with those made by technology; it also took him into a world of instruments not previously considered musical, such as the pots and pans he and his ensemble played as percussion instruments at the Museum of Modern Art in New York in 1943. He also began creating new instruments and new uses for older established ones. In 1938, for example, he invented the prepared piano, which is a regular grand piano into which Cage stuck foreign objects— such as wood, metal, and felt—between the strings, and from which came the sounds of a percussion orchestra, most notably in the *Sonatas and Interludes* of 1946–1948. Ultimately, with the help of both Indian philosophical doctrine and Japanese Zen Buddhist thought, Cage broadened his philosophy of art to accept and use not only noise but also silence, and sounds produced by chance, all the while looking for the next step, constantly exploring, and inventing with sound.

By the 1960s, however, what most people knew about John Cage, and what caused most of the controversy surrounding him and his work, was that Cage had become the first composer in the history of music intentionally and permanently to remove his ego—his personal likes and dislikes—from the process of writing music. He described it as letting sounds be themselves, and he accomplished it with the help of the *I Ching*, or Chinese Book of Changes, an ancient book of divination published in a new English translation by Pantheon Press in 1951 and given to Cage by composer Christian Wolff, whose father was the publisher. By creating a method for asking questions and making musical choices by chance procedures based on the tossing of coins and the consulting of the *I Ching*, Cage developed an indeterminate form of music created by chance. His first works in this new, nonintentional style were the *Music of Changes* for pianist and colleague David Tudor, and *Imaginary Landscape No. 4* for twelve radios, both written in 1951.

Fifteen years earlier, Cage had begun speaking publicly about the coming changes in music that he foresaw. In a now widely quoted talk given in Seattle in 1937, he said he believed the use of noise to make music would "continue and increase until we reach a music produced through the aid of electrical instruments which will make available for musical purposes any and all sounds that can be heard." Remember, this was 1937, long before magnetic recording tape or the instruments associated with the classic tape-music studios of the 1960s were available. In this same talk, Cage also suggested that the then-current dilemma among musicians over which sounds to call dissonant and which to call consonant would soon change to a disagreement between what was noise and what were so-called acceptable musical sounds. He continued that, once this happened, the use of harmony, with its self-limiting whole-steps and half-steps, would "be inadequate for the composer, who will be faced with the entire field of sound."[23]

As can be imagined, these ideas, as well as the music they inspired, were highly controversial and challenging to the very bedrock of Western musical assumptions. In "Four Statements on the Dance," written in 1939, Cage alluded to this controversy between music and noise in declaring that, "At the present stage of revolution, a healthy lawlessness is warranted."[24] Two years earlier, in "Credo," he had written that, "If this word 'music' is sacred and reserved for eighteenth- and nineteenth-century instruments, we can substitute a more meaningful term: organization of sound."[25] Continuing this redefinition, he suggested, in 1954, that, "If one feels protective about the word 'music,' protect it and find another word for all the rest that enters through the ears."[26]

The period of the late 1940s and early 1950s was critical in John Cage's development as an experimental artist. It began, according to him, when composer Lou Harrison—with whom he had given concerts of percussion music in San Francisco in the late 1930s and with whom he collaborated to write *Double Music* in 1941—suggested to him that the Indian concept of the function of music—to sober and quiet the mind, thus rendering it susceptible to divine influences—had been echoed by Thomas Mace, a seventeenth-century English composer. According to Cage: "I decided then and there that this *was* the proper purpose of music. In time, I also came to see that all art before the Renaissance, both Oriental and Western, had shared this same basis, that Oriental art had continued to do so right along, and that the Renaissance idea of self-expressive art was therefore heretical."[27] Because of this realization, Cage began exploring Oriental thought, and in a short period of time had attended the lectures of Ananda K. Coomaraswamy at the Brooklyn Academy of Music (1945); met Gita Sarabhai, whom he taught and with whom he studied Indian philosophy and traditional Indian music daily for six months (1945); and attended the lectures of Daisetz T. Suzuki on Japanese Zen Buddhism at Columbia University (1948–1951). Later, in the "Forward" to his first book, *Silence*, published in 1961, Cage said, "What I do, I do

not wish blamed on Zen, though without my engagement with Zen ...
I doubt whether I would have done what I have done."[28]

But this deeper understanding of Eastern philosophical thought brought about by these years of work and study had a more profound effect on Cage than that. In Coomaraswamy, he found the idea that the function of art is to imitate nature in her "manner of operation." And from Gita Sarabhai he took the idea that music is continuous, it is only we who turn away, plus an expanded understanding of the true purpose of music: to prepare the mind to experience the divine. Cage later defined a sober and quiet mind as "one in which the ego does not obstruct the fluency of the things that come in through our senses and up through our dreams."[29]

But it was in the Zen teachings of Daisetz T. Suzuki that Cage discovered the direction he would take artistically for the remainder of his life; the notion that sounds could be themselves, that is, exist as isolated events, interpenetrating but not impeding each other, each maintaining, all the while, its own uniqueness, beauty, individuality, and charm. And, in true Zen fashion, Cage ultimately came to believe that the true purpose of music was not the continued production of masterpieces that, when they were finished were already separate from life, but rather, "a purposeful purposelessness or a purposeless play." For Cage, however, this play was "an affirmation of life—not an attempt to bring order out of chaos nor to suggest improvements in creation, but simply a way of waking up to the very life we are living."

When one accepts the attitude that the highest form of responsibility to oneself is irresponsibility, implying the responsibility to transcend ordinary responsibility, and further implying "the calm acceptance of whatever responsibility to others and things comes along," then art becomes "a sort of experimental station in which one tries out living."[30] Consequently, "the highest purpose is to have no purpose," because it balances one with nature in her manner of operation. This belief by Cage—that art should imitate nature in her manner of operation, and that cause-and-effect thinking should be rejected—led him first to nonintentional music, produced through chance procedures but fixed thereafter, such as the *Music of Changes,* and later to indeterminate music, the outcome of which could not be predicted in advance.

The Happening (July 1952)

If the late 1940s was a time for Cage to reconsider and redesign the philosophical underpinnings of his artistic thought, then the early 1950s was the point when the new music inspired by this new aesthetic began to emerge. In the summer of 1952, Cage was invited to teach at Black Mountain College, a small experimental school located in the mountains of North Carolina that, since its founding in 1933, had stressed experimental, interdisciplinary work. The faculty included many of the finest contemporary creative artists, including the artists Willem de Kooning and Josef Albers (from the now closed Bauhaus), the poets Charles Olson and M. C. Richards, and the innovative thinker and inventor of the geodesic dome Buckminster Fuller. Cage, when on tour with dancer/choreographer Merce Cunningham, had been to Black Mountain once before in the summer of 1948, but only for a few days. Even so, he had managed to infuriate some of the faculty with a lecture unfavorably comparing Beethoven with Erik Satie, saying at one point that "Beethoven was in error" in thinking that musical structure should be based on harmony and not on time, and that his influence, "which has been as extensive as it is lamentable, has been deadening to the art of music."[31] Despite this controversy, in the summer of 1952—thanks to Lou Harrison, who was now the head of the music department, and to other faculty members who liked and supported Cage—he was invited back to teach the full summer term. And this time, not only did Merce Cunningham and David Tudor go along, but Robert Rauschenberg, a student at the college when Cage and Cunningham had first visited on tour, also returned.

That July, John Cage created what is now considered the first "happening." Calling his event *Theater Piece No. 1*, Cage enlisted Cunningham, Rauschenberg, and Tudor, along with Olson and Richards from the faculty, to begin simultaneous but separate artistic activities. During this forty-five-minute multimedia/theatrical event, Cage gave a lecture full of silences and Richards and Olson read poems, all while standing on stepladders; Cunningham danced in and around the audience; Rauschenberg hung his White Paintings (so-called because they consisted of a series of canvases painted white) from the ceiling and played records on an old windup Victrola; and Tudor played the piano; and throughout it all, slides and movies were projected on the walls. The formal structure of the event, if you could call it that, had been devised by Cage through chance procedures and the asking of questions, rather than by the making of ego-driven choices. The result was a continuously surprising juxtaposition of a multitude of unrelated elements, unfolding in a nonintentional but nevertheless structured manner, based on chance-determined lengths of time.

To better experience this unfocused performance, which took place in the school's main dining room, as well as to facilitate ease of movement by the performers, Cage divided the audience into four triangular sections, facing itself, with a small performance space in the middle, and a larger performance ring surrounding them on the outside. Aisles divided the four sections, allowing the performers to move freely back and forth. And because the action literally took place within the audience, Cage's *Theater Piece No. 1* was an early and important contribution to the 1960s avant-garde's attempt to weaken what they saw as the artificial art-music barrier between house and stage, audience and performer.

From the beginning, these "happenings"—as artist Allan Kaprow came to call them in the late 1950s—were difficult to describe and almost impossible to analyze with any degree of accuracy, not only because they were multifocused works incorporating simultaneous performance within a variety of genres but also because each "happening" was unique, shaped as much by the location of the event and the actions of the audience as by the performers. And because most "happenings" normally took place in nonconcert venues such as parks, industrial spaces, and people's lofts, the result brought together a sometimes startling juxtaposition of actions, objects, people, and unstructured events. Declaring the interaction between audience, artwork, and artist that became prevalent during the 1960s a new art form best described as "intermedia art," Dieter Daniels writes that its origins, "as inspired by John Cage and molded by Fluxus and Happening lie in the decision to replace an autonomous, finished work with an invitation to the audience to essentially self-determine its experiences with the artwork."[32]

Cage believed that theater was obligatory at this stage in the development of a new form of art, because not only do "changes in music precede equivalent ones in theatre, and changes in theatre precede general changes in the lives of people" but also that theatre is more representative of real life than the other arts, "requiring for its appreciation the use of both eyes and ears, space and time." He went on to say that audiences are seeing more and more works of art "which are not strictly speaking either paintings or music. In New York City they are called 'happenings.'" And he continued that "just as shadows no longer destroy paintings, nor ambient sounds music, so environmental activities do not ruin a happening. They rather add to the fun of it. The result, coming to the instance of daily life, is that our lives are not ruined by the interruptions that other people and things continually provide."[33]

4'33" *(August 1952)*

If Cage's intention was to allow the audience to determine its own artistic experience as a means of drawing its attention to the sounds of its environment—which he often said they might prefer to the "music" of a concert—he achieved this goal with his next work, *4'33"*, a piece in three movements during which no sounds are intentionally produced. Written a little more than a month after *Theater Piece No. 1*, *4'33"* (the title indicates the total performance time in minutes and seconds) consists of meticulously plotted-out lengths of time determined by chance. Cage said he was inspired to create this work by seeing Rauschenberg's *White Paintings*.

The first performance of Cage's "silent" piece, as it came to be called, was in Woodstock, New York, on August 29, 1952, in a one-wall-opened-to-nature concert space called Maverick Hall. It was performed by pianist David Tudor, who used a stop-watch to differentiate between movements of 33", 2'40", and 1'20" durations. In addition, he indicated the beginning of each movement by closing the keyboard lid, and the end of each movement by opening it. And although *4'33"*, according to Cage's instructions, may be performed by any instrument or combination of instruments, the charisma and personality of David Tudor, who gave the first three performances, has had the unintended effect of limiting it in most people's minds to a work for solo piano.

In the end, what is important about *4'33"*, of course, is that it is not a silent piece at all, but a piece in which accidental sounds inherent in the environment of the performance situation are allowed to be themselves and to be reflected on by the audience. It is this admission of environmental sound into musical sound that gives *4'33"* its importance—or, more correctly in Cage's view, the admission of music into life. Because, for Cage, silence is not silence, but the whole world of sound, presenting to those who will listen, nature in her manner of operation. Writing in *Media Art Interaction,* Dieter Daniels calls *4'33"* "the ideal 'open work,'" saying that "in it, nothing is fixed, everything depends on the conditions of the respective performance." Daniels also points out that "during the same period, Cage began to devise pieces that transferred the same principle of open interaction to the deployment of electronic media," citing as an example *Imaginary Landscape No. 4* of 1951, in which "twelve radios are used like musical instruments."[34]

Composition as Process

By the 1960s, Cage—by now universally regarded as the father figure, if not the founder, of a worldwide band of experimental artists of all disciplines loosely labeled the avant-garde—had fully accepted the notion that sounds should be brought into being and allowed to interact by chance. It became the only kind of music he wrote. He further believed that the audience, rather than silently sitting in rows, would often best be served by the experience of sound environments in which they were free to move around, make noise, and come and go.

And also having come to believe that "Art instead of being an object made by one person is a process set in motion by a group of people," Cage declared, "It isn't someone saying something, but people doing things, giving everyone (including those involved) the opportunity to have experiences they would not otherwise have had."[35] Ultimately, Cage came to believe that "the purpose of this purposeless music [and these purposeless events] would be achieved if people learned to listen. That when they listened they might discover that they preferred the sounds of everyday life to the ones they would presently hear in the musical program," a possibility that Cage said "was all right as far as [he] was concerned."[36] As he put it, "composing's one thing, performing's another, listening's a third. What can they have to do with one another?"[37]

Cage also proved to be something of a visionary about the technology of the future, in which his interests, by the mid-1960s, had become global. Writing in the first installment of his *Diary: How To Improve The World*

(You Will Only Make Matters Worse) in 1965, Cage reiterates RCA founder David Sarnoff's forecast of instant universal voice communication, instant television, and instant visual telephone service, and calls for a global communications system and a "reorientation toward a 'one-world concept of mass communications in an era marked by the emergence of a universal language, a universal culture and a universal common market.'" At the same time, he also voiced the need for "an utterly wireless technology" more than a quarter of a century before it became a reality.[38]

But in the end, it was the concepts of sound and silence, space and time, that engaged Cage's thinking the most. And throughout the span of his indeterminate compositions, composed over a period of some forty-plus years, we can see a continual development toward less control of the performer through greater ambiguity of the performance materials and the notations, and greater participation by the audience in the "creative" process—if not the actual decisions—of the performance. And Cage, always the optimist, was positive about the future of the indeterminate form of music he had begun. As he said, "There is no such thing as an empty space or an empty time. There is always something to see, something to hear.... Until I die there will be sounds. And they will continue following my death. One need not fear about the future of music."[39]

Brian Eno and the Landscaping of Sound

You may or may not recognize the name Brian Eno,[40] but it is highly likely that you have heard some of his work. Because Eno, the composer who can't read music and who often confuses his friends and foes alike with the comment that he is a nonmusician, wrote the startup music for the Windows operating system. If you have a PC you hear his work every time you turn your computer on. And that's significant in the context of virtual music because, like much of Eno's work, the Windows startup music exists in the background much like Satie's *Furniture Music*, influencing the surroundings, but not overpowering or controlling them.

As we consider Eno's complete body of work, we find that a sizeable portion of it was written not only with machines but by them. In fact, his method of composing is dependent on machines, first the reel-to-reel tape recorder of the 1960s (he owned thirty-one at one time and claims to have over one and one-half million feet of recorded tape), then the synthesizer of the 1970s and 1980s (he was partial to the older, less stable ones because they sometimes acted unexpectedly, and because he thinks "accidents" are often more interesting than the things he does intentionally), and now the computer. Furthermore, throughout his more than thirty years of activity, from the 1960s to the present, he has been one of a rare breed of musicians who considers the recording studio to be his primary musical instrument. He once said, "I'm very good with technology, I always have been, and with machines in general. They seem to me not threatening like other people find them, but a source of great fun and amusement, like grown up toys really."[41]

Now no matter how unorthodox this all may seem, when we consider the extent of Eno's accomplishments we have to admit that his "system" appears to work. Consider, for example, that Eno, along with Bryan Ferry, was a founding member of Roxy Music, the quintessential English rock band of the 1970s, for which he was the sound mixer and technical director. Or that from this beginning Eno went on to create more than twenty solo albums and singles of his own work; to collaborate with giants of the pop world such as Robert Fripp, David Bowie, John Cale, and Daniel Lanois, among others; and to produce albums for high-profile groups such as Ultravox, Devo, Talking Heads, and U2. Meanwhile, in a more experimental vein, Eno was also a major contributor to, if not the founder of, the ambient music movement of the mid-1970s, and, more recently, has been developing generative music, a term he coined to characterize a new computer-improvised musical genre he created in the mid-1990s using the Koan software. But how, exactly, did a composer with such impressive pop-world credentials also become a guiding light of the experimental music world?

Brian Peter George St. John le Baptiste de la Salle Eno was born in 1948 in Woodbridge, Suffolk, England. Between 1964 and 1966 he studied painting at Ipswich Art School, and credits the school's director, Roy Ascot, with establishing and encouraging an environment of experimentation and outside-the-box creative thinking. It was at Ipswich that Eno encountered John Cage's first book, *Silence*, through which he became interested in experimental music, and began to explore creating works using the tape recorder. Occasional visits to Ipswich by English avant-garde composers such as John Tilbury and Cornelius Cardew further convinced Eno that conceptual art, chance procedures, and the tape recorder constituted the proper methods and materials for his work. As he said in the mid-1970s, "my interest in music was in a set of ideas rather than in a set of techniques … it's the ideas that interest me." For him, the attraction of synthesizers "was that there was no code of playing any of this new equipment and recording studio technology developed so quickly that nobody could say 'This is the right way to play a synthesizer.'"[42]

After two years of study at Ipswich, Eno enrolled in the more traditional Winchester College of Art, but by this point his interest in experimentation was engaged, and he turned to underground activities to satisfy his desire to be creative musically. By the time Eno became involved with Roxy Music in 1972, his Cage-inspired, chance-derived work with tape recorders offered a cutting-edge new direction for the band to explore. It also offered him a venue outside the band, and his continuing success in this area became one of the primary reasons why Eno left Roxy Music in 1973; he was becoming more famous than its leader, Bryan Ferry.

Ambient Music

Although Eno had experimented with sound since the 1960s, the defining moment in the development of ambient music and his emergence as a true experimental composer came on the evening of January 18, 1975, when he walked in front of a taxi. And although he saw it at the last minute and tried to step back, the taxi, which was going about 40 mph at the time, ran over his legs and threw his head against a parked car. The result was that he was on painkillers and immobilized in bed for quite some time.

While he was convalescing, his friend Judy Nylon came to visit one day and brought him a recording of eighteenth-century virtuoso harp music. As she was leaving he asked her to put it on the record player in his room. But after she had left, and to his chagrin, it was raining and the volume was so low that the combination of the two meant that he could barely hear the music, catching only the loudest of isolated notes or the smallest flurries of sound. So there he was, unable to hear it properly, but also unable to adjust the volume or to turn it off because he was confined to his bed. As this forced listening continued, however, he said he "started to think that it sounded all right" and to wonder "why no music like this existed." He went on to say that the experience gave him "the sense of hearing the tip of something, and the knowledge that there was more beneath it." And as he continued to listen, he said he came to the conclusion that "I wanted my music to do this."[43] It was because of this experience that he resolved to make a commitment to experimental music and to take it more seriously.

Within a year after the accident, Eno recorded *Discreet Music,* the first of his records conceived as ambient sound, or as he described it, "music deliberately constructed to occupy the background."[44] *Discreet Music* is a collaboration with Robert Fripp, a guitarist with whom Eno had worked before. Eno's contribution to the project was to produce a "landscape" of tape-delay patterns created from a few notes on a synthesizer played at half-speed through a tape recorder, over which Fripp improvised. The result—a multicycling collage of tape loops truly made by machine—is a dreamy, ethereal, wash of isolated sounds: noticeable, but not imposing; hovering in the background, but easily ignored. Eno said he saw the process as one of removing his personality from the musical landscape. He also said that "one of the interesting things about having little musical knowledge is that you generate surprising results sometimes; you move to places which you wouldn't do if you knew better, and sometimes that's just what you need."[45]

If *Discreet Music* was Eno's first ambient work, *Music for Airports,* written three years later in 1978, quickly became the most famous example of the style. Eno said the inspiration for *Music for Airports* came when he was sitting in the Cologne airport waiting for a plane. His idea, he said, was to try and create music that would fit into the container of a functioning airport, and that "the underlying idea was to try to suggest that there were new places to put music, new kinds of niches where music could belong."[46] Remembering his experience when recovering from the accident, he said he tried to imagine the kind of music that would work in such a space; music that could withstand interruption because of the constant announcements that occur there.

Structurally, *Music for Airports* is based on the simple idea of repetitive loops, six in the case of the first piece on the album, each cycling for different amounts of time. Musically these loops consist of a few isolated pitches, some sung by three women plus Eno, others played on two pianos. These six sets of pitches—each on a different loop and repeating at irregular intervals because of their different lengths—when running simultaneously create incommensurable cycles, meaning that the six parts seldom, if ever, come back into original sync again. The experience, as Eno said, is one of hearing various clusterings and configurations of the same basic elements: "They stay the same. But the piece does appear to have quite a lot of variety."[47]

In describing *Music for Airports* in 1979, Michael Bloom, in his review for *Rolling Stone,* called it "aesthetic white noise."[48] Eno said he thought one of the things that ambient music could do was change our sense of time so that we don't really mind if things slip or alter in some way. For him, he said, the piece "was really about getting rid of people's nervousness."[49] Later, he said that he had been so impressed by this way of composing that he had made many pieces of music using even more complex variations of the looping technique, and that, in fact, all of his ambient music was based on the idea that "it's possible to think of a system or a set of rules which once set in motion will create music for you. Now the wonderful thing about that," he said, "is that it starts to create music that you've never heard before," concluding: "This is an important point I think."[50]

In addition to the obvious relationship of Eno's ambient music to Satie's furniture music, another underlying factor in Eno's ambient work is his interest in the chance procedures of John Cage, first discovered by him in *Silence* in the mid-1960s. In 1996, noting that much of his music is rules- or systems-based, and that he has always been interested in "ways of making music that went beyond the decisions I'd make based on taste," Eno said that "a big part of the thrill for me is to set in motion something that makes something you don't expect." Calling this way of creating music "out of control but not chaotic," he explained that his musical visions were always of interesting systems, never of final results.[51]

Now an obvious characteristic of Eno's ambient work, to anyone who has spent any time listening to it, is that it exists in a dimension of time all its own, floating by, as it does, one or two notes at a time. Eno has always understood and made artistic use of this quality, having recognized early that the tape recorder could collage time. He once commented that "the effect of recording is that it takes music out of the time dimension and puts it in the space dimension." As a composer, he said, it meant that he could "think in terms of supplying material that would actually be too subtle for a first listening." He also loosely quoted Marshall McLuhan, saying that the process of recording "makes all music present ... the whole history of our music [is] with us now."[52]

Generative Music

One of the first aspects of computers to capture Eno's artistic imagination were the screensavers, those "everchanging patterns on the screens of computers at rest," as Richard Williams labeled them in a 1996 article in the *Guardian*. His article was about Eno's latest contribution to musical invention, generative music, described by Williams as music "in which the process of creation is given over to the computer itself."[53] Starting in the mid-1990s, Eno began to create sets of "rules" for the computer so that it would create a musical composition that was recognizably the same and yet different every time it was played. As Eno described it in a 1996 talk given at the Imagination Conference in San Francisco, "Generative music is sensitive to circumstances, ... it will react differently depending on its initial condition." Calling these new generative forms "multi-centered," he continued that, "there's not a single chain of command which runs from the top of the pyramid to the rank and file below" but, rather, a three-dimensional complex of "web-like modes which become more or less active," a significant difference more in line with how the Internet works than with the traditional broadcasting model. In generative music, Eno said, "You never know who made it.... Am I the composer? Are you if you buy the system the composer? ... Who actually composes music like this?"[54]

If "who" composes generative music is an open issue, "how" it is composed is easier to explain. Eno uses the Koan software developed by SSEYO,[55] which gives him, or anyone else using the same program, control over some 150 different musical and sonic parameters. Calling this software something of a revolution in music, he said that although some of the computer "rules" deal with traditional musical decisions, such as pitch, rhythm, tempo, and harmony, others are more technical in nature and involve controlling the characteristics of the waveform itself (envelope, attack, and decay), whereas others are more structural and determine how the piece will unfold over time. Eno explained that these envelopes—more probabilistic than determinant in their effect—"create a multidimensional space, so the journey that the computer makes through [it] is very complicated and almost certain to never repeat."[56]

Eno doesn't claim to have invented the concept of generative music, only the name, explaining that there are many kinds of generative systems. The concept goes back at least as far as wind chimes, and certainly includes Steve Reich's tape pieces from the 1960s, *Come Out* and *It's Gonna Rain,* both of which create *moiré* patterns of sound as they overlay the same text on top of itself. In his San Francisco talk, Eno pointed out that the effect one hears in generative music, as in minimalism, "happens because of one's perception rather than because of anything physically happening."[57] He described it as the listening brain becoming habituated in a way similar to the way the eye does if we stare at something for a long time, saying the common information gets canceled out and we begin only to notice the differences. Eno does believe, however, that he has contributed significantly to the creation of something new, saying that "this new linkage [of generative music] with an increasingly commonplace technology [the computer] will make it a form in which many composers will wish to work," in the future.[58] And believing the generative idea to be a completely new concept of musical organization, Eno says it is one in which the material, with the help of the computer, organizes itself. Certainly, this is a major change from the way art is currently thought about and made.

In comparing generative music to classical music, Eno says that classical music "specifies an entity in advance and then builds it," unlike generative music that "specifies a set of rules and then lets them make the thing." Going further, he calls generative music unpredictable, whereas classical music is predictable; unrepeatable, as opposed to repeatable; and implicitly unfinished, as opposed to the "finished" classical score.[59] Growing more enthusiastic, he speculates that, "You'll eventually be able to have emotionally tunable music,"[60] in a future filled with "generative graphics, generative narratives, generative architecture—forms of culture that are evolutionary, [and] which somehow pay attention to your interests and modify themselves accordingly."[61] As Eno sees it, the interesting thing about computers is not that they can store and move large blocks of data around, but that they can "grow things from seed."[62] And noting that "the deeper significance of Generative music lies in the fact that it is supposed to exist only in real time, disappearing as it passes," he offers the possibility "that our grandchildren will look at us in wonder and say, 'You mean you used to listen to exactly the same thing over and over again?'"[63]

John Oswald and Plunderphonics

If Satie, Cage, and Eno set the aesthetic dimensions of interactive music, then John Oswald and Moby established the attitude. Because both—one famous, the other less so but equally talented—operate in that gray area of music, somewhere between plagiarism, appropriation, repurposing, and play. Unless their Web sites count, neither Oswald nor Moby are virtual musicians; their performances take place in clubs and on CDs. But their attitude about what's fair game when it comes to free use and appropriation, if not outright plagiarism, of other people's music as the raw material for the creation of their own work has become not only an art movement in itself, but also the prevailing attitude about who owns the music on the Web. One has only to consider the problems the recording industry has faced since the introduction of Napster in 1999, and its successors KaZaA, Morpheus, Grokster, and WinMX, to see how pervasive in our culture these attitudes of free-use and fair-game have become.

If any one person can be singled out as the prototype for this late-twentieth-century redefinition of "fair use," it is Canadian composer John Oswald (b. 1953),[64] who, since the mid-1980s, has been creating what he calls "Plunderphonic music" in which he uses entire songs by everybody from the Beatles, Bing Crosby, and Captain Beefheart, to James Brown, Beethoven, and Stravinsky, without permission, and with no attempt to hide or even disguise the source. He even plundered Satie's *Parade*, using it to accompany dancer Jennifer Mascall in a commission for the Expo '86 World's Fair in Vancouver. Oswald said he thinks he got the original idea for Plunderphonics from the science fiction writer J. G. Ballard, "who envisioned a future where people ingested Wagner's operas in seconds, at ultrasonic frequencies, and discussed the varying aural ambrosia of different performances."[65]

Oswald's work with Plunderphonics takes the art of sampling to an entirely new level, although he is quick to point out that what he does is only peripherally related to hip-hop sampling because, unlike the DJs, he generally deconstructs and recontextualizes the entire song. And also unlike hip-hop, which often quotes the work of others out of respect, Oswald's work, which in some ways can be considered musical collage, counts on a strong recognition of the original, otherwise his subverting of it would go unnoticed.

An experimenter who has altered the sounds of records since his childhood in the long-playing days of the 1960s, John Oswald, if nothing else, has demonstrated a quarter-century of commitment to a hands-on, interactive way of listening to the music most of us take for granted. Even today, he speaks of the beauty of having once owned a four-speed record player with 78, 45, 33, and 16 rpm from which to choose, saying he often liked songs better when they were played at the "wrong" speed. He also said his listening equipment never included a receiver, but a mixer instead, along with "an infinitely-variable-speed turntable, filters, reverse capability, and a pair of ears."[66]

By the late 1960s, Oswald had created his own band, consisting of a trumpet player, two bongo players, and him, playing records on his record player, almost always at the wrong speed. He said he eventually came to the recognition that he was really good at playing records, long before he realized that other people were doing it as well. And as analog and digital editing came along, Oswald got even better. He also said that listening to music at the wrong speed often gave him a better insight into the music itself, and he suggests that listening to Stravinsky's *Rite of Spring* at 78 rpm helped him understand what got people so upset in 1913, whereas listening to the Bebop saxophonist Charlie Parker at a slower speed helped him understand how Parker put his solos together.[67]

The controversy over Oswald's way of working—and the question of who "owns" what musically—began with a 1985 talk he gave to a group of fellow composers at the Wired Society Electro-Acoustic Conference in Toronto. Titled "Plunderphonics, or Audio Piracy as a Compositional Prerogative," it set not only the tone, but also the ground rules, for circumventing the U.S. and Canadian copyright laws in the name of art. Oswald said that he coined the term Plunderphonics "to cover the counter-covert world of converted sound and retrofitted music where collective melodic memories of the familiar are minced and rehabilitated to a new life."[68] Plunderphonic music is recognizable music that has been transformed in some significant way, making it both a new work of art and a comment on the original material.

In his 1985 talk, Oswald argued that using other people's music as raw material for new art was perfectly legitimate and, in fact, has a long history in both popular and classical music. In his own case, he credits both Italian composer Luciano Berio's *Omaggio a Joyce,* a 1958 transformation of singer Cathy Berberian's voice reading from James Joyce's *Ulysses,* and German composer Karlheinz Stockhausen's *Hymnen,* from 1967, which consists of electronic transformations of recorded national anthems from over 150 countries, as having had a strong and lasting influence on him early in his career. On occasion he also mentions Charles Ives as a composer he admires and who often made musical collages of popular and patriotic songs without hinderance, working as he did in an age before copyright issues were of much significance.

The success of Oswald's Toronto talk, particularly the audio examples, as well as his interest in having other people hear his work, led him, in 1988, to press a vinyl EP recording of four Plunderphonic pieces: *Don't,* which uses preexisting Elvis Presley material; *Pretender,* which begins with Dolly Parton's version of "The Great Pretender"; *Pocket,* using music from the Count Basie orchestra; and *Spring,* which takes as its starting point Stravinsky's *Rite of Spring.* A year later, in 1989, Oswald released his first Plunderphonics CD, a collection of twenty tracks, each transforming and reconfiguring the work of one musician or group, including such diverse examples as Michael Jackson's *Bad* and Beethoven's *Symphony No. 7.* Oswald said he likes to use "pop" sources that everybody knows, whether by rock stars or classical giants, because the recognition factor plays such a large role in the listening experience. He also offered that "there is a bridge between things that are often ghettoized as being extreme twentieth-century avant garde techniques and pop music," adding that, in his experience, "the two things can coexist."[69]

In each of his Plunderphonic pieces, Oswald uses the original recording as a starting point, altering it, not beyond recognition, but certainly far beyond what the composer or performer had ever intended or imagined.

Oswald's methods, in addition to changing the playback speed, sometimes drastically so, include older analog techniques such as splicing, over-dubbing, and filtering, as well as newer manipulative digital techniques possible with computers, samplers, and synthesizers. At times, he also enlists live musicians to play newly composed material over the top of the original. He said that when he first began creating Plunderphonic pieces he thought he would use these recording as prototypes from which he would then enlist live musicians to create the actual music, but that he came to see this approach as a compromise because this way of working never sounded as good as the original, even though he brought in excellent musicians like his friend, the guitarist Henry Kaiser. Furthermore, Oswald said that he didn't ask anyone's permission before creating any of his Plunderphonic pieces, feeling that if they said no he would have to honor that decision and not play it for people anymore, a prospect he didn't want to face. So as a way of ensuring "the maximum degree of self preservation" he said he "started to think that it wasn't even a good idea or a necessary thing to ask them" for permission to do what he was doing to their music.[70]

Perhaps if Oswald had left it at that there wouldn't have been much of a problem. But in creating the cover art for the CD he decided, over the objections of some of his friends, to morph Michael Jackson's head onto the body of a nude white woman, and that's where the real trouble began. He said he used the image because it was a visual representation of what the music sounded like, and because he hadn't compromised with the music and didn't want to compromise on the cover either. When the Plunderphonics CD was completed, Oswald made a thousand copies and began giving them away for free to friends, critics, libraries, and radio stations, believing that as long as he didn't sell the CD he would not get into trouble with the legal arm of the record industry. But altering Michael Jackson's image as well as his music proved to be the proverbial straw, and Oswald was quickly served with a cease-and-desist order from the Canadian Recording Industry Association. By that point, he had given away some seven hundred copies of the CD, and while he wasn't required to retrieve them he did have to relinquish the master tapes and the remaining three hundred CDs, and to agree not to make or distribute any more copies. But thanks to those seven hundred still-available copies, and to the persistence and determination of some of the people working in the area of sampling, all twenty pieces from the banned CD are now available on the Web.

Although Oswald was forced to take his Plunderphonics CD off the market (free though it was), his plan to make his music better known proved to be a success. Within less than a decade after releasing it he received commissions from Elektra Records to create *Rubaiyat* (a fortieth anniversary tribute to the company based on material in their catalog), the Kronos String Quartet to create *Spectre* (a work for their 1993 album *Short Stories*), the composer John Zorn to create *Plexure* (an entire album of Plunderphonic music for his Avant label), and the Grateful Dead to create a double CD based on material from their vault. The result of this last commission, titled *Grayfolded* and based on one of the Dead's signature songs, "Dark Star", was selected by the *Toronto Sun* as the #1 International Recording of the Decade, and appeared in the "Year's Best" lists in both the *New York Times* and *Rolling Stone*.

In 2003, however, Oswald told interviewer Paul Steenhuisen that he saw a potential long-term problem for Plunderphonic music, noticing as he had that for the younger generation "historical perspective extends only to a couple of years," and that they seem to have "a very narrow sense of history." As an example, he mentions Bing Crosby's "White Christmas," the most recorded and broadcast popular song for almost half a century, lamenting that "there's a whole generation of people who seem not to recognize it now."[71] And because the Plunderphonic method of composing is dependent on previously recorded music, and successful listening to the style requires a knowledge of this source material, the apparent lack of historical memory, if continued in future generations, could have serious consequences for the longevity of the genre.

How this all may develop long term, of course, only time will tell. But in the meantime, a new style of sampling called mashup, in which DJs play the melody of one song over top of the accompaniment of another, has emerged. Oswald says that much of his own work from the past thirty years seems "to flow directly into that category," adding "I guess I'm a mash-up pioneer, although as far as I know, none of the mash-up people have heard of me."[72] And as for the charges of plagiarism that have plagued Oswald throughout his career, he has had a ready answer for that since his 1985 talk in Toronto, in which he cited John Milton, who wrote that piracy or plagiarism of a work occurs only "if it is not bettered by the borrower." And he also reminded his audience about Stravinsky's famous quote that "a good composer doesn't borrow, he steals."[73]

Obviously, the issue of sampling is central to Moby's concept of how to make music. And the pros and cons of that debate, we should realize, are not as simple as they may first appear. One way of thinking about it is that both John Oswald and Moby are the perfect embodiments of the artist-as-consumer, loop digging, or mining for samples as it has come to be called, from the entire history of recorded sound. But it is also worth remembering that the appropriation of other people's music as one's own is not unique to the late twentieth and early twenty-first centuries. It was common for Renaissance composers to add a fourth line to a three-voice piece, or a third part to a duet, and call it their own. This, after all, is how King Henry the Eighth came to be called a "composer." Plus, as the primary materials for making music change more toward the digital realm, the methods used to make this music will, of necessity, have to change.

Moby and the Concept of Play

If John Oswald represents the renegade wing of experimental music, then Moby is the representative from the mainstream pop world. And if, at the turn of the century, John Oswald's Plunderphonics CD was difficult to locate, Moby's CD, *Play*, appeared to be everywhere. Because not only did *Play*, released in 1999, sell ten million copies worldwide, but each of the eighteen pieces on the album was commercially licensed to advertisers, movies, and television shows, months before the CD became available in stores. There was, or course, no reason for anyone associated with the project to believe that this kind of success was possible. Even Moby, before its release, said that he hoped *Play* might sell as many as 250,000 copies. And looked at logically, that was optimistic, given the fact that none of his previous records had sold over 150,000. So why did *Play*, Moby's fourth album for a major label after earlier releases on Instinct, Elektra, and Mute, become such a financial success, reaching, as it did, platinum status in over twenty-five countries? In some ways the answer is unknowable, involving, as it does, the whims of mass attention and public taste. But from what can be known, the answer includes everything from Moby's concept of "play," to his attitude about sampling, to his desire to create "hits," an obsession that keeps him listening to the same track from a best-selling CD, over and over, trying to figure out what blend of musical ingredients combined to make it a success.

Born Richard Melville Hall in 1965 to two Columbia University students living in Harlem, and nicknamed "Moby" by his parents because of the family's distant relationship to Herman Melville (the author of *Moby Dick*), Moby grew up primarily in Connecticut. By the age of fourteen he had started his own band, covering such songs as "Money" by Pink Floyd and "Birthday" by the Beatles. The following year, in 1980, he started his first new wave/punk rock band, eventually settling on the name Vatican Commandos, and covering songs by the Clash and the Sex Pistols, as well as writing some songs of his own. By his senior year of high school, Moby had obtained his first four-track cassette recorder and, as he says, "realized that I could finish songs by myself and that I didn't need to be so reliant upon other musicians."[74] And after less than a year as a student at the University of Connecticut, he dropped out in 1984 and began DJ-ing, first at the Beat in Port Chester, New York, then at other clubs throughout the Northeast. Moby said that it was from DJ-ing that he came to understand that "no song is an island," meaning that in order to keep people dancing he had to take into consideration long sequences of songs and how their rhythmic development over time might drive and inspire the crowd. He immediately saw the beauty of this structural control—a shape that goes far beyond dancing— and that he came to see and appreciate "how sound and rhythm work on people physically."[75]

Moby moved to New York City in 1989 and began DJ-ing in such clubs as MK, Mars, and the Palladium. By the following summer he had given his first electronica performance at MK, and again a short time later at the Palladium for five thousand people. Almost simultaneously, his second single, "Mobility," was released in the winter of 1990 and sold two thousand copies, while his third single, "Voodoo Child," released the following winter, sold double that amount. But it was his fourth single, "Go," released in the spring of 1991, that caught the crowd's attention, becoming an international dance-club hit, and eventually selling over a million copies. As described by Gerald Marzorati in the *New York Times*, "Go" combines "the eerie string motif of the theme from David Lynch's TV series *Twin Peaks* with a jubilant bass line, thumping beats and a sample of a crowd yelling the song's title."[76]

By the mid-1990s, Moby's music was constantly charting on the UK's Top 40 Singles chart ("Go" reached #10), and he was touring not only with such acts as Orbital and Aphex Twin but also with Lollapalooza and the Red Hot Chili Peppers. By 1997, Moby was also writing music for film, including the "*James Bond* Theme," which reached #8 on the UK singles chart. Still, as exciting as all of this was, it did not project future sales of ten million. To comprehend the success of *Play*, it is necessary to understand both how Moby creates his music, and how the results of this approach affects his fans.

For Moby, composing is "play" in all its senses: the fun of doing, the usurping of material, the constant tinkering that can produce five or six versions of hundreds of songs in a relatively short amount of time. At the beginning of each new project, his first step is generally to collect what he calls "a cappella sounds," by which he means short, unaccompanied solo riffs (both vocal and instrumental), sometimes of only a few seconds in length, that already exist on other people's records. By enlisting his friends and record company personnel to scour record stores and cutout bins in various parts of the world, he usually collects several hundred of these solo moments for each new project he undertakes. His next step is to separate these sounds electronically from the songs they are a part of, and to store them digitally in his computer, creating what he calls his "sonic palette," saying that he likes this palette to be as broad as possible before he actually begins to work.

In *Play*, the most memorable of Moby's a cappella moments are taken from father and son folklorists John and Alan Lomax's field recordings, made in the Deep South in the 1930s and 1940s of blues and gospel singers, voices that commingle in *Play* with sampled beats from funk and disco, guitar licks, a melody on a keyboard, and Moby's own musical contributions, both instrumental and vocal, both played live and added later in the mastering. Marzorati says that this compositional format is Moby's way of "recapturing the popular past," rendering it "at once novel and strangely familiar, the alchemy that somehow makes for that sound that says *now*."[77] Ethan Smith, writing in *Wired*, calls *Play* "music that sounds cool—but not too cool ... music that sounds both underground and accessible at the same time." He also mildly criticizes Moby's music as "toe-tapping sonic wallpaper ... that works as well in restaurants, aerobics classes, and movies as it does in clubs."[78]

Once Moby has his sonic palette chosen and catalogued in his computer, he begins to lay down tracks, building the mix one track at a time. Working primarily in ProTools, a state-of-the-art digital audio recording program that allows him to cut and paste sound samples inside his computer without the need of a mixing board, and with the further possibility of altering the waveforms and adding a multitude of effects, he builds his mix, track by track, until it sounds the way he imagines it. Some of the tracks he plays live, others he sings, but at the core of the mix are the samples he has mined from other records. At various stages of the project he becomes the composer, the performer, the producer, and the engineer, creating, along the way, nearly everything associated with the sound of the CD by himself. According to Moby, the technology exists, as does the recorded music, and his combining of the two is how music is best written today.

Like John Oswald, Moby makes little or no attempt to hide or disguise the source of his samples. Some of them, such as the Lomax field recordings, are brought to the forefront, making of these blues and gospel singers soloists out of time and place, singing along to beats and electronic sounds they could never have imagined when they were alive. Other samples are obscured through mixing and overdubbing, but that is a byproduct of the process, and not an attempt to hide the source. And unlike Oswald, Moby and his record company meticulously clear and license all of his samples; with sales of ten million, clearance is a necessity. Nevertheless, and in spite of the clearances, Moby jokes that on his records he is not only a composer, musician, and engineer, "but also a plagiarist and a thief."[79]

As surprising as it may seem, not all musicians, or even record company executives, take exception to having their music "stolen" through sampling. The more regional, less well-known bands, as well as the independent labels themselves, often welcome it, correctly sensing that both sampling and file sharing on the Web are vehicles for making their music more readily available and them more widely known. Mark Gage, an electronica/techno producer and remixer who works under the name of Vapourspace, spoke for more artists and labels than you would guess when he told *Keyboard* magazine, "I think you're not really famous until you've been ripped off."[80]

2
UNSILENT NIGHT:
A CASE STUDY IN MOTION

If any one piece of music can be said to represent the technically sophisticated, but non-Internet related, world of interactive music of the 1990s, it
is Phil Kline's *Unsilent Night,* a forty-minute, genre-blurring, musical tour
de force employing dozens, if not hundreds, of boom box tape players
carried by the audience as they parade through and perform in the streets
of downtown New York. The resulting artistic spectacle that these march-
ing musicians create is a living, moving, boom box sound sculpture;
something Kline is fond of calling a "city-block-long stereo system."[1] Now
a recurring event in a number of American and European cities at Christmas time each year, *Unsilent Night* has become, since its first staging in
New York's Greenwich Village in December 1992, the quintessential
nonsinging electronic caroling party, or, if you prefer Kline's characterization, the "archetypal outdoor mega-boombox event" of the holiday
season.[2] In 2003, outdoor performances of *Unsilent Night* took place in
Atlanta, Philadelphia, San Diego, San Francisco, Tallahassee, and
Vancouver, in addition to New York, where the yearly event has become a
recurring cult-classic Christmas tradition. In 1999, Kline staged a performance of *Unsilent Night* in the New York offices and hallways of MTV,
and in 2000, he organized and directed a New Year's Day performance in
Berlin.

A downtown New York composer/guitarist with impeccable experimental music credentials, Phil Kline was born in Pittsburgh, Pennsylvania, but grew up in Akron, Ohio, where, he says, his earliest musical training "came from listening to records and playing guitar in garage bands."[3] After moving to New York and graduating from Columbia University with a major in English Literature, he enrolled in the Mannes College of Music, emerging a few years later as a composer and drifting into the downtown New York club and rock scene. He said later that the one thing these educational experiences taught him was the value of continuing to buy and listen to more records. Along the way, Kline also became a member of the Glenn Branca Ensemble (an orchestra of microtonal electric guitarists and rock drummer), touring internationally and recording with them for a number of years. In the 1980s, he cofounded the no-wave art punk band the Del-Byzanteens with the filmmaker Jim Jarmusch, who played keyboard and sang; the writer Luc Sante, who wrote the lyrics; and the painter James Nares, who played drums; Kline played guitar and sang. During this same period, he also provided soundtracks for film and video projects by such prominent artists as Nan Goldin and Wim Wenders.

The Boom Box Orchestra

In 1990, Phil Kline began to write the music for which he would become best known: a continuing series of works for orchestras of "massed boom box tape machines," many of the pieces designed to be performed in public spaces. These works, which include his early *Bachman's Warbler* for harmonicas and twelve boom boxes from 1990 (premiered at the Bang On A Can Marathon in New York in May 1992), not only take as their starting point but attempt to create an organic synthesis of "the tape loop and phasing techniques of Brian Eno and Steve Reich" with "the sound mass experiments of Glenn Branca." Kline says that, whereas in another life he might have learned to play the violin, joined the orchestra, and became an orchestral composer, in this life "the first instrument I learned to play really well was the tape recorder."[4]

For Kline, the reel-to-reel recorder that he first began to compose with was not only cumbersome and heavy, but the very process of working with it had a daunting physical presence as well, requiring, as it did, the actual splicing of tape and the draping of it around mic stands "like the cables of suspension bridges" to produce the tape loops he preferred to use in his music.[5] But the discovery of the boom box cassette recorder changed all that for him. Precision-cut, "endless" cassettes were readily available that would loop the musical material recorded on them over and over without pause, and without the need for splicing, extra audio equipment, or the draping of tape on microphone stands. Kline said he didn't even need electricity with boom boxes as long as the batteries would hold out.

When he first started writing his boom box pieces, Kline said he thought of the boxes as the basic instrument of his performances, and that he began "making live tape loops in sequence to produce clouds of over-tones and feedback." Later, he started to see the boxes "as players in a virtual orchestra," and to write his music directly onto the cassette tapes, which he then played back in unison, creating "dense yet pliant sonic textures that could be moved around in open spaces." Kline quickly came to see the boom boxes as the ideal electronic instrument for his work, because they were not only handy and relatively inexpensive, but "the best independent sound sources I could buy dozens of."[6] Currently, he owns over forty boxes of various kinds, some of which he lets people without a box of their own use at his outdoor boom box events. Kline also shunned the isolating, for-your-ears-only quality of the portable Walkman, choosing instead the community-building, territory-establishing public statement made by the ghetto blaster boom box.

Musically, Phil Kline says that what he first liked about multiple boom box performance pieces was that they would repeat and manipulate the sounds "with a kind of precision that was not exactly precise," explain-ing that each performance was "colored by the vicissitudes of the mecha-nisms [of each machine] and the subjectivity of a particular space and time." This made the recording and playing back of a boom box piece an active musical process, rather than an automatic or passive one, with the finished product yielding "surprising phenomenological results," as well as suggesting "certain philosophical questions."[7] Kline told *Wired* magazine in December 2001 that in his massed boom box performances, "You're constantly moving in and out and around a crowd, so there's a dynamic you can't anticipate," adding: "It's a part of the piece I have no desire to control."[8]

Kline generally begins composing a new piece for his boom boxes by selecting and creating the basic sound sources he plans to use in the new work. Referring to his loops as the plainchant and fugal subjects of his tape-generated music, Kline said that, at first, his goal was to produce pieces that utilized a large number of loops capable of being manipulated in real time. Beginning with a group of boom boxes lined up and playing identical-length endless cassettes, he said he would record and rerecord the same musical material, in the manner of Alvin Lucier's *I Am Sitting In A Room* (1969), until it produced "spiraling waves of phase patterns which gathered room tone and distortion as they accrued."[9] With *Unsilent Night*, the first of his large "orchestral" playback pieces written two years after he began to work with multiple boom boxes, Kline said he created a multichannel master tape from which he then recorded separate strands of the musical material onto a series of individual cassettes. This musical material combined preexisting Christmas hymns, English carols, and Gregorian chants—the traditional music of the holiday season—with the sounds of bells, harps, mallet percussion, and synthesizers that Kline had composed and then recorded onto the master tape. The result of combining and then looping these various sounds in this way creates what the writer Tom Bickley describes as "a mostly tonalist minimalist pitch content … [flowing] gradually from one timbre and texture to the next."[10]

A Living Sound Sculpture

For the first performance of *Unsilent Night* in December 1992, Kline said he got several dozen of his friends together in the spirit of a holiday Christmas party, asked them all to bring their boom boxes along, gave each of them a cassette tape with some individual strand of the music on it, and told them all to push "play" in unison. As this boom box pickup "orchestra"—consisting of both professional and amateur musicians, as well as many of Kline's nonmusical friends—snaked its way through New York's Greenwich Village, home to thousands of New York University students, holiday visitors from various parts of the world, and more than a few down-on-their-luck panhandlers, Kline said the audience for the performance, aside from the participants themselves, became anyone who was standing on the street or just happened to be passing by.

As an experiment, *Unsilent Night* worked beyond anything Kline had ever expected or even imagined. The music spread and filled the air in a way that made it impossible to tell where it was coming from, even if you were standing in the middle of the "orchestra." The sound mass seemed to come alive because of the blurring and oscillating of the music caused by the slight variations of the playback speed of each machine. Kline explained that "a constantly evolving polyphony was created ... as one heard individual machines suddenly coming into focus, then receding back into the overall cloud of sound."[11] During the time he has been working with massed boom boxes, Kline says he has developed a sense of what simple sounds, multiplied by one hundred, might sound like, and that he has begun to use "sliding harmonic movements" so that even street traffic, truck horns, and police sirens will sound as if they are a part of the music, not unlike Eno's ambient music, but on a more physical scale.[12]

As the December performances of *Unsilent Night* continued in New York throughout the 1990s, a ritual emerged of Kline's mobile symphony circling the fountain in Washington Square Park, a village landmark, and then parading to Tompkins Square Park in the East Village, a mile or so away. Over the decade, the number of performers, as well as the onlookers who marched along with them, became larger and larger each year. In recent years, the performance has drawn hundreds of both participants and spectators; in 2003, for instance, the parade "included more than 500 people and 100 boom boxes" according to the *New York Post*.[13] And since *Unsilent Night* is a piece of music that does not require trained musicians for its success—basically, anyone with a boom box can make the band—the range and type of people who participate is infinite. Tom Bickley reported that the crowd in New York for the 2003 performance "included youthful anarchists, art students from nearby NYU, parents with their children and more than one gentleman in a suit and tie."[14] Bickley, a self-confessed veteran of a number of protest marches over the years, says that what he appreciates about the experience Kline offers is "the lack of verbal rhetoric" that, in some unspoken way, provides "a gracious atmosphere of community gathered in pleasure rather than in anger." And calling *Unsilent Night* "an effective witness for inclusion and democratic participation," he observed that, in 2003, at least, "Everyone seemed to be listening!"[15] Eve Beglarian, a New York composer who has participated in a number of Kline's outdoor events, including his late September 2001 tribute walk through lower Manhattan, says that as Kline's music unfolds—"spread out spatially by the walkers, and in time by the vagaries of the individual cassette mechanisms"—it creates "the most beautiful musical public art I know."[16]

Sonic Plasticity

In considering the social and aesthetic implications of Phil Kline's *Unsilent Night,* it might be useful to recall John Cage's suggestion that if people want to reserve the word "music" for the melodic and harmonic sounds composers made during the common practice ("classical") period that extended from Bach to Brahms, they should reserve it, and assign another name to the sounds that enter through the ears today. Just don't make the mistake, he warned, of letting one's definitions get in the way of one's experiences. Now that we are able to look back on the emergence of experimental music with the beginnings of hindsight, Cage's concern for definitions may, as so much of what he said and wrote, prove to be prescient. Because music for Cage *was* changing, and in ways that took it far from the common-practice norm. Furthermore, most of these fundamental changes, first introduced by Cage in the middle third of the twentieth century, have continued and grown more important over the years as succeeding generations of younger composers have come to embrace them.

With today's experimental music, even the most basic of assumptions about what we can expect to hear during a performance, how the sounds may come to be made, what we, as the audience, may be asked to contribute to the process, or even what the social, if not the political, ramifications of the music's "message" may imply, may not be appropriate, or even sufficient, to describe, anticipate, and consider the music that might actually occur. But more important, the traditional analytical tools many of us were taught to employ in the analysis of music may not even apply when dealing with these newer ways of creating and combining sounds. There are entire genres of new experimental music, particularly the interactive kind, that are not written to be played within prescribed blocks of time, or meant for presentation in specially designed halls by experts who have spent years in training, to an attentive audience sitting patiently and expectantly.

As Cage's music continued to change, he began to believe that a new form of musical analysis and criticism was needed to deal more accurately and directly with this new music that he and others had invented, a music in which the rules are still changing and new genres still emerging, with active audience involvement as opposed to passive listening, and featuring the intentional blurring of the traditional composer-performer-listener roles. This music, of which interactive music is a part, requires a new set of observations, new methods of analyses, a new group of definitions, and a new form of understanding from those analytical techniques that helped to explain the traditional music of the past. And although we are only now beginning to develop an historical understanding and appreciation of interactive music (a type of music becoming, if not "normal," at least closer to the "norm") we must start now to allow these new questions to shape the dialogue, and to focus our discussion beyond the key centers, repeating themes, and recognizable sonic architectures that informed classical music. Because if interactive music is to be allowed to make its case, it must do so on its own terms, within its own set of defining parameters, and be judged for its contribution and lasting worth to the milieu it actively creates and sustains, a milieu as far removed from the concert hall, after all, as a classical violin sonata is from group-improvised, street-band, Dixieland jazz.

In the case of *Unsilent Night*, Phil Kline's first artistic decision was to create an open-ended musical structure that would accept the unexpected aspects of chance, yet simultaneously offer a multidimensional, controlled infrastructure capable both of holding the experience together artistically, and of giving the participants—musicians and nonmusicians alike—a successful sense of contribution and accomplishment. In developing this through-composed, democratic, sound environment, Kline's goal was to control the overall sonic shape of the experience but not the moment-to-moment interactions—neither the minute intermingling of sounds between the members of the "orchestra," nor the social connections and interactions between the "orchestra" and the audience on the street. In fact, there are parts of *Unsilent Night* that Kline says he never wants to control—just as Cage said that one of the reasons he turned to chance procedures to write music was because it allowed him to create a palette of materials and a simultaneity of events that would never have occurred to him otherwise.

As for the actual musical material in *Unsilent Night,* beyond what Kline wrote himself, there are the aesthetic considerations concerning his use of preexisting music—the hymns, carols, and chants—which he employs in the manner of John Oswald and Moby, albeit, in Kline's case, the music is wholly in the public domain. Nevertheless, this use of musical appropriation as a compositional technique signifies an aesthetic stance concerning what constitutes appropriate source material, as well as a prevailing attitude about copyright and fair use that is at the heart of the compositional process today, not only in experimental music but in many popular styles as well. With interactive music, the need to identify the composer is less specified and more generalized. And although *Unsilent Night* does not tread very far into this territory, it does broach the question.

For both the listener and the performer, *Unsilent Night* is outdoor ambient music, echoing against the buildings, and altering and transforming the landscape as it passes by. The environment it creates is not so much a ghetto-blasting invasion of space as it is a moving cloud of sound, with the ability to float, linger, and establish pockets of sonic energy and focus—a sound, in other words, that feels alive. And in a sense, it is alive, because of the people who physically move it around, creating, as they go, a soundscape that from place to place, and from year to year, always seems familiar, yet never sounds quite the same. The end result is a constantly changing sonic perspective that, ultimately, is not dependent on whether one moves in and out of the crowd, or simply stands still as the music moves along.

And just as there is no one perfect place to be situated within the "orchestra" when performing *Unsilent Night,* there is no one optimum location from which to experience it. The music appears to be everywhere, it comes and goes, the sounds not dependent on location for their enjoyment. Instead, the music shifts and turns and snakes through the crowd, focusing on first one group of boom boxes locked briefly into sync before moving on to another, as it hovers in the air and slowly floats by. As Kline points out, these clouds of sound are a living example of the German electronic music composer Karlheinz Stockhausen's forty-year-old unrealized concept of sonic plasticity, containing within them, as they do, the ability to move about physically in space. (Stockhausen, one of the founders of the electronic music movement in Europe in the 1950s, used the term "sonic plasticity" to refer to the ability to move sound around during an actual performance by physically moving the loud speakers, thus creating a plyable sound environment.) And throughout it all, the music crosses aesthetic boundaries at every turn—from classical to ambient to electronica—whereas the unanswered questions of "Who is the audience?" and "Who are the players?" hover in the air.

Ultimately, of course, the success or failure of interactive art in general, and *Unsilent Night* in particular, is dependent on the people involved: the audience of willing participants, as well as the casual users of the street who may just be passing by and decide to become involved. This willingness of people, musicians and nonmusicians alike, to agree to come together in community and participate in an art project—to offer their full-body involvement in the art work, as it were—is central to the success of interactive art. Equally important for its success is the ability, built in by the composer, for this group of participants to feel good about their contribution in a nonhierarchical, nonjudgmental way. There is, after all, no ascending scale of performing ability with a boom box, and no one person's "technique" at playing it is better than that of anyone else.

In *Unsilent Night*, there is no star of the show; everyone is a part of a larger whole, playing a role in an "orchestra" in which all are simultaneously a leader and a member of the team. This, in turn, builds a sense of community, both musical and otherwise, seldom found in traditional Western music. The overall sonic and social experience this creates—an experience unavailable in the concert hall—is a result of the combination of the immediacy of the street, the blurring of the line between listener and performer, and the changing perspective that, as Kline describes it, offers "a paradigm of listener experience, attention and focus in which participants could wonder (as they wandered) what (and where) the piece was and what it sounded like even as they were listening." Kline speculates about whether it was "the central information on the individual tapes, the hectic counterpoint one heard when walking in a small group of players, or the great rounded buzz one felt from the periphery" that constituted the core of the piece?[17] There are, of course, no definitive answers to these questions, or, to be more precise, there are as many answers as there are participants because of the multifocused, multidimensional aspects of the work.

Ironically, Phil Kline's success with outdoor events has brought him invitations to perform indoors in some of the best concert halls and art galleries in New York City, including Alice Tully Hall at Lincoln Center and the Whitney Museum of American Art. And as much as it is possible to capture the sound of a moving sound sculpture, a recording of *Unsilent Night* was released in 2001, containing sections of the performance with such titles as "The Crossing," "The Milky Way," and "Angels of Avenue A."[18] There is also talk of upcoming performances of *Unsilent Night* in England next season and at the Winter Olympics in Torino, Italy, in 2006. Kline, drawing on a literary analogy to explain it, says achieving this level of success brings to mind "the notion of the boom box as a Trojan Horse." And characterizing the boom box as "a cultural crossover messenger working both sides of the street," he exclaims, "ghetto-blasting indeed!"[19]

3
THE *BRAIN OPERA*:
A CASE STUDY IN SPACE

The idea that there is a mutual advantage to be gained through the marriage of art and technology is not new. It dates back at least to the Renaissance, where it was thought that science and art were two of the pillars that established the enlightened mind, if not to the ancient Greeks and the scientist-artist-philosopher model of humanity that developed there. In the twentieth century, however, these two modes of thought became mutually suspicious of each other; some educational theorists even went so far as to suggest that these two approaches resided in different sides of our brain. But with the emergence of the avant-garde in the 1960s, the idea that it might be advantageous to recombine science and the arts was given a significant boost by two American scientists: Max Mathews at Bell Labs in New Jersey, who gave many early computer music composers access to the emerging digital technology being developed there, and Billy Kluver in New York, who, along with fellow scientist, Fred Waldhauer, and artists Robert Rauschenberg and Bob Whitman, founded E.A.T. in 1967.

E.A.T., or Experiments in Art and Technology—an outgrowth of the "Nine Evenings: Theater and Engineering" series of performances organized by Kluver and Rauschenberg at the 69th Regiment Armory in New York in 1966—was established as a nonprofit organization with the goal of bringing artists and scientists together in the service of art. Kluver, a physicist and electrical engineer who had been uniting art and science since 1960 (when he assisted the Swiss sculptor, Jean Tinguely, to design his self-destructing machine, *Homage to New York,* which, when turned on, proceeded to take itself apart in the sculpture garden of the Museum of Modern Art), has, in the intervening years, offered scientific expertise and technical assistance to a great number of artists and musicians including Jasper Johns, Andy Warhol, and John Cage. Although E.A.T. represents one of the first instances in mid-twentieth-century America in which artists and scientists were brought together formally for artistic purposes, it did not prove to be the last time that such formal connections occurred. In fact, E.A.T. set the standard for many such partnerships that were still to come.

Since the 1960s, there have been any number of centers established throughout the world where artists and scientists are brought together and their collaborations aesthetically encouraged and financially supported. Places of particular significance to experimental musicians include the Institut de Recherche et Coordination Acoustique/Musique (IRCAM) in Paris, designed and run by French composer and conductor Pierre Boulez, and the Media Lab of the Massachusetts Institute of Technology in Cambridge, the home institution of American composer Tod Machover. It was at the Media Lab—where Machover has worked since 1985—that, for several years during the mid-1990s, the full resources of this artist/ scientist confluence were turned toward developing and implementing Machover's multimedia opera of the mind, the *Brain Opera,* a walk-in, interactive model of the musical brain.

From the time of his childhood growing up in Mount Vernon, New York, Tod Machover (b. 1953) has maintained dual interests in both music and technology, thanks in part to his mother, who taught piano and was interested in musical pedagogy, and to his father, who was a computer scientist and an early expert in the field of computer graphics. A cellist as well as a composer, Machover studied composition at the Juilliard School with Elliott Carter and Roger Sessions from 1973 to 1978, receiving both bachelor's and master's degrees, and even beginning the doctoral program in composition. Machover put his studies at Juilliard behind him in 1978 and accepted an invitation to go to Paris as the Director of Musical Research at IRCAM, a position he held for seven years until he left to go to the M.I.T. Media Lab. Machover told Frank Oteri, editor of the American Music Center's *NewMusicBox* online magazine, that, in addition to his lifelong interest in music and technology, he went to IRCAM because he was also "fascinated by Pierre Boulez's music and the whole European avant-garde tradition." In 1981, while still at IRCAM, Machover composed *Fusione Fugace,* one of the first pieces of music designed for live performance on a real-time digital synthesizer. As Machover described the piece, the specially designed keyboards, buttons, and slider boxes he created "allowed three interconnected performers to control all aspects of a complex evolving timbre."[1]

Machover left IRCAM in 1985 and began working at the M.I.T. Media Lab, where he is currently Professor of Music and Media, as well as the head of the lab's Opera of the Future group. Once at the Media Lab, Machover said he "became interested in adding 'intelligence' to the computers sitting between [the] performance controllers and [the] MIDI sound output devices." By 1986, he and his team at the lab were beginning to develop what they called "hyperinstruments," which they defined as computer-connected "interactive instruments that gave performers enhanced expressive capabilities." Machover first used these new instruments in his 1987 opera *Valis*—commissioned for the tenth anniversary of the Centre Pompidou, the Paris home of IRCAM—in which hyperkeyboard and hyperpercussion instruments allowed two performers "to shape and control a whole evening's worth of complex electronic sound."[2]

A second stage of hyperinstrument development began in 1991, when Machover and his team began creating "intelligent" hyperinstruments for such well-known musicians as Prince and Yo-Yo Ma. The hypercello he created for Yo-Yo Ma had complex physical sensors attached to both the cello and the performer that allowed each extended performance to be shaped differently by measuring the nuances of performance expression and then using this information to expand the instrument's capabilities. Machover said that, paradoxically, as the hyperinstruments became more virtuosic, he began to see ways to adapt them so that they could be played by amateur musicians and even by children. This, he said, led him to think about building an entire orchestra of hyperinstruments for the general public, and that, in turn, led him to create the *Brain Opera.*

Basically, the *Brain Opera* is a three-part work that features a new generation of hyperinstruments. Using these instruments, Machover is able to incorporate the musical contributions of both live and online audiences into the piece. The three parts of the *Brain Opera* include:

1. The Mind Forest, described by Machover as "a complex space filled with hands-on experiences that turn body gesture and voice input into music ... and images"[3]
2. The *Brain Opera* performance itself, where three trained performers using specially designed hyperinstruments called Sensor Chair, Rhythm Tree, and Digital Baton create a fifty-minute uninterrupted three-movement concert presentation combining musical material written by Machover with material previously created by the audience in the Mind Forest
3. Net Music, that, in the third movement of the piece, brings in material contributed by people on the Web through an online instrument called the Palette, which is activated for each performance

During the development of the *Brain Opera* in the mid-1990s, Machover said that his highest priority was "to create musical experiences and environments that open doors of expression and creation to anyone, anywhere, anytime." He added that this type of "active music" could become "one of our most powerful tools for discovering the unity and coherence that underlies the chaos and complexity of everyday life."[4]

The Mind Forest

A complete performance of the tripartite *Brain Opera* begins in the lobby of the theater, or more likely, a large open space or room close by where Machover and his team can assemble a maze of hyperinstruments with names like the Singing and Speaking Trees, the Rhythm Tree, Harmonic Driving, the Melody Easel, and the Gesture Wall. The space itself was designed by architect Ray Kinoshita, a member of the *Brain Opera* team, and Machover says it is intended to give the impression of walking into a giant musical brain. The purpose of designing and deploying all of these instruments was to involve the audience in "contributing to, performing, and helping to create the piece itself," by giving them a hands-on interactive experience with the various individual parameters of music, that is, melody, rhythm, harmony, and so on.[5]

The Singing Trees create a sonic accompaniment, or aura of sound, around sung pitches, measuring the purity and calmness of the sound and responding in kind. The Speaking Trees do the same for spoken words, whereas the Melody Easel allows users to draw melodic shapes and fragments with their fingers. These melodies, which are taken from the core melodic fragments Machover composed for the *Brain Opera*, change timbre, articulation, and embellishment at the slightest touch of the hand. The Rhythm Tree, consisting of 320 touch-sensitive pads and accommodating up to 50 players at any one time, contains both percussion sounds and spoken voice samples, allowing users to create combinations of word chains and rhythms. The instrument also allows Machover to measure the collective behavior of its users. The Harmonic Driving hyperinstrument, by contrast, is much like a video game, complete with a steering wheel, joy stick, and foot pedal, with harmony, structure, articulation, and visuals all controlled by the steering and tilting of the mechanism. And the Gesture Wall, containing sensors attuned to every movement of the user, allows audience members to control musical timbre and engage in "word painting" with some of the core fragments of the text of the opera. Machover's goal with all of the Mind Forest experiences was not just to let people contribute sounds to the *Brain Opera* but also to cause them to reflect on the deeper meaning and greater significance of these experiences.

In all, the Mind Forest contains some forty of these new interactive musical hyperinstruments, all designed and arranged in ways that encourage participation by highlighting their user-friendliness and disguising their high-tech, space-age internal characteristics. The ultimate function of all of these hyperinstruments is to give each person in the audience the ability to sculpt their own individual musical experiences in a way that is, at once, both personal and collective. At the first series of performances, which took place between July 23 and August 3, 1996, at the Lincoln Center Festival in New York, eight performances a day were given, with as many as 175 audience members able to participate each time. May Lee, writing for *CNN Interactive*, called the Mind Forest a "high-tech musical wonderland," and referred to its creator, Machover, as "part Einstein, part Beethoven, part Bill Gates."[6]

The *Brain Opera* Performance

If the experience in the Mind Forest is individual and fragmentary, with each person able to create their own path of unique sounds as they move through the maze, the actual concert performance portion of the opera is an attempt at integration, or as Machover says, "an attempt to create a new kind of balance between the ordered complexity of Bach and the exuberant chaos of Cage, with a touch of The Beatles ... thrown into the mix."[7] Once inside the concert space, multiple projections fill the walls, floor, and ceiling, while three performers, one of whom is Machover, combine the raw materials previously created by the audience in the Mind Forest (and saved as sound samples on computer) with musical material that Machover wrote ahead of time. The instruments they perform with—the Sensor Chair, Rhythm Tree, and Digital Baton—are all hyper-instruments that, through a complex array of sensors, take detailed, subtle readings of body positions and motions, and apply this information to the database of sound samples in the central computer.

Machover tried to create a structure with the *Brain Opera* that would let each member of the audience "play with the individual elements of the music, get to know them, add to them, and then see the fragments fit together like a giant puzzle."[8] The overall musical shape of the piece is based on a reworking of the six-part "Ricercare" from Bach's *Musical Offering*. And although the three movements of the *Brain Opera* are performed without pause, they each exhibit unique characteristics that clearly distinguish them from each other. The first movement is the most improvisatory and free-form of the three, focusing on and incorporating many of the sound samples created by the live audience—sounds that can change significantly from performance to performance. Moving in the general direction of words to sounds to music, Machover's overall plan takes the movement from free association of sounds to the sounds of a more structured environment, and from the sounds of everyday life to that of transformed experience.

At the conceptual heart of this first movement is the "text" for the opera (libretto is not the right word), created by Machover from his many discussions with Marvin Minsky. Minsky is an M.I.T. professor and pioneer in the field of artificial intelligence, as well as a friend of Machover's since his Juilliard days of the 1970s. Best known for his book *The Society of Mind*—which models the activity of the human brain as an orchestra of free agents and unconnected mental processes operating without a centralized conductor—Minsky is known for asking questions that appear "so basic that they seem naïve, yet so perceptive that no one has yet answered them," questions such as "Why do we like music?" and "Why does music make us feel?"[9]

Machover conducted a series of interviews with Minsky between 1993 and 1996, and used short statements from them—rather than a traditional story with a plot, or even a linear narrative—to create his nonnarrative text for the *Brain Opera*. A few of these individual statements include "The mind is too complicated to summarize.... Each emotion is just a kind of thinking.... You never do anything in just one way."[10] Machover designed the *Brain Opera* to cause the audience to consider such questions, and, hopefully, to look further into the music and reflect on how independent fragments of sound can form layers that, in turn, coalesce into complex yet unified musical images. On a larger scale, this integration of diverse sonic sources is an attempt "to present an exploration of how our minds turn fragmented experience into coherent views of the world."[11]

The second movement of the *Brain Opera* employs very few of the audience-created samples. Instead, it consists of melodies and sometimes text (both spoken and sung) from the core pitch and text fragments users were given to play with in the Mind Forest. The music in this section is, therefore, completely composed, although there is a lot of room for interpretation because of the nature of the hyperinstruments the three performers use. The general musical shape of this movement is as one continuous arc, growing faster and faster to the end.

Net Music

The third movement of the *Brain Opera* brings in players from home on the Internet and allows them to "solo" in an improvisation they control collectively by their manipulation of the Palette, a Web instrument originally developed in the Media Lab by graduate student John Yu as a part of his master's thesis. Essentially, the Palette, which is activated only during a live performance of the *Brain Opera,* is a multiuser, Java-based musical hyperinstrument that allows users to manipulate three intuitive musical qualities that Machover labels Energy, Coherence, and Style. These words appear on the 3-D interface of the Palette, and by sliding one or more of them up or down in the nature of a three-channel mixer, the user is able to send real-time musical information to the *Brain Opera's* centralized computer system, where it is translated into MIDI sounds and added to the live performance mix. During the performance of this movement, Machover and the other two live performers have the ability to focus on the contributions of one Internet performer, combine them into groups, or include them all, as well as the ability, through their own hyperinstruments, to send back information that will allow the sounds of the individual Palettes to "follow the changes in the live music."[12]

Technically, the Palette consists of a set of Java applets that makes available a Web-based version of a hyperinstrument. These applets, which were designed by members of the *Brain Opera* team, have names such as Sound Memory, Cyber-Metal, Groove Net, Web Choir, and Minsky Text Games. And although the multiuser Palette hyperinstrument is available online only during an actual *Brain Opera* performance, a single-user version, or practice Palette, is always online. This practice version of the instrument allows users to listen to and remix a previous *Brain Opera* performance, including a composite of that performance's Internet contributions.

As the third movement of the *Brain Opera* performance draws to a close, Machover creates a grand finale by bringing all of the various elements of the opera back together again: the contributions that the live audience created in the Mind Forest; the sounds coming from the online contributors; the music that Machover composed; the text fragments that he developed with Minsky; and the real-time manipulations by the three live hyperinstrument performers. At the end, Machover even rolls out a Sensing Carpet hyperinstrument (complete with Doppler Radar sensors) to add yet another strand of sound to the mix, and encourages the live audience to move about in what Richard Dyer of the *Boston Globe* characterized as a "cosmic dance."[13] Machover called the overall result a "surprising synthesis and collaboration of forces."[14]

For a composer who began his musical life admiring the formal complexity and rigid serial control exhibited in the music of Pierre Boulez, there certainly seems to be a lot of Cage-inspired chance scattered throughout the *Brain Opera*. Machover told Frank Oteri in 1999 that when he first went to Paris in 1978 to work at IRCAM he had little interest in the music of John Cage, or the experimental tradition he represented. However, the longer he stayed in France, the more he came to value those unique aspects of American music and the more he came to love the music of Cage, as well as Charles Ives. And although Machover is quick to point out that there is a significant difference between Cage's philosophy of music and his own, he acknowledges that "Cage has been the biggest inspiration" for his public-oriented, interactive works.

As for including this amount of freedom in the *Brain Opera*, however, Machover noted that it was, for him, "an extreme case" of allowing the public to help shape and manipulate the final result.[15] As it finally transpired, Machover estimates that he wrote about 60 percent of the music for the *Brain Opera*, and left about 40 percent of the sounds to chance. More important to him, however, is the changing mix of precomposed and chance-derived elements that occur from section to section; he notes that "there are at least twenty different models ... of how pre-existing music and audience/performer modification can be combined." Machover's team employed such a large number of mixing combinations in developing the *Brain Opera* because each model had a different musical feel to it and, combined, they created a real sense of progression and continuity.

The House of Music

By the time it was completed in 1996, the *Brain Opera* had involved a team of more than fifty artists and scientists from the M.I.T. Media Lab, and, according to Richard Dyer of the *Boston Globe*, cost over $3 million.[16] In addition to Machover, the composer and project director, the Web documentation lists fifty-seven additional contributors, some with job descriptions such as Electronics Fabrication, Software Director, and Digital Baton Hardware Design. On the completion of its initial run at the Lincoln Center Festival, the *Brain Opera* undertook a two-year tour with performances at the Ars Electronica Festival in Linz, Austria, the Electronic Cafe International in Copenhagen, the NexOpera Festival in Tokyo, the Festival Acarte in Lisbon, and the Kravis Center in West

Palm Beach. In 2000, it was permanently installed in the House of Music in Vienna. Located in the historic Archduke Karl Palace, the House of Music is five stories of "interactive musical adventure" combining, according to Marcy Mason of the *Chicago Tribune,* "the classics with the future of music in a techno-modern setting."[17]

For the opening in Vienna, Machover and his team added a new feature to the work that he called the Future Music Blender, an instrument that "allows visitors to choose and blend their favorite music into *Brain Opera* music, using a specially designed Sensor Chair to steer and shape the ongoing, collective music composition."[18] For this permanent installation, the Future Music Blender is, in a sense, a substitute for the *Brain Opera* performance. Even from his first dreams of the *Brain Opera,* Machover imagined it as a "never-ending, always-changing stream of music" that would then be "added-to and shaped by [future] audiences," a function, he pointed out, that was served originally by the *Brain Opera* performances and the three hyperinstrument performers who manipulated and guided the final mix. And whereas his dream of an "ongoing, participatory music" that exists without performers, and is "created and extended by anybody and everybody" was not possible for a touring production, it could be achieved when the *Brain Opera* reached its permanent home.

In the House of Music, after experiencing the "complex, multi-layered, festive atmosphere" of the Mind Forest, visitors move to the "more concentrated, calm, continuous, and unified" atmosphere of the Future Music Blender located in a separate room some fifty-five meters square.[20] Once inside the Future Music Blender, visitors first listen to a selection of music and sounds contained in an onsite music/sound database—sounds that they have just made, others from Machover's composed samples, and some contributed by Internet users (when the site is active)—choosing those they like by selecting small physical objects containing passive ID tags linked to them. By tossing these ID-tagged objects into the "blender," the audiences, as they come and go, continually remix, or blend, the ongoing music, through specially designed "blender" software "capable of parametrically defining a musical composition, adding to it, and altering it in various ways."[19] But whereas a group of twenty or more people may be in the room together, only one visitor at a time is able to sit in the center of the room, on a raised platform, commanding the newly designed Sensor Chair, and steering the music of the *Brain Opera* into the future.

This individual and personal shaping of the music is made possible by the Sensor Chair interface, which combines precise measurement with freedom of movement. Designed by the Media Lab team just after they had created the hypercello for Yo-Yo Ma, the Sensor Chair was originally created for magicians Penn & Teller. The chair works by measuring the subtle upper body movements of the user, analyzing expressive gestures from the precise hand and body movements that it can sense, and translating these movements into sound. In the Sensor Chair that is installed in Vienna, three foot switches on the chair platform allow the user to select a Mixing, Soloing, or Steering mode of performance. In the Mixing mode, the music is generated internally by the Blender's computer while the person sitting in the chair is able to alter the sound quality and sound processing, articulation, and balance. In Soloing mode, the automatic music ends and each individual gesture of the user produces one individual sound. When in Steering mode, the player takes control of all of the Blender's parameters and, literally, steers the music through a musical landscape of their own imagination and invention.

Interactive Space

For all its high-tech gadgetry and range of individualized experiences, the *Brain Opera* is a work of art firmly and permanently rooted in time and place. To experience it, a listener must join with other members of an audience in physically attending a performance that always begins at a certain hour and lasts for a specified amount of time. This was true for the Lincoln Center Festival premiere in 1996 as well as for the performances that took place during the subsequent two years that it toured the world, and especially today, now that the *Brain Opera* is installed in its permanent home in the House of Music in Vienna. One must always go *to* the *Brain Opera;* it does not come to you. In this regard, little has changed since the time of Mozart and Beethoven, whose music was heard in Vienna under similar circumstances some two hundred years ago. But although the *Brain Opera* is designed for an attending audience—general and nonspecialized though it is—it is not intended for the passive audiences of Classical and Romantic music of either that time or today. In fact, the opera begins as soon as visitors step into the lobby and are confronted by a whole host of Mind Forest hyperinstruments with which they are expected to interact. Experiencing the *Brain Opera* is more comparable to the interactive, experiential, and somewhat blurred audience/performer model of Phil Kline's *Unsilent Night,* but to an even greater extent than Kline's work was ever designed to be.

To fully experience and appreciate the *Brain Opera,* audience members must not only present themselves at a specified time and place, but they also must become an active part of the piece itself, developing, if you will, a physical and tactile relationship with the hyperinstruments, and through their use, making pitch and rhythmic contributions to the basic musical content, an action that, in turn, affects the overall shaping of the work itself. In essence, visitors are expected to turn their own body gestures and vocal sounds into musical material. It is these many hands-on experiences taking place in the Mind Forest that ties the work together, both formally and artistically, in the minds of many people, because they can see, over time, how this material is incorporated and finally comes to fit together.

To Machover's credit, the hyperinstruments he and his team have developed are not high-tech toys and games but sensitive, sophisticated musical instruments that encourage even audience members with little or no musical training to interact with them, and that respond directly and subtly to being touched, sung to, and manipulated in ways that reinforce this hand/eye/music symbiotic relationship. And although Machover composed some of the sounds that occur in the Mind Forest, these sounds are not pieces of music but, rather, core melodic and rhythmic fragments that are to be altered by the audience before being incorporated into the piece. Machover noted in 1999 that he could envision an entirely new generation of hyperinstruments that would help to take the "focus off physical virtuosity and the ... athleticism of learning to play an instrument"—an activity normally requiring great amounts of time and effort—and put it, as much as possible, directly onto "the mental and emotional activities of music." He suggested that if this happened, "not only would the general level of musical creativity go up, but you'd have a much more aware, educated, sensitive, listening, and participatory public."[20] The hyperinstruments of the Mind Forest are a significant step toward this goal, opening, as they do, doors of expression and creation for users of all abilities.

Some years earlier, Machover described the experience he was aiming to engender in visitors to the *Brain Opera* as "the voyage of each audience member through the maze of fragments, thoughts and memories, to collective and coherent experience."[21] Ultimately, this experience—despite all of its group-oriented activities centered in the performance component of the work—strives from the beginning to be a personalized physical activity, offering a solo path through a forest of interactive instruments that, if they don't think, at least respond in thoughtful and intelligent ways, and yielding, as Machover intended, a hands-on experience with the parameters of music and, metaphorically at least, a walk-in interactive model of the musical brain. Furthermore, this musical walk-through of touching the instruments and, by doing so, creating musical moments that are incorporated into a greater whole some minutes later, has the effect of blurring the distinctions between composer and performer, as well as between physical navigation and artistic content. And although there is a high degree of chance and unpredictability within the tightly controlled structure of the *Brain Opera*, Machover's goal—to encourage as much unity and coherence as possible to emerge from beneath the multiple layers of complexity and chaos with which the work begins—is a goal not unlike what Phil Kline aimed to achieve in *Unsilent Night*.

If the Mind Forest is Machover's attempt to allow the audience to play physically with individual elements of music, and by doing so become familiar enough with them to feel comfortable making a gestural/musical contribution of their own, the *Brain Opera* performance is an attempt to integrate and synthesize these fragmentary experiences and sounds into a giant, coherent, musical mosaic, one that Machover hopes will cause audiences to think about order and disorder in both music and life. Moving from words to sounds to music as the first movement does, and from the sounds of everyday life to those of transformed experience as the complete fifty-minute performance is structured to accomplish, Machover, as the performance progresses, begins to combine into the music his own written material with the contributions previously created by the audience, and reduces the amount of audience control from approximately 175 separate

inputs down to three experienced hyperinstrument performers—profes-
sional musicians—who are responsible for manipulating and guiding the
final mix of *Brain Opera* performance sounds. Furthermore, if *Unsilent
Night* is low tech and localized in its performance ambitions, the *Brain
Opera* is high tech and more universally oriented, particularly when the
Web component of the performance is introduced. Not only does the Net
Music section of the *Brain Opera* represent a linking of real with virtual
spaces, but the physical contributions made to the performance by the
audience's trip through the hyperinstruments in the performance space is
echoed in the individual use of the Palette over the Web by each listener
contributing from home.

Once the *Brain Opera* was installed in Vienna, and the Future Music
Blender replaced the concert performance and the trio of hyperinstrument
virtuosi who controlled it, the music of the opera became the ongoing,
always changing, participatory experience that Machover had originally
envisioned. Although the audience is still given some degree of input and
control through the contributions that come in over the Internet, the
experiences in the Mind Forest, and the audience's individual decisions
regarding music to put into the "blender," the real control of the sounds of
the opera shifts from the many to the few to the one: the audience member who, at any particular moment, is sitting in the Sensor Chair. If Kline,
in *Unsilent Night,* uses his performers as agents, or carriers (in both a
physical and a metaphysical sense), for the regeneration and evolution of
his music—music that is dependent on his agents but whose components
are not chosen by them—as they physically carry his sounds from one
location to another, Machover, through the Sensor Chair, allows the
actual body of his individual users to become a human joy stick, or whole-
body controller, making physical decisions that affect the actual sound and
formal shape of the music. From the many voices that are given artistic
input at the beginning of the *Brain Opera,* to the three professional hyperinstrument players controlling it during the actual performance, the continuing development of the music focuses on the individual control of one
person, sitting in the Sensor Chair in Vienna, driving the *Brain Opera*
through the living and evolving database of sounds, into the uncharted
and unknowable sound world of the future.

4
MUSIC ON THE WEB IN THE TWENTIETH CENTURY

Today, most people take their personal computers for granted. Loaded with memory and operating at near warp speed, the average PC of the early twenty-first century can now send and receive everything from color photographs and live music to book-length manuscripts and feature-length films. The only question that concerns most of us is not whether a file is too big to send but, rather, how long it might take to download it. And with the continued development and expansion of cable modems, broadband, and Internet2, combined with the exponential increases expected in the operating power of future generations of PCs, speed, storage space, and general ease of use are only expected to grow greater in the years to come.

A quarter century ago, by contrast, when personal computers first entered the consumer market, this was not the case. Then, PCs were small and slow, with little in the way of power or memory to recommend them. Requiring a hobbyist's enthusiasm and tenacity to operate successfully, these early PCs were anything but the user-friendly models of today; *coaxing, tinkering,* and *nurturing* are operative words that come to mind. And certainly, these PCs of the late 1970s were no match, musically, for the large mainframe computers that many university composers had access to and used to create their sounds. So in some ways, it is surprising that experimental composers embraced the new small, inefficient PCs so quickly, writing musical algorithms for them to play, and performing with them live, almost from the start.

Nowhere was this trend toward creating music with the PC more active and lively than with the experimental composers of the San Francisco Bay Area. Living in close proximity to what soon would be called Silicon Valley, and operating inside an artistic climate that encouraged experimentation—not only in new classical music but in rock and jazz as well—these Bay Area composers worked with some of the first commercially available PCs. Two related groups of these musicians—first formed as The League of Automatic Music Composers (1978–1983), and then reformed (with some of the same personnel) as The Hub (1986–1997)— became "the world's first computer network bands," exploring, as they did, "the unique potentials of computer networks as a medium for musical composition and performance."[1]

The League of Automatic Music Composers (1977)

At a time when most academic computer-music composers were working in relative isolation from each other on university mainframes, striving, as they were, toward rhythmic and timbral complexity, and seldom, if ever, considering the possibility of performing live, The League of Automatic Music Composers not only played their computers in concert, but they hooked them together and played interactively, allowing the musical algorithms written for one computer to interact with and influence the output of other computers real time, during an actual performance. Strictly noncommercial, and coming from a variety of experimental backgrounds, these Bay Area composers maintained an aesthetic centering on "compositions that changed with each performance, textures that emphasized a simultaneous multiplicity of voices, and a practice based on collaborative, communal or group-oriented activities." And with a defiant do-it-yourself attitude, evoking the experimental spirit of earlier West Coast composers Lou Harrison, and Harry Partch, The League of Automatic Music Composers began a process that stretched the boundaries of interactive, networked computer music all the way to the Web.

The earliest commercial PCs, known then as microcomputers, were little more than a single circuit board about the size of a sheet of paper, with a keypad for entering data and a connection to an external audiocassette player that was used for storage. The microcomputer of choice among the Bay Area composers was the KIM-1, released in 1976. Originally priced at $245, the KIM-1 was created by MOS Technology (acquired by Commodore in 1976), and was a forerunner of the Commodore 64 (1982) and later the Amiga 1000 (1985). Unlike today's PCs, with their vast amounts of memory and storage capacities, the KIM-1 had an eight-bit microprocessor with one kilobyte of RAM (1 K), running at one megahertz (1 Mhz). Because there were no programs commercially available to run on the KIM, composers had to write their own, in this case in 6502 machine language, entering them into memory through the hexadecimal keypad, and saving them on audiocassette. (Saving programs on paper tape was also an option.) Because of the relatively slow speed (1 Mhz) and data width (8 bits) of the KIM, high-quality sound generation—which requires high bandwidth and lots of memory—was not a possibility.[2]

Nevertheless, in 1977, and within a year of the initial release of the KIM-1, Bay Area composers Jim Horton and Rich Gold linked their KIMs together and gave a networked performance at Mills College in Oakland. Early the following year, John Bischoff and Horton began working collaboratively on a computer-to-computer linkage that Bischoff remembers always took "hours to develop and debug" before they could even begin to think about creating music. Later, during the spring of 1978, Horton, Bischoff, and Gold performed as a networked trio at an artist-run space in Berkeley known as the Blind Lemon, and in November of that year, they were joined by composer David Behrman, newly arrived from the East Coast, in a "Micro-Computer Network Band" performance, again at the Blind Lemon. Somewhere along the way, this loose collection of musicians with a common interest in networked computer music became known as The League of Automatic Music Composers, a name Bischoff says referred partly "to the historical League of Composers started by Aaron Copland and others in the 1920s," and partly to acknowledge "the artificial intelligence aspect" of their performances, because they considered "half the band as 'human' (the composers) and half 'artificial' (the computers)."[3]

In describing the music that was produced through this man-and-machine convergence, Bischoff says that The League didn't actually write individual compositions but, rather, created entire concerts of music;

concerts without titles that the composers thought of as "public occasions for shared listening." In fact, in the earliest performances of The League, the composers allowed the networked computers to run on their own, trading algorithms unattended, whereas the composers themselves became members of the audience. But before long, the desire to tweak the performance became too compelling and the composers began sitting around the equipment table, performing with the network, adjusting various parameters on the fly, according to Bischoff, "in an attempt to nudge the music this way or that."

The Hub (1986)

The League of Automatic Music Composers disbanded in 1983, partly as a result of the continuing health problems of Jim Horton, the person around whom the group had originally gravitated. But various former members continued to explore the possibilities of live networked performances. One enduring problem The League had encountered was that every time they rehearsed or performed there were "a complicated set of ad-hoc connections between computers that had to be made." Not only time consuming, these early computer-to-computer connections were fickle, and prone to failure, making it difficult to invite outside musicians to perform inside the network. But for a concert at the 1986 Network Muse Festival, John Bischoff and Tim Perkis (also a former member of The League) networked their two computers through a third computer that they dedicated to using as a mailbox, and through which they could then communicate and post data (musical algorithms), making each composer's individual algorithms always accessible to the other player, and serving as a common memory for the group. Bischoff and Perkis called their performance "The Hub," and said this concert was the beginning of the band of the same name.

About the same time that The Hub was forming in the Bay Area, New York composers and producers Phill Niblock and Nic Collins began discussing the possibility of linking their two venues in a simultaneous concert. This idea of performing in two spaces at once, linked by a modem, was Collins's idea. Collins, then programming a concert series at The Clocktower in downtown Manhattan, said he approached Niblock, whose Experimental Intermedia Foundation was located only a few blocks away, to coproduce the event; together, they invited The Hub to create a performance that would link their two venues.[4] Because of this invitation, The Hub quickly solidified into a group of six—John Bischoff, Tim Perkis, Mark Trayle, Chris Brown, Scot Gresham-Lancaster, and Phil Stone—and began working together as a band. For the New York performance, which took place over two warm spring nights on June 6 and 7, 1987, so that the audience could have the opportunity to visit both spaces, The Hub decided that they would perform as two trios, each with its own distinctive sound. Bischoff, Perkis, and Trayle—who had performed in the Bay Area as a trio called Zero Chat Chat—performed at EIF, while the other three composers formed the trio that played at The Clocktower.

Each trio had an identical computer-driven hub, newly built for the occasion. These hubs could communicate with each other automatically, using a modem and a phone line. The computer used to create these second-generation hubs was the SYM-1 by Synertek. The SYM-1 contained the same 6502 processor as the KIM, but had 2 K of RAM, as well as a 6850 ACIA (asynchronous communications interface) chip for serial communication. And whereas these twin hubs were capable of communicating with each other at a rate of up to 9600 baud, most modems could only support a rate of 1200 baud, so that was the rate used for the New York performance. But even that was a relatively fast speed, considering that the original first-generation hub had communicated at a rate of 300 baud.

During each of the two New York concerts, The Hub played three networked pieces that used "the modem network to create the acoustically divorced, but informationally joined sextet," and three other pieces that were independently performed in each location, and that could "take full advantage of the improvisational predilections and local interactivity of each ensemble." Kyle Gann of the *Village Voice*, who heard the concert in both venues, said "the oblique correspondence of identical pieces" played between the two spaces over two nights made for a somewhat "peculiar" experience, particularly because "the two audiences did not hear the same sounds." Although each group fed information to the other one, the basic musical materials were different in the two spaces, and the end result was noticeably different, creating what Gann described as a "sonic conceptual butterfly: same body, wildly different wings." Gann thought that, for the listener, the real interest and excitement lay in the reemergence of music as process, and in the giving up of individual control in favor of group decisions, the result becoming "a sonic entity larger then the sum of its members ideas," in effect, a music with a life of its own.[5]

The success of the two New York performances was the beginning of a decade-long career for The Hub. During the early 1990s, the band undertook a series of national and international tours, including concerts in the Hague, Eindhoven, Brussels, Ghent, and Berlin. They networked their computers through a new MIDI-based hub, and, at times, collaborated with acoustic musicians, using pitch and amplitude trackers to collect data from the acoustic performers that was then distributed to the members of The Hub to manipulate. These musicians included the saxophonist Larry Ochs, the violinist Nathan Rubin, and the pianist/composer Alvin Curran, whose performance of his *Electric Rags III* created data for The Hub's composers to use in various ways as they improvised along. During this time, The Hub also released their second CD, *Wreckin' Ball*, in 1994; their first, simply titled *The Hub*, had been released five years earlier in 1989.[6]

In 1997, The Hub was in residence at the Georgia Center for Advanced Telecommunications Technology, a state-of-the-art, high-tech concert hall with Ethernet connections at every seat, located on the Georgia Tech campus in Atlanta. Chris Brown said that for their performance in this space "a special on-stage hub Web server funneled audience preferences about the on-going music to the group, while a video projector displayed a score, indicating progress through the piece."[7] Later that year, The Hub also participated in a live, Web-based performance linking musicians at Arizona State University (ASU) in Tempe, Mills College in Oakland, and the California Institute for the Arts in Valencia, over the Internet. Called "Points of Presence," and sponsored primarily by the Institute for Studies in the Arts at ASU, the performance called for two members of the six-member Hub to be at each of the three locations. Control data was sent by each member over the Internet to operate various pieces of software in the three locations, as well as the laptop-to-laptop communication of algorithmic programs that ran the Hub protocols. But things did not quite go as planned. Brown said the problems they experienced in this performance were not so much the time-delay latency of the Web, which he estimated as 100ms within the United

States and 300ms to Europe, but rather difficulties of debugging the software "on each of the different machines with different operating systems and CPU speeds in different cities." As a result, the full network functioned for only about ten minutes, and most of the performance, particularly in Arizona, was spent describing to the audience what they should have been experiencing. The band itself, always far more interested in "performer interactivity, algorithmic complexity, and the web of mutual influence that the network provided," felt that the technology had finally begun to defeat the music, and shortly after this performance the members of The Hub decided to disband.

NetJam (1990)

As the Internet began to take shape and coalesce, one of the first aspects to develop widely was a series of e-mail discussion groups. First called Usenet News, later shortened to Usenet, these groups were originally established by UNIX operating-system users as a rapid access method of sharing information about possible fixes for programming bugs and news about the availability of new applications and releases. But Usenet groups quickly expanded to include almost any topic anyone might want to discuss. And unlike LISTSERVs, which automatically send regular, if not daily, postings to every computer on the "list" (some moderated, others not and thus forwarding everything that shows up, no matter how mundane), Usenet was established as a client-server system, meaning that it allows users to subscribe to one or more specialized discussion groups, scan the titles of all recent postings, read or download only those messages on topics that interest them, respond with follow-up material if desired, and even create their own messages on entirely new topics. John Naughton, in his *Brief History of the Future,* characterizes the Usenet system as "the world's largest conversation," and says that beginning with an estimated 3 sites in 1979, 15 in 1980, and 150 in 1981, Usenet discussion groups expanded to more than 11,000 sites by 1988.[8]

Music, as might be expected, was one of the topics that quickly made its presence felt in both LISTSERVs and Usenet groups, with postings and discussions on everything from alternative tuning systems, algorithmic composition, and music theory, to Roland samplers, Korg Wavestations, synthesis technology, women's issues in music, and how to play the didgeridoo.[9] In one of these groups (rec.music.synth), a discussion began in early 1990 about starting a news group dedicated to musical collaboration over the Internet. Spearheaded by Ruita Da Silva from the University of California at Berkeley and others, this group quickly agreed on the use of Standard MIDI Files, or SMF, as the data format for music representation (because it was already so pervasive), and they discussed at some length various schemes for data compression, file formats, and transfer protocols. By April 1990, K. Richard Magill of the University of Michigan at Ann Arbor had established a "NetJam list" as a way to distribute messages and files among these participants, and within days of his service becoming active, three collaborative pieces had begun. But Magill's original effort was short-lived, and by late May or early June of that year the collaborations had ceased and the list had gone dormant.

This slowdown didn't last for long, however, and by the summer of 1990 the idea of jamming together on the Web was revived by Craig Latta, a student at Berkeley pursuing concurrent bachelor's degrees in music and computer science. Using the NetJam protocols developed in Ann Arbor by Magill as a starting point, Latta created an automated mail system that would handle everything from subscribing to the list, to the submission of MIDI data, the translation of this data into a format compatible with each user's home equipment, and the retranslation and redistribution of the data back to the originator plus any others who might be working on the piece. In addition, Latta's NetJam design was both platform independent, thus allowing users of Macintoshes, PCs, Amigas, Ataris, and machines running Unix-variants all to communicate with each other, as well as protocol independent, meaning that it would work with the wide variety of MIDI-controlled devices in use throughout the world.

The actual process of becoming a group member of NetJam was simple and required only that participants have a computer, an Internet connection, a means of data compression, and some type of MIDI synthesis equipment. Upon joining NetJam, each new member was first asked to describe themselves—musical interests, influences, philosophies, and so on—and their equipment. This information was then put into a permanent database and made available to other members looking for like-minded collaborators. Latta says that a new piece of music would begin when someone worked out "a progression, a riff, a rhythm, some lyrics, sonorities [or] algorithms for doing any of the preceding," and sent it to the moderator as two separate kinds of files.[10] The two files consisted of the actual MIDI data file, plus a README file describing the music, the compositional process, and the MIDI material. These early collaborations on NetJam did not take place in real time but, rather, existed as MIDI files sent by e-mail, which were downloaded, altered, or added to in some way, and then reposted. As first one and then another collaborator added to the piece, they altered both the data and the README files to reflect the changes that they had made. Slowly, the music evolved as it passed from person to person. Latta says that in 1995, there were 134 active participants collaborating on pieces worldwide.[11]

From its initial support of Standard MIDI Files as the basic data format, NetJam quickly branched out to support software and hardware beyond SMF sequencers, such as C-sound, digital audio data, and Opcode *MAX* patchers. Latta says they began real-time collaboration experiments on NetJam as early as 1991, "when Kurt Pires, then on academic leave from Berkeley (and a member of the experimental Computing Facility), wrote a MIDI client and server in Perl." The idea was that collaborators with the proper equipment and connections could began to send MIDI data real time through a common server, which, in turn, would send the synchronized composite data out simultaneously to all the collaborators, enabling everyone to take part in a "virtual jam session" over the network. Unfortunately, according to Latta, it never really had much of an impact because, at the time, "we couldn't find anyone else with MIDI gear connected to Net-connected machines."[12]

As each collaborative NetJam piece neared completion, the inevitable questions of "Who says it's finished?" and "Who owns the copyright?" would arise. Latta's solution was to give "the initial composer-instigator" the most creative control in both the assembly of the "final product" and "the phrasing of the copyright(s)." His own personal suggestion, however, was that the music resulting from all NetJam collaborations be put "in the public domain," pointing out that "the original idea, after all, is to jam."[13]

Rocket Network (1994)

In the mid-1990s, the two fundamental factors hindering real-time, online collaboration on the Internet were limited bandwidth and lack of speed. All sound files, with the exception of MIDI files, contain hundreds of kilobytes, if not megabytes of data. Depending on their size, some files could take considerable time to upload and download, particularly back when a 28.8 kbps modem was considered fast. And although NetJam was one of the first to make remote jamming on the Internet a reality, creating, as it did, a virtual space for musicians from anywhere in the world to come together and make music, it was never able, despite its desire and attempts, to enable this music making to take place in real time. With the exception of a few experiments, remote collaboration on NetJam was always asynchronous, with the actual creation of new tracks occurring offline, at home, somewhere between the downloading and the uploading of the files—a roundtrip of data that, depending on how fast the composer wanted to work, could take anywhere from a few minutes to several days to complete. But no matter how fast one worked, there was never any illusion that the music was happening in real time; the excitement was that it was happening at all.

If NetJam took the first step toward remote online jamming, the next step was taken by Rocket Network. First established as ResRocket Surfer in London in late 1994, its Vortex Jamming software made online collaboration *appear* to take place in real time—even if it really didn't, and even if it was still MIDI-only for the first four years.

To jam on ResRocket, one began by opening an account and downloading the free ResRocket client/server music software—officially called the Distributed Realtime Groove Network (DRGN) but unofficially referred to as Dragon (Version 1.0 appeared in early 1996). To hear the music, Macromedia's Shockwave media player also was required. The public jams were free; when the private studios appeared later they were rented for varying amounts ($10 a month or $100 a year was the original fee), depending on how many megabytes of storage space a particular project might require. Once on the ResRocket site, users found a combination of music sequencer software and chat room functionality, with an Information/Help section about the basic characteristics of the program; a Who/Where/Rooms section indicating who was currently logged on, where they were on the site, and which rooms were currently available for jamming; and a Chat section that allowed all connected users in a room to communicate with each other.

By entering an online ResRocket "virtual studio" called MUSE (Multi-User Studio Environment), and working within the "chat room" concept—with different free public rooms and leased private studios available for creating styles of music as diverse as classical and rap—users in these rooms could continuously and simultaneously audition a composite loop of the music being created, write tracks for this loop, upload them, and have them appear in the composite loop almost at once, giving the impression of a real-time recording-studio experience. In 1998, *Business Week* said ResRocket had attracted some fifteen thousand musicians playing in "a virtual music studio that bills itself as 'the biggest band in the world.'"[14] Occasionally, these virtual bands included the contributions of well-known musicians such as Elton John, Sinead O'Connor, and Thomas Dolby;[15] Dave Stewart of the Eurythmics also was said to sometimes play along.[16]

The ResRocket Web site and proprietary DRGN software resulted from a chance Internet encounter between two British rock musicians—Willy Henshall of Londonbeat and Tim Bran of Dreadzone—and two Northwestern University graduate students in Evanston, Illinois—Matt Moller and Canton Becker—who liked both music and computers. All four shared the goal of creating "a way for musicians to work together online."[17] Henshall, who had been on the Internet with his Atari since the early 1980s, had, by the early 1990s, formed, with Bran, "an online collective of about 600 musicians, connected through the Usenet newsgroups for the exchange of MIDI-triggered samples."[18] The group became so popular that Henshall and Bran eventually had to move it off Usenet and establish a dedicated FTP server and Web site to handle the ever-increasing traffic. The members of the new site democratically chose the name ResRocket, reportedly one of ten possible names randomly generated by a computer.[19] Initially, what attracted Henshall and Bran to Moller and Becker was that, according to Henshall, they "were developing what was to become Res Rocket's DRGN software," adding that Moller had "written an online MIDI looping application" and was working with Becker "on the server end." Henshall said that when he and Bran first logged on in their West London studio using Moller's software and heard the beats of a bass drum mapped to a General MIDI drum kit coming through, they thought, "That just came from Chicago!" Henshall said, "Tim and I were speechless."[20]

Although certainly the industry standard during the time of its existence, ResRocket was not without a certain amount of competition. In 1998, the Interactive Technologies Group at Ruksun Software Technology released the Alpha version of LiveJam, their new online music software designed specifically for live musical interaction on the Web, and made it available for free download.[21] Ruksun, headquartered in Pune, India, believed that their emphasis on real-time jamming, and their successful efforts toward improving the live streaming of musical data, would differentiate them from their competitors, primarily ResRocket. At the time, both companies were "complimentary," according to Ruksun spokesperson Anmol Chawla, by which he meant that both LiveJam and ResRocket encoded their sound files in Standard MIDI Format. According to Chawla, ResRocket's services were designed primarily for composers, who created offline, and only then got online to upload their work, whereas Ruksun's LiveJam focused on facilitating real-time interactivity. Ruksun was able to focus their efforts toward live jamming because of their new proprietary software, Olympus. Basically a generic community server platform for Internet-based multiuser applications, Olympus, according to Chawla, allows users "to share data across the Internet in as close to real time as intelligently possible."[22]

But ResRocket, which had begun in 1994 as a MIDI-only place to jam for free online, became Rocket Network in 1998, and with the name change came a number of significant musical and corporate changes. The new goal, stated as "achieved" on the Web site in 2001, was to establish Rocket Network as "the industry standard, global production network for audio production and session management."[23] But creating an online studio capable of professional-quality recordings by live musicians required a significant redesign of the software to incorporate digital audio, as well as making available significantly more data storage space to contain these larger sound files. Now located in San Francisco, and with the financial backing of Microsoft co-founder Paul Allen's Vulcan Ventures, Rocket Network developed Rocket Power, a new proprietary software that connected digital audio sequencers to the Rocket Network system and allowed digital audio files to be sent over the Internet "in a bandwidth-efficient manner." *Electronic Musician's* Peter Drescher, writing in April 2000, said that "the resulting speed and transparency [of the audio compression codec] create the illusion of a real-life recording session," a virtual studio experience that was "poised to change the paradigm of multitrack recording."[24]

Almost immediately, the new Rocket Network corporation began seeking out strategic partnerships with various audio companies, offering to lease them Internet Recording Studios in return for being allowed to "Rocket Power" their products, that is, make them compatible with the Rocket Power software, an arrangement everyone involved saw as the emerging of a new kind of Internet-collaboration technology. The first product to sign on was Steinberg's Cubase, followed by Emagic's Logic Audio. In describing the arrangement in 2000, Sara Perkins, Rocket Network's public relations manager, said: "We sell groups of studios as studio centers to our partners, who are basically online resellers, and they can brand the Internet Recording Studio and sell or lease them to their existing community of users." As Rocket Network CEO Willy Henshall described it to *Internet Audio,* "Think of AT&T.... AT&T doesn't really care what kind of phone you use. They sell air time. That's what we do. We sell bandwidth, and we sell storage, and we sell added services."[25] Dave Froker, President of Digidesign, who signed ProTools on (beginning with Version 5.2), said he believed the Internet would "greatly expand collaboration between audio pros in completely new and exciting ways," adding that "our strategic investment in Rocket ensures that our customers will have access to the world's best tools and technology for high quality collaboration with other ProTools users—anywhere, anytime."[26] Writing for *Electronic Musician* in October 2002, Gary S. Hall gave a brief list of the firms with which Rocket Network had established functioning Rocket Network Studio Centers, including Digidesign, Emagic, Futurehit.com, Musician.com, Music Player Network, NetStudio, Rittor Music (Japanese language), Sorinetwork (Korean language), and Steinberg.[27]

The beauty of the new Rocket Power software, of course, was that it would work with any operating system and with any sound file—MIDI, MP3, WAV, AIFF, even proprietary formats. And although the digital files had to be uploaded and downloaded, being too big to be streamed and altered in real time, even at 56.6 kbps—the new modem standard by the late 1990s—they *could* be worked on simultaneously, because the master version of the project was held on a Rocket Network server, whereas local copies were provided to everyone involved. Any change was dynamically updated and mirrored to the other musicians as quickly as it was posted. Users of the Rocket Network/Logic Audio interface, called Rocket Logic, for example, had sixteen MIDI tracks and, depending on their home or studio computing power, up to four digital audio tracks at their disposal. As Sara Perkins characterized it, "You can do anything you want with the tracks once they're up there. It's like working in your normal studio.... What happens here is you have a central arrangement on a central server which is one of the Rocket Network services and you could all be working on that same project at the same time."[28]

At its most dynamic and expansive, Rocket Network had three levels of user accounts: Private, Pro-User, and Free. Private users were the only ones who could create new projects, identify the other collaborators, and define each person's level of access. The Pro-Users could not initiate new projects, they could only contribute to existing ones, while the Free users could experiment only in the public sessions, which couldn't be saved. Pricing for the Private-level accounts could run as high as $1,200 a month, depending on the size of the storage space and the amount of data transfer needed; Pro-User accounts cost a one-time fee of $29.95.

But the line between hobby and commerce, enthusiast and entrepreneur, blurred quickly on the Web. The metamorphosis of ResRocket Surfer into Rocket Network is a prime example. At the end of the twentieth century, everybody who had ever thought about it thought that there was money to be made on the Web—but that was before the economic Internet bubble burst. And unlike many such Internet startups, which folded at the first sign of trouble, Rocket Network actually stayed in business until early 2003. By that point, however, the reported "inherent costs of both data storage and requisite bandwidth for data transfer" caused it to close. According to a May 8, 2003, article from the online Audio Recording Centre, Avid Technology, Digidesign's parent company, acquired the assets of Rocket Network, intending "to incorporate Rocket's collaboration and delivery technologies into a LAN- and WAN-based system for ProTools." The Recording Centre announcement speculated that

Digidesign's intention was "to link together ProTools systems within a single studio complex or post-production facility, as opposed to a long-distance, web-based system."[29]

Beatnik (1993)

Not all Internet endeavors failed when the Internet stocks collapsed. A select few of the smaller, highly focused, Web-oriented businesses like Thomas "Dolby" Robertson's Beatnik—online as Headspace since 1993, incorporated as Beatnik in 1996—came through, thanks to a coherent business model, more than adequate venture-capital funding, and the lofty goal of "sonifying" the Web.

As Dolby saw it, the Internet of the early 1990s was a "silent movie," and his job was to supply the sound. And to his credit, Dolby was quick to understand that sound and music on the Web could be far better in both quality and means of delivery than what was currently available. He wanted the tools for making music on the Web to be as sophisticated as they were for making music for the movies. After all, digital sound, thanks to the shift from LPs to CDs during the 1980s, had already reached a level of development that other forms of digital art, such as gaming, movies, and virtual reality, were still striving to attain. Furthermore, Dolby recognized that regardless of what final form the digital data might take, from audio to video, "it's all going to come to the same terminal, down the same pipeline."[30] Not only did Dolby want to improve the status of audio on the Web, he wanted to improve, if not revolutionize, the way that audio was produced and delivered, not only to make it sound better, but to enable it to be more reliable, as well.

Better known as Thomas Dolby when he was topping the pop charts in 1983 with his first techno-pop hit "She Blinded Me with Science" (complete with a self-directed video in heavy rotation on early MTV), Dolby transformed himself, in the 1990s, into a "musician for the interactive age," as *Entertainment Weekly* said[31]; the *Washington Post* called him "an apostle of Internet music and sound."[32] Fascinated by technology since childhood, and nicknamed "Dolby" by his schoolmates for his interest in high-tech music and toys, Thomas Morgan Robertson quit school at sixteen, experimented with synthesizers as a pop star, took his nickname as his stage name, and learned computer programming on his own.

By the early 1990s he was off the pop charts and extolling the virtues of the Internet on television as the technology correspondent for VH1.

In 1993, Dolby founded Headspace, an Internet company based in San Mateo, California, dedicated to bringing music, sound, and interactivity to the Web. Dolby was fascinated by virtual reality, and he realized quickly that "the moment there was any kind of audio attached [to it] … it really improved the experience." Feeling the need to push the envelope toward VR, Dolby said "my role now is to shift into the next set of tools, which is virtual reality and interactivity."[33] He thought it was important for artists to be involved from the beginning, because they do things imaginatively; the dreamers, Dolby said, must be given the opportunity to experiment with the Web. One reason he started Headspace was to "bridge the gap between composers and technicians," and to facilitate a little more cooperation "between the artists and the people with the technology."[34]

The problem with high-quality audio on the Internet is the size of the sound files and thus the amount of time they take to download. Even though the new compression schemes available by the mid-1990s, such as Real Audio and MP3, alleviated the problem somewhat by facilitating real-time streaming of the sound, they didn't solve the problem and they weren't, as Dolby pointed out, "interactive the way a Web page is." Taking his cue from Hypertext and its ability to control the various aspects of a Web page and its linkage to other pages with a single command, Dolby designed Beatnik. He noted "in effect, what we created at Beatnik was Hypermusic as a concept…. Beatnik allows you to basically weave music and sound effects and voices into the Web page itself."[35]

Hypertext Markup Language, or HTML, is the reason Web pages look and act the way they do today: the colors, the images, the text fonts, the bells and whistles—all of these and more are controlled by HTML. Instead of sending all of this digital data over a server every time a new request is made, HTML only sends the *code* for rearranging bits of information that are already installed in each local computer. Furthermore, because only the code and not the much larger data file is being sent at each request, HTML allows each new page to load much faster than it otherwise would. Music, with its sequences of pitches, durations, volume, and instrumentation, lends itself to a similar type of bit separation and compression. Dolby was able to create Hypersound to compress sound in the same way that Hypertext compresses text. Beatnik's Hypersound information—such as instructions to the General MIDI instruments, or to the digital audio data (which has already been compressed and sent in bits to the home computer)—causes the data to be reassembled according to the instructions of the new HTML code. Dolby once told a BBC reporter to think of it like trying to send a wedding cake over the telephone, saying, "you can't really send a wedding cake … but you can send the recipe if you have flour, water and eggs at the other end."[36]

The basic elements of the Beatnik system are a General MIDI-compatible software synthesizer called the Beatnik Player, which is a free and downloadable sound-engine plug-in that allows reassembly and playback of the sounds at the user end; and the Beatnik Editor, which is software that facilitates the creation of custom samples as Rich Music Format (RMF) files. RMF, Beatnik's proprietary software, combines both MIDI and audio file data and compresses both. The Beatnik Editor, which allows sounds to be embedded in Web pages as HTML code, is licensed by Beatnik to designers and developers, who then create custom sounds for their clients that can be played interactively at the user end. Once a browser is equipped with the Beatnik Player, the Player will read the HTML code, tell the computer how to reassemble the various parts of the music, and create high-quality sound in something close to real time. On some "sonified" Web sites, users can even mix their own versions of the music located there, using mouse clicks to control what they hear. The most well-known early example of this form of interactivity is probably the version of David Bowie's hit single "Fame" that could be found on the Beatnik Web site in the late 1990s. The page itself contained the lyrics, and by clicking on various buttons on the page, each listener could add or subtract individual lines of the music—bass, guitar, background, vocals, drums—to create their own unique mix of the song.

Although the Beatnik Player and Editor are designed to handle both MIDI and digital audio files, many of Beatnik's Web sounds are made from the General MIDI instruments that are native to most computers. In addition to the 128 instruments in this sound bank, Beatnik offers a second set of 128 customized sounds, made from the first bank, but with a different set of parameters applied, giving the developer or programmer a palette of 256 built-in sounds from which to choose. And because both the audio and the MIDI files are compressed, the already small MIDI files (some now under 3K each), work perfectly as background music and button rollover sounds. Furthermore, through the use of JavaScript, the musical controls operate in near real-time, with notes triggered, volumes raised and lowered, tempos changed, and instruments substituted on demand. By mid-1998, the BBC News Online reported that the Beatnik Player plugin had been downloaded over 1.5 million times; the total is far greater today.[37]

Because Beatnik software was not only designed for the Web but also maximized for it, it quickly became the sound engine of choice powering the audio content of the Web sites of online giants such as Netscape, Oracle, Sun Microsystem's JavaSoft, MTV Online, and Microsoft's WebTV. Beatnik also was instrumental in developing Yahoo!'s music site, and Beatnik software created the musical experiences found on the Disney, Columbia-Tristar, Universal Studios, and PBS Web sites, as well. After a successful merger in 1999 with Mixman Technologies, a maker of groove-oriented remix software, Beatnik could boast of revenue streams coming from a variety of sources, including the sale of software, the "sonifying" of Web sites, and the licensing for everything from gaming gear to WebTV.

Individual artists and musicians have always had a place on the Beatnik Web site—to create music, remix tunes, or just explore—but online jamming was never the company's goal. The Beatnik site was designed primarily as a destination for Web developers and their clients, the online professionals best able to help Beatnik attain the level of market penetration needed in order to truly "sonify" the Web. During the 1990s, Beatnik targeted its resources and technology primarily toward the Web sites of radio stations and large corporations. But by early 2001, it began to focus on supplying and facilitating the multimedia audio content for the rapidly emerging wireless technology. The goal was not only "to enable a rich, personalized, immersive audio experience" for mobile phone and PDA users but also "to promote a universal format" for its delivery. Beatnik said its contribution would be to provide "the core audio engine technology, application programming interfaces [APIs] and tools."

Now in use for several years, the Beatnik Audio Engine (BAE) is second-generation software that enables the playback and mixing of all popular audio formats, including several developed by Beatnik. It then integrates these results with everything from mobile phones and PDAs to digital cameras and TV set top boxes. Furthermore, because BAE is optimized for wireless mobile devices, it enables developers to create "enhanced structured audio" for everything from gaming sound effects, to ring tones, to multimedia messages, "using extremely small data file sizes."[38] Although the wireless mobile devices of today don't exactly provide the virtual reality experiences dreamed of and worked toward by Beatnik and others during the previous decade, they are, with their Internet-based multiple features and enhanced audio capabilities, a significant step along the way. Once we do finally arrive in that virtual world in which all our senses are engaged, the chances are good that Thomas Dolby will be waiting there for us with a new generation of Beatnik sounds. As he once told *Entertainment Weekly,* "If you're wearing a VR helmet, you're totally at my mercy; I can hit you with amazing sounds and you're there."[39]

MusicWorld (1997)

One of the more intriguing threads of development running through the long-range planning sessions at Beatnik and other Internet companies during the 1990s was the promise of virtual reality (VR): that feeling it encourages of being *there* even though, in fact, you're still *here*. By 1997, the industry giant Microsoft was involved, through its Virtual Worlds (V-Worlds) Group at Microsoft Research, a computer science research organization within Microsoft that began in 1991. Concentrating on VR between 1997 and 2000, this research team not only built a working computer infrastructure called the Virtual Worlds Platform for "the deployment of online 3D virtual worlds," but they, and others, also created a number of V-World projects and prototypes using this platform. These ranged from the British Telecom-developed Ages of Avatars, a multiuser journey through the virtual worlds of birth, growth, power, and spiritual enlightenment, to the in-house-created Fred Hutchinson Cancer Research Center Project, which deployed "an online social support virtual world" linking the patients and their care givers in Seattle with their families via the Web.[40]

From its inception, the Microsoft group had intended that the Virtual Worlds Platform "be easy to use and build on," constructing it in such a way that only a knowledge of Dynamic HTML and Visual Basic Script were needed to succeed. In February 2000, Microsoft Research released the code for the Virtual Worlds Platform (Version 1.5), allowing developers worldwide to experiment with their source code in building their new worlds.

One of the V-World prototypes that emerged thanks to the release of the Virtual Worlds Platform code was called MusicWorld. Described as "a graphical collaborative musical performance environment," this imaginary online world used avatars to explore three different soundscapes, allowing them, as they moved about, to mix sounds and compose patterns to "a live, online 'album' of multiple songs."[41] MusicWorld was originally designed by Sean Kelly and Christopher Sung when they were both graduate students at NYU, after Kelly had completed a summer internship at Microsoft Research. Their first idea as students was to use the Virtual Worlds platform to link together people listening to the same CD. However, before the project was completed, Kelly was working at Microsoft Research, and "a dynamically changing, [online] environment where avatars could be [musically] expressive and change their world in real-time" had emerged.[42] Kelly said he wanted MusicWorld to be "personal and persistent," by which he meant that any changes he made not only should be noticeable but also should linger and remind others of his presence, even after he was gone.

MusicWorld offered three soundscapes through which the avatars could wander: a black-and-white rendering of New York City; a tropical scene with green palm trees; and a dark starry sky with white eyes drifting by. In this world, clicking on an eye would change the tune. Within each soundscape, avatars were offered different styles of music that they could mix individually, their changes instantly shared with everybody. In all three soundscapes, clicking on one of several colored globes controlled some aspect of the music, such as the bass line or the drums. The tempo could be changed by clicking on pulsing rings running up a tall purple tower. Personalized sound clips could also be blended into the mix, with those, too, shared in real time. All of these attributes—plus the volume, number of repetitions, and pitch—were under the control of the avatars wandering through the Soundscapes. Dave Vronay, a user interface design engineer with the Virtual Worlds group, noted that although playing alone in MusicWorld was not much fun, playing with others was. According to Vronay, "that type of interaction is very compelling, it's like a new activity."

The avatars themselves, although a bit too cartoonlike for such a dungeons-and-dragons world, came in a variety of choices, thirteen in all, ranging from a middle-aged woman named Sylvia who always carried her dog, to Martin, a naked green extraterrestrial. And if you didn't like any of these, you could add one of your own design. The avatars had a range of "eleven built-in emotions, from smiling and laughing to posing and frowning." Vera, the busty vampire, had a frown that was said to be "particularly nasty," which she might be forced to use if the music took a turn she didn't like.

For all of its apparent success, the Virtual Worlds project, and Music-World, only had an active life at Microsoft Research of about four years. John P. Young of the Peabody Conservatory in Baltimore, writing in 2001 about "Networked Music" in the English journal *Organized Sound,* said that although MusicWorld exhibited several important characteristics of a distributed musical environment, it was limited "by its emphasis on literal representations and incompatibility with non-Windows platforms." Nevertheless, and citing Rocket Network and *Cathedral* as similar examples, he said that MusicWorld "may have progressed the farthest" in attempting to network music by "bridging real and virtual space."[43]

The Internet Underground Music Archives (1993)

Three other early Web ventures deserve to be mentioned: The Internet Undergound Music Archives (IUMA); Cinema Volta; and WebDrum. All three began as small, independent, arts-related sites. Although IUMA greatly outgrew Cinema Volta and WebDrum, all speak to the equalizing power of the Web, and the ability, once online, for the "little guy" to coexist with organizations of far greater resources and size. Although it may sometimes appear that the Internet has been taken over by the corporate world, even today an individual with a good idea can still succeed.

Jon Ippolito, writing in the March–April 2000 issue of *artbyte* magazine, said that "in 1995, eight percent of Websites were produced by artists," adding that "this growing cyber-avant-garde has remained at the leading edge ever since."[44] If you include the fan clubs, museums, concert halls, galleries, and artist-support sites springing up around the world, 8 percent may be a conservative estimate. After all, Web sites dedicated to a single person, purpose, or idea have always been around; some of the oldest sites on the Web were put there by the artists and their fans.

In 1993, California guitarist Jeff Patterson formed a garage band called the Ugly Mugs and, with the help of some friends, put up a Web site to support the new band and, hopefully, get a few gigs. Designed in such a way that other bands also could be featured, Patterson's Web site—with the unwieldy name of the Internet Underground Music Archives—gave each band its own URL in their own name (http://artists.iuma.com/IUMA/Bands/Ugly_Mugs/), with a Web page on which to post tour dates, lyrics, and MP3 files; sell their CDs, records, and T-shirts; and make contact with their fans—all for no charge. At the beginning, when file size and bandwidth always had to be considered, IUMA artists were given space for one five-minute song and a twenty-second excerpt, two pages of text to hold everything from lyrics to bios, and a two-image limit for photos and cover art. IUMA handled the merchandising on consignment, and, for a small fee, provided artists with extended services, such as the ability to add more songs to the site, post a video clip, or get the latest stats on their progress up or down the IUMA charts.

Committed to the independent, unsigned musician, IUMA's mission, idealistic as it was, was to let the music speak for itself, and the artists speak directly to their fans. The commitment, as IUMA's PR put it, "was to bring the talented artist chasing their dream together with the many music fans who would never otherwise hear their music."[45] Ultimately, this was the first successful attempt to promote and distribute music online, and the beginning of a seismic shift in music retailing. IUMA saw its mission as no less than "empowering the unsigned musician through a reinvention of the music industry."[46]

The IUMA Web site was (and still is) easy for band members to navigate and casual listeners to explore. That was always its strength. From somewhere near the home page, bands and solo artists could register, sign up for the free services, check their sales figures, and scan the charts, while listeners could choose a musical genre, sample it with Real Audio, and, for a small fee, download anything they liked as an MP3. Also located on the home page, IUMA Radio allows listeners to sample their favorite genre (with bands randomly selected), and play it in the background as they work. By 1999, IUMA was hosting millions of page views per month, and featured over thirty-five hundred solo artists and bands on individual Web sites, each with their own unique URL. IUMA made money through the fees, selling merchandise for the bands, offering enhanced services, and selling advertising on the Web site, a big-ticket item in 1999.

In June of that year, as the Internet stock bubble continued to inflate, EMusic.com acquired IUMA, which until then had been a privately held California company located in Santa Cruz. At the time, EMusic.com billed itself as "the premier destination for high-quality downloadable music in MP3 format" on the Web. The acquisition of IUMA allowed EMusic.com "to offer Internet music fans a logical continuum of music," from well-known name artists to up-and-coming new talent, according to Gene Hoffman, EMusic's President and CEO. IUMA's Jeff Patterson saw the acquisition as providing his artists with the opportunity "to gain significant visibility and attract the attention of independent labels."[47]

Although IUMA became, in effect, a subsidiary of EMusic, it continued to operate as an independent Web site, with the ability to integrate its promotional efforts, when appropriate, with EMusic.com. This was significant for IUMA's unsigned bands that now stood a better chance of gaining the attention of one of EMusic's more than ninety independent label connections, including Epitaph and Rykodisc. The best of these bands could even look forward to being "called up" to the EMusic.com site and distributed commercially from there. And some, such as Gangsta Bitch Barbie, Soul Chasm, and Clark W Griswald, actually got recording contracts with major labels, and became, if not household names, at least "wannabe" poster-bands.

At the end of the twentieth century, money for Web-related projects was really flowing fast. Neither the Web development companies, nor the sites they created, were actually making much money, but they appeared to have a lot, and were spending it in ways that today can seem bizarre. The money itself was coming in from venture capitalists, who expected a profitable return; advertisers, who saw a new market emerging; and IPOs, to let the rest of us in on the company's stock. By November 1999, even IUMA could afford to act flush, announcing that, henceforth, all IUMA artists would receive 25 percent of the total ad revenue generated by their individual IUMA sites. Jeff Patterson said that sharing advertising revenues with their artists was something IUMA had always wanted to do, and joked that the fact that his band, Ugly Mugs, had recently made an appearance on the Top 40 IUMA charts had nothing to do with the timing of the decision. Both EMusic and IUMA said they wanted to demonstrate their commitment to give artists fair and accurate compensation for their work, and to encourage other companies to act more responsibly.

Unfortunately, venture capital money for Web projects, as well as money from Web site ad revenues, was not as plentiful once the century turned. By February 2001, EMusic's resources and cash flow had shrunk so severely that they could no longer sustain IUMA's expenses, much less fund its growth. An e-mail sent to their artists by IUMA President Patterson and General Manager Antony Brydon on February 7, 2001, described the situation as "an amazing and painful time for the music industry," and said that "the rules that govern what we do change on a daily basis."[48] IUMA had to suspend operations; there was no money left to pay the staff. But although IUMA no longer accepted new artists, sold merchandise, or gave customer support—the transactions that required human interaction—some of the staff volunteered to maintain the Web site so the artists already on IUMA could continue to make modifications to their Web pages. At the time operations were suspended, IUMA was hosting over twenty-five thousand artists and was the repository of more than one hundred thousand digital music files.

Fortunately, this chapter in IUMA's history has a happy ending. In less than two months from the suspension of services, IUMA signed an agreement to be acquired by Vitaminic, the leading digital music distributor in Europe (founded in April 1999 and headquartered in Milan). Within weeks, IUMA's core staff was rehired, and the Web site relaunched with a full range of artist and fan services, including Artist Uplink, the A&R affiliate program, bulletin boards, statistics, charts, and IUMA radio. And although the ad-sharing program remained suspended, given that the advertising market on the Internet had crashed, it was considered a small price to pay to keep the site alive. In the end, Jeff Patterson, a guitar player—an individual—got everything he originally wanted from the Internet: a Web site to support unsigned artists, and a Top 40 appearance by his band, whereas an untold number of other unsigned artists got encouragement, worldwide exposure, and a chance to further follow their dreams.

Cinema Volta (1994)

Cinema Volta is John Maxwell Hobbs's umbrella title for all of his creative work, but it applies particularly to his work involving music on the Web. He took the name from the original Cinema *Volta*, which was Dublin's first movie house, founded by James Joyce in 1909. As he put it, "Cinema Volta just sort of grabbed me."[49] With Cinema Volta, Hobbs created an umbrella broad enough both to cover his record releases and be the name of his band, but Cinema Volta is primarily known as a long-lived Web site. The Web site's first online incarnation began as early as 1994, under the name "Dog Solitude," but then it only contained links to audio clips of some of Hobbs's recordings.

John Maxwell Hobbs has been actively involved with the Internet since, at least, his days as the Producing Director for New Technologies at The Kitchen, New York City's premiere downtown space for video, music, dance, performance, film, and literature, and a cutting-edge center for the artistic display of new media and technology. Hobbs, who was a member of the staff from 1991 to 1996, created The Kitchen's first Web site. Begun in early 1994, it contained over two thousand separate files, including a comprehensive history of The Kitchen from its beginning in 1971, and a video distribution catalog of over six hundred titles of video art; it also was one of the first of its kind on the Web.[50]

In November 1994, The Kitchen became the New York site of the Electronic Café International. The Electronic Café was started by telecollaboration artists Kit Galloway and Sherrie Rabinowitz as a seven-week component of the 1984 Summer Olympics Arts Festival in Los Angeles. The purpose was to support "artists migrating toward a new order of art making," as their 1984 manifesto, "We Must Create At The Same Scale As We Can Destroy" made clear.[51] By 1994, the Electronic Café International had become "a unique international network of multimedia telecommunications venues with over 40 affiliates around the globe," and was, as Galloway and Rabinowitz described it, "the mother of all cybercafes." Using analog telephone lines, digital ISDN lines, video, and sometimes the Internet, the idea was to give artists the ability to explore "co-creation and collaboration in real-time networked environments."[52]

The Electronic Café inspired Hobbs to think of using technology to develop multisite performances. One event was the Virtual Abbey, developed and produced with David Hykes, leader of the Harmonic Choir, a vocal group specializing in microtonal overtone singing. Because Hobbs much preferred natural reverberation to a digitally produced artificial one, particularly with the type of music Hykes's group would be singing, he suggested that they combine the Harmonic Choir's performance at The Kitchen in New York with the acoustics of Hykes's favorite performance space, the Thoronet Abbey in the south of France, in essence, transporting the acoustic environment of a twelfth-century abbey into a venue in twentieth-century New York. To accomplish this feat, during the performance—which occurred in November 1995—"the voices of the Harmonic Choir were digitally transmitted to the abbey, [and] the reverberation of the abbey was then transmitted back to New York in real time, where the audience had the same acoustical experience as those who were in the real abbey in France."[53]

Thanks to the worldwide contacts and connections provided by association with the Electronic Café, The Kitchen, through its executive director Lauren Amazeen, was able to bring French Telecom on board to provide some of the funding and install ISDN lines in the Abbey; Hobbs, with the help of Michel Redolphi and Luc Martinez at CIRM (Centre International de Rencontres Mathématiques), was able to locate the low-latency audio codecs needed to send a stereo audio signal over phone lines at 128kbps. Hobbs said that the 70-ms delay inherent in the phone transmission between The Kitchen and the Abbey "closely duplicated the natural pre-delay of the Abbey itself."[54] For the performance, French TV sent a video crew to transmit pictures from inside the Abbey back to The Kitchen.

Audiences in both locations heard the moving about and coughing of each other, thanks to microphones that allowed these crowd noises to trigger reverberations of their own. Hobbs said it gave the New York audience "a strong sense of actually being in the Abbey themselves." During the second performance, which occurred at 3 A.M. in France and, thus, had no audience of its own, the Abbey felt both empty and full all at once, alive, as it was, with the sounds of the New York audience that wasn't (physically) there. According to Hobbs, the tech crew in the Abbey called it an "eerie experience" to be in an empty church and hearing the sound of two hundred people milling about, "almost as if it were an audience of ghosts."[55]

As for John Maxwell Hobbs's own Web music, Cinema Volta really began in late 1995 or early 1996, when its most significant component, Web Phases, went online. (Hobbs says now that he isn't certain of the date.) A complex and compelling idea, hidden behind a deceptively simple interface, Web Phases explores each user's emotional relationship with, and physical connection to, the Web. Hobbs calls it "an interactive musical composition that incorporates chance and randomness of Internet traffic."[56] Visitors to Web Phases find a silent site with four frames at the top of the page with the word "Silence" written in each of them. Hobbs says the frames "function as *targets* for the musical tracks listed in the pull down boxes" below. The four pull-down menus have the same eleven sound loops, each one of a different length—including, drums, Reggae drums, bass and drums, two kinds each of drones, phases, and pianos, plus piano and strings—all of it music that Hobbs has written. Some of the loops fit together perfectly, some of them don't. Selecting a track for one of the four frames will cause that sound loop to begin to play. A musical piece emerges from the user's choice of different loops for the other three frames, plus the fact that these choices, whatever they are, "will constantly change over time."[57] This change occurs not only because each of the musical loops is of a different length, but because each loop's starting time is affected by the amount and nature of the Internet traffic that exists during the actual time it is being downloaded. Hobbs says that "essentially, the composition being generated contains a picture in sound of the state of the Internet and the connection to it at that moment."[58]

Hobbs later said that he had two reasons for creating Web Phases. First, he wanted to explore his own ambivalence toward "interactive" Web music, feeling that "most of these pieces are neither truly interactive nor specific to the Web," because they "only give the illusion of user participation and freedom," adding that "the hand of the artist very tightly controls the users, no matter what choices are made." The second reason was that he wanted to work "toward the creation of a musical equivalent of hypertext." But the overall desire, he said, was "to create a piece that would allow a user a satisfying experience with a minimal amount of participation, yet allow a deeper involvement if desired."

By 1998, Web Phases was beginning to attract wide attention. It was named a winner in the Web Design category of the Digital '98 ASCI competition (Art & Science Collaborations, Inc.), and was featured as a "Quick Hit" on July 10, 1997, in the *New York Times Online*. Earlier that year, Kyle Gann, writing in the *Village Voice*, had described Web Phases as operating "on a noticeably higher artistic level" than the earliest tape-music and computer-music pieces, concluding that "the potential for social reorientation is even more incredible," and predicting "we'll look back and say 1998 was the year our relationship to music entered a new era."[59] Hobbs, more succinctly, said, "Sound in the real world is a rich source of information. Why should cyberspace be silent?"[60]

WebDrum (1997)

For a number of reasons, Phil Burk's WebDrum[61] is a good site with which to conclude this tour of the development of music on the Web— a digital David with a virtual instrument, if you will, toiling among the online corporate Goliaths. But thanks to the leveling effect of the playing field that the Web provides, Burk's story, too, is a success. And although neither WebDrum, nor SoftSynth—the company Burk founded in 1997, and a leading provider of audio software for Java and the Web—can boast of the impressive growth and hit count that Beatnik or IUMA can, Burk can take credit for creating good products, weathering the downturn, and keeping his virtual drums going online all the while.

Burk's WebDrum, which also began in 1997, is an online multiplayer drum machine that can be played either alone or with up to seven other people per session. Users, when they jam, may also chat with other players in a text field at the bottom of the screen. Basically, WebDrum is a Java Applet that "allows multiple users to share the editing of a drum pattern" by turning on or off notes on a grid.[62] To begin, players must download and install the free Softsynth-developed Jsyn audio plugin—technically a Java Audio Synthesis Application Programmer Interface—and select one or more of the virtual instruments available from a menu. According to Burk, three types of drums are there for people to play: regular drums with a simple pattern editor; melodic drums with a pitch-time grid; and envelope drums that allow users to control a synthesizer.

Once logged onto WebDrum, users may choose to join an existing drum session, or create a new one of their own. As they jam together, each player, individually, has the ability to alter not only the parameters of rhythm and tempo, but also those of pitch and sound color.[63] Any particular drum may be "owned" by only one player at a time, meaning that only that user may edit it. Any of the other players, however, can, with a click, take over a drum that someone else owns and make it their own. So in a typical session, rhythms are created, sound colors change, parameters are adjusted, and drums freely, or not so freely, change hands, all, more or less, simultaneously. It can get rather lively at times. Recognizing that WebDrum may not be the most heavily trafficked site, and that users may find no one there to jam with when they arrive, Burk offers a feature whereby players can, in advance, schedule a session for a "tele-jam."

Phil Burk's work with music, computers, and the Web dates back to the late 1980s and early 1990s, when he was a lecturer and researcher at Mills College in Oakland, California. Along with fellow faculty composers Larry Polansky and David Rosenboom, Burk designed and developed the Hierarchical Music Specification Language (HMSL), an object-oriented language that provides music-related tools to experimental musicians. Designed as a programming language for experimental music composition and performance, HMSL is normally used for live interactive MIDI performance, although "composed" pieces also have been archived as MIDI files. Some of the composers who have used HMSL in their work include John Bischoff, Chris Brown, The Hub, Phil Corner, and Nick Didkovsky for Dr. Nerve.[64]

In 1997, with the release of Jsyn, Burk's SoftSynth became one of the first companies to provide a real-time audio synthesis API for Java, which is one of the primary Internet programming languages. According to Burk, Jsyn functions for Java as an audio toolbox "that can synthesize high fidelity music and sound effects directly on the user's computer without having to download large sound files."[65] In addition to Jsyn, SoftSynth also developed TransJam, a generic server for multiuser games and music performance. In a talk to the International Computer Music Conference in 2000, Burk said he developed the TransJam software to overcome the two main obstacles to improving the sound of online audio: "the lack of good high fidelity sound generation in the default browser" and the fact that "Java Applets running in a web browser need a way to find each other, and exchange musical information." TransJam, he said, "was designed to address those needs," whereas the WebDrum "was designed to test the capabilities of the TransJam server," creating, in effect, an interactive musical proof-of-concept for a SoftSynth product.

In that same 2000 talk, Burk spoke in some detail about his artistic aims, saying that his development of TransJam "was inspired by the work of the pioneering network band, 'The Hub'"—returning us to that early experiment in interactive performance. Burk's hope was to provide a server that would "enable composers to create networked compositions in the style of The Hub … on the web."[66]

5
CATHEDRAL:
A CASE STUDY IN TIME

John Cage once said that if you ever get a good idea, you had better act on it quickly, because you may not be the only one who has it. When a good idea emerges, it is in the air, ready to be taken and acted on by anyone who can read the signs. That was pretty much the way it felt in the spring of 1997, as Nora Farrell and I hurried to finish the music and make the art that would become *Cathedral,* a work, not for live concerts, but for the virtual stage of the World Wide Web—a never-ending display of music and art that anyone, anywhere, anytime, could hear. Because it was destined for the Web, there was *a lot* to do: Web pages to design; animations to create; and music files to shrink sufficiently small to actually stream. As the launch of the site approached, we were working day and night. Of course, I had some concerns about entering the new world of Web composition, not the least of which was worrying that, in moving my work to the Web, I might no longer be thought of as a composer of music for acoustic instruments. But that fear—unfounded as it turned out—was overshadowed by the lure of new artistic territory to explore, and the certainty—yes, certainty—that our path was right.

Nora and I date the beginning of our artistic work together on the Web to Amsterdam and March 1996. We were there for a week to investigate a new MIDI device being developed at STEIM, which is a government-sponsored center offering artists technological expertise.[1] The plan was to create an evening-length multimedia event, already named "Cathedral," using their MIDI device to position our sounds three dimensionally inside the performance space. But, during that week, we actually spent more time in the cafés talking about the Internet, how fast it was growing, and how we might begin to use it in some kind of artistic way. Gradually, we both came to realize that the multimedia "Cathedral" that we were designing for the stage could be transformed into *Cathedral,* a work for the World Wide Web. While still in Amsterdam, Nora and I committed to making *Cathedral* a Web piece, not only because we recognized the vast artistic potential of the Internet but also because we could see the possibility of creating an entirely new musical and social experience online, one that would give our listeners the opportunity to become actively and creatively involved in an ongoing, worldwide-accessible work of music and art.

Even during those earliest café discussions, we envisioned *Cathedral* as an interactive Web site with Web-based musical instruments that anyone could play, as well as a place on the Web to hear acoustic music through a regular series of live webcasts and performances online. It's worth noting, incidentally, that most of these plans were impossible to realize given the state of Internet technology in 1996, but we were fortunate that its rapid development paralleled our development of the project, and we were soon able to realize everything that we had imagined that week.

When *Cathedral* went online June 10, 1997, there were fewer than a million actual (as opposed to registered) sites on the World Wide Web, and less than 2 percent of those made any sounds at all. This first version of the *Cathedral* site included streaming audio, streaming video, animation, images, and texts; at the then top speed of 56kbps, less than a minute of music would play before most home computers would go silent momentarily to rebuffer the file. At that point, our goal was to create an imaginative, ongoing artistic experience by blurring the distinctions separating composers, performers, and audiences, and inviting everyone who visited the *Cathedral* site to be a creative participant, expanding, as we saw it, on a process begun by John Cage in the 1950s, if not by Erik Satie fifty years before that. Ultimately, our intent was to offer each individual listener the ability to create his or her own unique musical experience online, an experience that we hoped would help to build community and reawaken an active interest in individual involvement with the artistic process.

Although *Cathedral* is a multidimensional work with multiple layers of meaning, in its most fundamental form it consists of three primary components: a Web site; a PitchWeb; and an Internet Band. The Web site features a variety of interactive musical, artistic, and text-based experiences; the virtual instruments—including the Web-based Pitch-Web—allow listeners to participate actively and creatively; and the Cathedral Band, which gives periodic live performances and offers listeners focused moments in which to come together and play music in community online.

The Web Site

As a Web site, *Cathedral* is a work of music and art that lives and grows in the virtual concert space of the World Wide Web.[2] The title is related to Gothic cathedrals only in the sense that although they took centuries to build, they were put to use long before their completion, becoming gathering places for the spiritual and artistic ideas of the times. But unlike the Gothic cathedral, which was rooted in time and place, this new *Cathedral,* built as a virtual edifice online, is always available, and accessible anywhere, to anyone with Internet access. And although it can be experienced in a number of different ways, one of our intentions was that the *Cathedral* Web site be a place where visual and aural meditations are both facilitated and encouraged.

Conceptually and thematically, *Cathedral* is the story of five mystical moments in time. These moments—which we call the Building, the Bomb, the Pyramid, the Web, and the Dance—represent for us significant points of human creativity and collective actions. Specifically, these moments refer to the building of Chartres Cathedral, the first detonation of the atomic bomb, the building of the Great Pyramid at Giza, the founding of the World Wide Web, and the inception of the Native American Ghost Dance religion. For Nora and me these five moments signify events of continuing importance for the future, because they raise unresolved issues of religion and spirituality, power and self-destruction, lost civilizations, the future of individuals and societies, the natural and supernatural, and, by extension, the fate of the indigenous people of the world. In a way, these points in time are the windows—and the mirrors—in and through which we chose to see and express ourselves. On the *Cathedral* Web site—in an area dedicated to the "Moments"—there are thirty-two experiences designed, not as answers, but as points of reflection and contemplation for these five moments. For our listeners, the intention is that these moments will provide visual and aural points around which to attach meaning and extend narrative, creating for them a multilayered artistic form, and encouraging a return to mythic thinking and the reintegration of sonic materials.

In addition, the Web site contains a Codex that housed the thirty-two basic texts that are the inspiration for *Cathedral.* These texts, collected between 1994 and 1996, include the words of poets, prophets, mystics, psychics, seers, chiefs, and medicine men from throughout the ages. There is also a Chronicle that is a reflection on *Cathedral* and its five moments in the form of a hypernovel, and a Stage that only appears when the Cathedral Band touches down in physical space to perform, which temporarily establishes a physical moment, and a bridge between the audience and the performers: a portal, lobby, and gathering place, all in one. There is also a set of three Virtual Instruments called Sound Pool, Chaos, and PitchWeb.

There are four basic types of music on the *Cathedral* site:

1. Computer music written specifically for the Web and existing as either sound, MIDI, or MP3 files that are streamed from the site and heard in real time
2. Acoustic music written for traditional ensembles (some using one or more of the virtual instruments), and incorporated into the site through the live webcasts and the archives
3. Rhythm beds for the improvised music performed live and online by the Cathedral Band
4. Interactive music, which is played live by the listeners on the virtual instruments, sometimes with the band

In all, there are some forty-nine composed pieces associated with *Cathedral,* including thirty-two computer works, twelve chamber pieces, and five orchestral works, including one for gamelan.

The Virtual Instruments

In deciding to create new instruments for the Web, our goal was to give listeners an active role in the creative process by encouraging everyone who visited the *Cathedral* site to take part. In considering the design, we felt it was important to develop instruments with scalable levels of musicality so that people of any musical ability could play them. Additionally, by making these instruments both freely available and as technologically inclusive as possible—as well as by periodically presenting live and online concert experiences using the PitchWeb—we hoped to engage large numbers of people in the process of making music online, encouraging, as we are, everyone who visits the *Cathedral* site to be not only a listener but also a performing "member of the band."

The Sound Pool was the first of the virtual instruments to appear online.[3] Created by Charles Wood, our programmer during the first two years of *Cathedral,* from source code written by Nina Amenta and Mark Phillips at the University of Minnesota Science and Technology Center, it went online in December 1997. First-time visitors to the Sound Pool encounter a silent, black screen that mouseovers and mouse clicks will activate into a geometric, polyphonic, image/sound collage. Technically, the Sound Pool is an interactive sound plot, in which each line, or file, of music in the Pool is triggered individually by clicking on hidden nodes in a growing web of multicolored geometric patterns, allowing users to trigger the sounds and images into a musical mosaic of their own creation. The sounds in the Pool also may be supplemented by listeners who may contribute their own sound files to be woven into the Pool, played online, and integrated into future performances. Additionally, these lines of music change location randomly among the nodes. The overall result is that a combination of random user clicks, the computer's reshuffling of the sounds, and the charms of chance all contribute to stirring the Pool. Our intention is that listeners will never experience, either visually or aurally, the same Sound Pool twice.

The most interactive of our virtual instruments is the PitchWeb, which is a Web-based multiuser instrument with text chat capabilities that can function in both live and online concert events, plus has the ability to create and host its own "sonic chats."[4] Users play the PitchWeb by selecting and manipulating shapes that are mapped to sound samples contained in multiple banks of sixty-four sounds each, moving them to the playing field, and playing them in any order and combination through movements of the computer mouse. Playback also can be automatic, or by directly playing on the computer keyboard. These sound/shapes also can be resized and overlapped to create polyphonic passages, and in the CD-ROM version of the instrument, which I play on stage, the resulting sound patterns can be saved and reopened at another time.

In its most complex form, the PitchWeb may be played directly on the computer keyboard in real time, like a synthesizer. With the online multiuser version of the instrument, performers can affect the composite sound individually, by having their changes updated instantly across the network and heard by everyone at the same time. On a simpler level, PitchWeb users also may create music by typing in words or phrases in any language and having the instrument itself automatically convert them into musical sounds.

The PitchWeb's multiple levels of performance allows each user to design their own unique experience—from passive listener to active performer or contributor—and interact with the music, and each other, in a "hands-on" way. The PitchWeb also encourages players of all abilities to participate in *Cathedral* by performing either alone (as a solo or with accompaniment provided by the instrument), with one another in groups, or live with the Cathedral Band during one of its ongoing series of webcasts.

The earliest version of the PitchWeb was debuted online from The Franklin Institute Science Museum in Philadelphia in October 1998, during the premiere of *Dreaming Dances, Round & Square,* when it was played with the *Relâche* Ensemble by me, as well as by audience members on their laptops and on computer terminals stationed around the hall. During the performance, my computer screen was projected onto a screen above the performers, and the audience was able to watch as I played.

The multiuser version of the instrument went online in December 2001, when PitchWeb bands in Boston, New York, and Atlanta performed during a forty-eight-hour *Cathedral* webcast. It was featured again in July 2002 during a week of Cathedral Band performances and online activities at the Mini[ ]Max Festival at the Brisbane Powerhouse in Australia. And in May 2003, the TAMA Tokyo PitchWeb Band, a group of over twenty-five university students organized by Professor Akihiro Kubota, performed live with members of the Cathedral Band in a webcast from TAMA Art University in Tokyo. During most Cathedral Band concerts, either Nora or I mix our online PitchWeb players directly to the stage on which we are performing. We have found that this adds a new dimension to the experience, because we can converse with members of the online band through text chat even as their sounds are appearing live. It gives us, and them, the impression of simultaneously being on stage and online.

The Cathedral Band

As I mentioned, one of my concerns, as a composer of music for acoustic instruments, was that Web music would not be perceived as exclusive, either of the music that came before it, or the music happening around it. Rather, virtual music, by the very nature of its geographic scope, must be inclusive and embrace the sounds of multiple cultures. Thus, the Cathedral Band was created as an Internet band—playing both in concert and online— that would bridge the gap between the live acoustic worlds, both concert and traditional, and the online virtual world of *Cathedral*. Through periodic live performances that allow worldwide PitchWeb users to perform along with the musicians onstage, the band is the aspect of *Cathedral* that most incorporates live performance, and the physicality of the five moments, into the Web site.

The members of the band—who can vary from performance to performance—always includes DJ Tamara from Seattle who plays drum'n'bass and ambient samples, plus the PitchWeb and the PitchWeb MUD, or multiuser domain, which allows us to bring in players worldwide. Our first performance as a band—which took place in Seattle in August 1999 on DJ Tamara's weekly Groovetech Web radio show— included Tamara playing records, me playing the PitchWeb, and Stuart Dempster, the "first trombonist" of the avant-garde, playing trombone, toys, and didgeridoo. Since then, a core group of musicians has expanded to include "Blue" Gene Tyranny on keyboards (an original member of Iggy Pop and the Stooges, as well as a regular in the ensembles of a number of avant-garde musicians including Robert Ashley), Abel Domingues on guitar (a former member of Blondie), and the Australian didgeridoo virtuoso, William Barton, a band regular since our first performances together in Brisbane in 2002. The rest of the band varies depending on the location of the concert and their availability.

One of the goals of the Cathedral Band is the uniting of multiple cultural streams within a dialogue of structured improvisation, with each performer preserving his or her own uniqueness, identity, and voice. We have, from the beginning, developed associations with musicians from many cultures, to create a kind of international *Cathedral* "family." So far, we have performed with electric guitar, trombone and toys, mixed and toy percussion, Tibetan folk, Chinese pipa, Hindustani and Japanese vocalists, and Australian didgeridoo.

Arthur J. Sabatini, as the Chronicler, is the voice of *Cathedral*. In performance, the Chronicler tells the story of one of the five moments, expanding, although not explaining, its references and associations. The Chronicler establishes the connections between today and these five mystical moments in time. Since 2003, we also have worked with Shadows of the Chronicler—storytellers translating and responding to the musings of the Chronicler into other languages. These Shadows have included F. Math Lorenz working in Polish and Farsi at our Tisch School webcast from New York University in March 2003, and Fukutoshi Ueno working in Japanese, beginning with our performances in Tokyo in May 2003. Most of these performances are archived on the *Cathedral* site.

Musically, the band is coanchored by the DJ and the PitchWeb. Generally, a Cathedral Band performance is semi-improvised and reactive, with the onstage performers working within a general thematic and rhythmic framework, and sometimes developing a dialogue of musical motifs out of the material generated by the worldwide PitchWeb band. Our intention in incorporating the online PitchWeb players into the live performances is to let people join the band, as it were, and experience live music in a hands-on rather than a passive way. We have discovered that combining the Web experience with live concert events is both engaging for the audience and challenging for the professional musicians who play in the band.

Our live *Cathedral* webcasts began in 1998 from the Spoleto Festival USA in Charleston, South Carolina, with a performance of *Ghost Dance* by the Festival Orchestra with John Kennedy conducting. It was also the first webcast that the festival had participated in. From 1998 to 2001, the *Cathedral* webcasts continued from The Franklin Institute Science Museum in Philadelphia, Groovetech Web radio in Seattle, Roulette and Galapagos in New York, and Kiva in Phoenix. More recently, *Cathedral* webcasts have occurred in Australia at the Brisbane Powerhouse (2002), at TAMA Art University in Tokyo, Japan (2003), and from The Cutting Room, LaMama, and the Winter Garden in New York City, all in 2004.

The 48-Hour Webcast of 2001

In December 2001, the *Cathedral* Project—as Nora and I had begun to label the overall endeavor—produced a forty-eight-hour webcast streaming thirty-four concerts live from five continents, and, in the process, creating the largest festival of Internet music held to date. Arrangements for the festival had begun as early as our 1996 trip to Amsterdam, where our original discussions had suggested plans for *Cathedral* to culminate with a forty-eight-hour webcast in 2001. Ultimately, although we decided to leave *Cathedral* open-ended, we retained the idea of a forty-eight-hour webcast as a celebration of the completion of the first stage of development.

During the online festival, which took place between November 29 and December 2, our listeners experienced Tanzanian folk songs sung by Jonathan Hart Makwaia; the pipa playing of Wu Man; an audio tour of Krakow and Chicago; keyboard performances from Tokyo and Buenos Aires by Tomoko Yazawa and Walter Frank; Australian birdcalls and poetry from New Zealand performed by Warren Burt; as well as the collective contributions of PitchWeb bands playing day and night. In New York, the epicenter of the event, the Cathedral Band, joined by other groups and composers, performed throughout the weekend at Galapagos and Liberty Science Center, while the New York PitchWeb Band played at Harvestworks, a digital media center for the arts.[5]

Incidentally, one thing that we learned pretty quickly about putting music online is that webcasting an actual concert being performed in a "real" auditorium is not the same thing as creating a concert for the Web. A concert for the Web is a different auditory experience altogether; it's much more personal and more intimate. There is far less of a sense of being in a communal space in cyberspace, as there is, say, when sitting with other people inside a concert hall. On the Web, it is just you and your computer, everywhere and yet nowhere, at the same time. In that environment, music streamed in real time, we've found, is an intimate, up close, and in-your-head experience.

Internet Time

Artistically, what does this all add up to: a Web site, a PitchWeb, and an Internet band? What's different, formally and perceptually, from musical experiences of the past? Certainly, as a work of art, *Cathedral* is unlike any previous concert or theatrical model. To mention the most obvious reason why, the form of *Cathedral* is not expressed linearly in time; in fact, it's highly nonlinear. Time is no longer a factor in a piece of music that is always available; that has no beginning, middle, or end; and that no two people experience in the same order, or for the same length of time. If nothing else, *Cathedral* is a basic reconfiguration of the relationship between musical time and space, or in this case, cyberspace.

On first glance this may seem to create artistic chaos, because *Cathedral* can only be experienced in fragments, and, furthermore, appears to have "centers everywhere and boundaries nowhere," to borrow a phrase from Marshall McLuhan's last book *The Global Village*. But what we've found in the years that we have been doing this work is that there are new unifying artistic forms unique to cyberspace that can be intuited, and that the true identity of a work like *Cathedral* is *only* comprehended over time, through its many personalities. In cyberspace, these musical experiences appear like a series of worlds unfolding in real time. There is obvious order, but no real map, and no "correct" way to go forward, because development is unfolding in all directions at once, creating an interactive matrix of possibilities, and causing a plurality of forms to occur, all of which are individual, none of which are, in any sense, alike. Or, to look at it in yet another way, as musical space transforms in cyberspace, the artistic perceptive abilities of people will need to expand in order to comprehend three-dimensional thematic pathways that are to be taken with different pacings and different understandings of the "flowing" of time.

The result is a structure that is, at once, "simultaneous, discontinuous, and dynamic," to borrow another McLuhan phrase. McLuhan, who distinguished between different modes of viewing the world with this phrase, believed that a simultaneous, discontinuous, and dynamic structuring of information can plunge man "into a new form of knowing, far from his customary experience tied to the printed page," and that knowing itself is being recast and retrieved in this newer, nonlinear, 360-degree, acoustic form.[6]

As early as 1992, Marcos Novak, a transarchitect, artist, and theorist currently at UCLA, suggested in an essay titled "Liquid Architectures in Cyberspace" that on the Web "time itself may pulse, now passing faster, now slower"; it is the infinite possibilities of relating forms that drives Internet time. Novak thinks that we should abandon the metaphor of a flowing river of time in favor of the concept of metamorphic liquidity, architectures that, in his words, "breathe, pulsate, and transform from one form to another."[7]

Dante Tanzi, who is a member of the technical and musical staff in the Laboratory of Musical Information at the University of Milan, and who has been considering the questions of musical form and time on the Web since the early 1990s, believes that "the mobile and immaterial architecture of cyberspace leads communication away from a sequential and linear style, compelling subjective time to flow again and again around decisions already made." On the Web, "the differentiation between [the various] forms of time, [the] accumulation of performances, and [the] presence of decentralized configurations of subjectivity, upset not only [our] ideas of [musical] object and musical process but also [alter] the subjective point of view from which those ideas have been drawn."[8] In an essay written in 2000, Tanzi goes even further in saying that the impermanence of contexts and the pluralities of time forms on the Web establish new conditions for musical awareness, leading to diverse types of imaginative and symbolic operations. He observes that "we are asked to change our attitude towards the identification of musical events when music becomes a space inhabited and manipulated by many people, although the result is still to be perceived as a single process."[9]

The common theme running throughout all of these scenarios is the emerging of a new type of information exchange, one that encourages nonflowing musical time. The Web has created a new communications model that is more liquid that linear, and has multiple points of access and a seemingly infinite number of communication paths. Certainly, this model is more directly related to the functioning of a neural network than the "music as sonic artifact" concept of the past. Furthermore, the nonlinear, time-curving nature inherent in these new Web technologies and techniques, when distributed in large-scale throughout the network, offers, at least in principle, a new metaphor for consciousness, and a new format in which to create entirely new kinds of art.

But what kind of time does *Cathedral* explore? A. T. Mann, in his book *Sacred Architecture*, quotes the astrologer Robert Hand as saying that, spiritually, there have always been two ways to interpret time. The first, which Hand calls Type 1 religions, have a cyclical understanding of time, with a wheel of reality, implying reincarnation, liberation, enlightenment, and nirvana. Type 2 religions, by contrast, have a linear understanding of time, and they imagine a paradise at a definite time and place at some point in the future.[10] The philosopher Suzanne Langer, by contrast, writing in *Feeling and Form* (1958), said that there are three ways to experience time: clock time, by which she means time as sequence; lived or experienced time, which is the feeling of the "now" turning into the "past"; and virtual time, by which she means those musical moments when, focused on sound with a single sense—the sense of hearing—"sonorous forms move in relation to each other—always and only to each other, for nothing else exists there." She continues: "Virtual time is separate from the sequence of actual happenings as virtual space from actual space," calling it "an image of time measured by the motion of forms that seem to give it substance, yet a substance that consists entirely of sound."[11]

At its best, *Cathedral*, because of its Web-based, multidimensional nature, is capable of reflecting a combination of these "images" of time. If time is altered in *Cathedral*, then the space it exists in is altered, too. In *Unsilent Night*, for example, the audience is everyone who is physically in and around the boom box orchestra as it moves through the street. In the *Brain Opera*, the audience enters an individualized interactive environment but quickly becomes involved in a group-oriented, collaborative activity that is space bound. Whereas *Cathedral*, online and instantly available to everyone, always has an audience of multiple levels of one, at home alone, no matter how many other people also may be logged on. In a sense, *Cathedral* exhibits the sonic plasticity of Phil Kline's *Unsilent*

Night, but on a virtual level. And as visitors to *Cathedral*—by selecting their own unique paths through the content—engage in their own personalized version of our interactive story, the piece, in effect, folds back on itself, less monolithic and more like a Hoberman sphere. Because it unfolds in this nonlinear manner, it is up to the audience to reassemble it in space and time—thus creating their own order, and leaving with their own impression of what *Cathedral* is. Because each visitor to *Cathedral* creates a unique event, their visit is a moment in time—cybervisitors, as it were, come to reflect on five mystical moments in time. We are, after all, all bound by time. Fortunately, there are a few ways that we can momentarily escape, or at least suspend, this limitation; experiencing art is one of these ways.

6
CELL PHONES AND
SATELLITES

Alexander Graham Bell received a patent for the telephone in 1876; two years later, Thomas Edison received one for the phonograph. Bell's first phone call was to his assistant in the next room; the two machines were connected by a copper wire. Edison's phonograph recorded by having a vibrating stylus scratch the sound waves onto a sheet of tinfoil wrapped around a rotating cylinder. Although neither invention exactly qualifies as a new form of art, their widespread acceptance and further development over the next 125 years provides a good metaphor for both the extent of the technical innovations that took place in the twentieth century, and the equally innovative but still unimaginable ones yet to come in the twenty-first. In the same way that the mechanism of the phonograph has evolved from tinfoil and a stylus to iPods and surround-sound CDs, and the telephone has morphed into a wireless miniature of itself, complete with color screen, speed dialing, text messaging, and caller ID, continued wide-ranging innovations, coupled with new inventions, can be expected to further alter the technology that surrounds us, and that, in turn, will allow us to create new forms of art.

Consider the cell phone, for example. Couple it with global positioning satellites and the Internet, and then project it forward fifty years, and the combination appears capable of altering forever how we may "travel" through our daily lives. Already, new works of art involving sound, technology, and mass communications, developed through various combinations of the Internet, the cell phone, and the Global Positioning System (GPS), have taken place in various parts of the world. Simultaneously, on the political front, Smart Mobs, armed with cell phones and e-mail, are changing the way mass protests are staged and handled. Flash Mobs—those hundreds of people who show up simultaneously and unannounced at a given location (often a commercial store), stage a minidrama for perhaps ten minutes (generally involving an absurd plot and calls on cell phones), and then disappear—are brought together by e-mail, organized by cell phone, and documented and recruited on the Web.

The use of the telephone to transmit music and pictures, or even to create art, is not a new idea. Somewhere around the turn of the previous century, an opera was sent live over the telephone to New York as it was being performed in Philadelphia. In 1906, Thaddeus Cahill unveiled his Telharmonium, a 60-foot-long, 200-ton instrument intended to broadcast music to restaurants and hotels, as well as wealthy private homes, over the telephone lines, creating early Muzak, or the first important electronic-music machine, depending on your point of view. And in 1933, a live stereo broadcast of a concert was sent from Philadelphia to Washington, DC. Even the transmitting of photographs has a history dating back to 1927 and Herbert Hoover, whose picture was sent from Washington to New York. But it wasn't until composer Max Neuhaus began his series of *Public Supply* radio call-in works in 1966, and those regionally located works yielded the nationally organized *Radio Net* in 1977—performed by people across America over National Public Radio's network of 190 participating stations—that significant numbers of people became involved in performing music, collectively and interactively, over the telephone.

Radio Net

Max Neuhaus[1] began his musical career as a solo percussionist, one of the best. He was born in Beaumont, Texas, in 1939, and grew up outside of New York City. He once studied with the legendary swing band drummer Gene Krupa. During the heyday of the 1960s avant-garde, he played and toured with such giants as the German composer Karlheinz Stockhausen and the French composer and conductor Pierre Boulez. But in 1968, just as his first solo recording was about to be released, Neuhaus gave it all up; he quit performing, and became a composer himself, focusing much of his energy on creating sounds for public spaces, which often became the long-running, if not permanent, sonic architecture of the place. Examples of his work in this style include *Times Square,* a sound installation that, since 1977, has existed under a subway ventilation grate in a traffic island in the middle of New York's Times Square; and his 1968 *Listen* excursion, in which he bused his audience on one of his new-music "Field Trips Thru Found Sound Environments," this one to a New Jersey Power and Light Power Plant in South Amboy, to hear it as a work of art.

Since the mid-1960s, one of Neuhaus's primary interests has been utilizing public utilities in the service of art. Beginning with *Public Supply I,* performed over New York's WBAI in 1966, he combined a radio station with the telephone network to form a two-way "aural space"—in this case some twenty miles in diameter—in which listeners could interact and create a dialogue with sound simply by making a phone call. What interested Neuhaus was "the challenge of making a live work from unknown materials," and that the concept of all his broadcast works "is gathering lay people together to make music … music as an activity rather than a product," a group experience that he thinks has been largely lost in Western society.[2]

The first *Public Supply* piece began as a request for an interview from WBAI, but Neuhaus convinced the station's music director to allow him to create a work of art instead. Installing ten telephones at the station, he built a switching and mixing system, as well as a semiautomatic answering system to handle the calls. (It is worth remembering that neither telephone answering machines nor live radio call-in shows existed in 1966.) As the sounds came in over the phone lines, Neuhaus didn't alter them, but rather mixed and combined them, forming subgroups to be put on the air and adjusting their individual levels according to the types of sounds they were making. He even allowed the delayed feedback caused by people who called in while sitting beside their radios to go live, saying it "made a nice texture to the work." Calling the variety of sounds people contributed "much more than you could ever imagine," he explained that one person read a long poem, giving the piece momentary continuity, whereas others offered shorter sounds, some personal, a few mundane.[3]

Over the next eight years, Neuhaus recreated his interactive *Public Supply* piece at radio stations in other cities, including CJRT in Toronto (1968) and Chicago's WFMT (1973). It was the group activity that these pieces generated that gave him his real motivation, a process where people made sound together, listened to it, and adjusted what they were doing according to what they were hearing. This community dialogue was the heart of the musical process. Neuhaus considers the broadcast/telephone concept a musical form, calling it an "activity" rather than a finished work of art.

Reflecting on his *Public Supply* pieces, Neuhaus said recently that he chose the radio and telephone to focus on even though, at the time, they may have seemed like primitive technologies with which to make music, because they were, and still are, "the most widely used forms of live communication technologies we have." Labeling the global telephone system "the biggest machine we have ever made"—connecting some five hundred million different places on earth—Neuhaus says that "the telephone forms a two-way virtual space in the aural dimension," and points out that "we function in it aurally as if we were in one real space, but this space doesn't physically exist." What fascinated Neuhaus about radio was that it could give us a completely electronic "live ear view into a space which can be anywhere or nowhere." Referring to both the telephone and the radio as "single-dimensional virtual spaces," he points out that they extend our real world, rather than engulfing us in more multidimensional virtual realities, the way, for instance, that television does. For Neuhaus, single-dimension virtual aural spaces "reproportion, focus and stimulate imagination rather than becoming a substitute for it," creating virtual architectures acting as forums open to everyone interested in the evolution of musical sound.[4]

In 1977, when Neuhaus developed his telephone/broadcast concept for National Public Radio (NPR) on a national scale, he wanted to create a situation in which the callers would "do the mixing and grouping for themselves." This decision came partly from artistic reasons, and partly from practical ones. Neuhaus created five regional call-in centers for *Radio Net* and, obviously, couldn't be in all five places at once to mix and group the participants as he had in *Public Supply*. His solution was "to remove [himself] completely from that process and implement it as an autonomous electronic system."[5] Neuhaus configured the broadcast into five loops, one for each of the call-in cities—New York, Atlanta, Dallas, Minneapolis, and Los Angeles—all five passing through the central hub at the NPR station in Washington. At this time, NPR radio programs were distributed in a round robin system, meaning that telephone lines connected all the stations in a large loop stretching all the way across the country. Any station in the NPR system could broadcast nationally by opening the loop and feeding their program to all the others. Neuhaus "saw that it was possible to make the loop itself into a sound-transformation circuit" by closing it and inserting a frequency shifter so that the sounds would circulate, creating "a sound-transformation 'box' that was literally fifteen hundred miles wide by three thousand miles long." As sounds from individual callers came in and circulated, they became mixed and layered with the sounds of the loop. Referring to each loop as "in a sense a living thing" with its own characteristic sound, Neuhaus saw his role as tuning the loop, that is, constantly adjusting the gain, the mix, and the shift, a process he described as "holding the balance of this big five-looped animal with as little movement as possible."[6]

In Neuhaus's previous *Public Supply* pieces he had allowed the individual callers to decide the nature of the sounds they would make, but in *Radio Net* he decided to ask all the participants to whistle. He did this in order to give himself a body of pitched material with which to work. As the sounds came into each city, they passed through the self-mixers he had created and distributed to each of the five stations, and began to loop. Each cross-country pass created additional layers of sound that overlapped and slowly died out as new sounds took their place. By maintaining a continuous conference call with the engineers in the five cities during the broadcast, Neuhaus could hear each loop and could request that changes be made to one or more of them in frequency shift and/or gain.

During the course of the two hours on the Sunday afternoon that the program aired, ten thousand people called in and whistled their sounds. The writer and critic John Rockwell said that "what one heard at home was a subdued whistling cacophony that any listener with sufficient imagination could feel part of."[7] Neuhaus said that the people making the sounds were the real composers of the piece, and that his role was to be "the catalyst for the situation," setting up, as he did, the mechanism to make it all possible. He concluded, "maybe that's a new concept or role for a composer."[8]

Dialtones (a Telesymphony)

If Max Neuhaus's work represents the beginnings of interactive telephone music, then Golan Levin's *Dialtones (a Telesymphony)*, or *The Cell Phone*

Symphony as it is now more commonly known, represents one of its most recent and inventive manifestations. Unlike Neuhaus, who was dependent on his listeners' willingness to call the hub cities, Levin—thanks to the technological advances of the past quarter-century—is able to create his music by calling his participants directly. Employing hundreds of telephones, all at once and in the common space of an auditorium, Golan Levin (b. 1972) creates music of both charm and substance, arranging and spatially placing his sounds through the choreographed dialing and ringing of his audience's own mobile phones, an audience that is seated in a prearranged grid. Levin's creation is not a cacophonous jumble of ring tones, all going off at once, as you might imagine. It is a subtle, sophisticated organization of sounds, which, at times, may resemble a forest (with bird calls and sonic patterns snaking through the crowd), waves of harmonic progressions, or the canonlike ringing of polyphony, all plotted in space and time as carefully as a Mahler symphony, or a 3-D ride at Disneyland.

Levin has undergraduate and graduate degrees from the MIT Media Laboratory where he studied in the Aesthetics and Computation Group. He is quick to point out that one in ten people on the planet owns a mobile phone, giving him a ready stock of "instruments" for all of his performances. *Dialtones* represents Levin's "personal inquiry into abstract communications protocols"; he creates "new communications systems to explore such protocols," using them "in performances which strive to be both demonstrative yet sublime."[9] Although Levin is not particularly fond of the traditional sound of the telephone, saying "one cellphone sounds kind of horrible, but in unison, they can sound quite pretty,"[10] he does appreciate the telephone's high level of mechanical and design sophistication, pointing out that "the mobile phone's speakers and ringers make it a performance instrument … the buttons make it a keyboard and remote control … [and] the programmable rings make it a portable synthesizer."[11]

Levin achieves this degree of musical sophistication with an everyday appliance by being involved, both technically and artistically, in all aspects of the planning and performance of *Dialtones*. His first step, made with the help of his small team of programmers, is to design the customized ringtones, over one hundred different ones for each performance. Then, when the audience arrives at the concert, Levin asks each of them to register their mobile phones into a networked database (both the calling number and the model number), at special Web-based terminals located in the lobby or near the hall. Simultaneously, a seat is assigned to each participant and a new customized ringtone is encoded in RTTTL format (ringtone text transmission language) and downloaded to each user's phone using SMS, or short messaging service, which sends text messages between cell phones in a manner similar to e-mail. During the actual performance, which normally lasts some twenty-eight to thirty minutes, Levin's small group of programmer/performers activate the audience's mobile phones *en masse* by dialing them using a specially designed interactive graphical software interface that draws on the database of phone numbers collected before the concert. Because both the audience's seating positions and ringtone sounds are known in advance, Levin's musicians are able to create unique spatially distributed melodies and chords, as well as more novel textural phenomena such as waves of polyphony and roving clouds of sound that Levin categorizes as "a diverse range of unprecedented sonic phenomena and musically interesting structures."[12]

As a piece of music, *Dialtones* consists of three large subsections or movements, each some ten minutes in length. Additionally, the overall thirty-minute structure is overlaid by a group of fifteen "sound-textures," each about two minutes long. The first section consists entirely of these kaleidoscopic sound-textures produced through the ringing of various combinations of the audience's mobile phones. The second section is a solo movement performed on ten amplified cell phones by one of the *Dialtones* staff members. And the third movement is a combination of soloist and ensemble, ending with a climactic crescendo in which increasingly greater numbers of phones are rung. Although the maximum number of telephones that can be rung simultaneously with Levin's custom-designed software interface is sixty, a combination of almost instantaneous round robin dialing and the replacing of quieter rings with louder ones makes it appear that all of the audience's phones are ringing together. Levin created this three-part structure "to introduce the contrasting aesthetic possibilities of virtuosic real-time cell phone performance ('mobile phone jockeying') on the one hand, with coordinated-ensemble handheld-music on the other."

To support the spatial characteristics of the sound, and as a means of adding visual and diagrammatic dimensions to the performance, Levin also created two visual subsystems for *Dialtones*, one that casts a small overhead spotlight on the person or persons whose phone is being rung, the other a series of small red LED keychain lights that flash when they are held within one meter of a ringing phone. According to Levin, the combined effect of the ringing phones and the synchronized lights is "to render each participant as an audio-visual pixel," and the group as a simultaneous "audience, orchestra and (active) score." During the first two performances of *Dialtones*, both of which took place at the Ars Electronica Festival in Linz, Austria, on September 2, 2001, the two hundred people in each audience were arranged in a 20 × 10 seating grid. For the next seventeen performances, which occurred during May and June 2002 as a part of the Swiss National Exposition, each audience of ninety-nine participants was arranged into a 9 × 11 grid. For these performances, Levin estimates that somewhere between five thousand and eight thousand phone calls were placed.

Although *Dialtones* may sound like a highly programmed and controlled sonic experience, there is an element of Cagean chance involved because, ultimately, the exact realization of the piece is a function of both the sounds planned by the project's staff, in particular Scott Gibbons and Gregory Shakar, and the actual cell phones brought by the audience to the performance, phones from some thirteen different countries in the case of the two Linz performances. This is where the element of chance comes in, because not all cell phones can have their ring modified. For about one third of the phones in the audience, not only could Levin's team not change the ring, but also they had no way of knowing what sound these phones might make, an element of chance that influenced their planning and composing of the concert.

Golan Levin wrote *Dialtones* in the hope that experiencing a performance could "permanently alter the way in which its participants think about the cellular space we inhabit," inverting "our understandings of private sound, public space, electromagnetic etiquette, and the fabric of the communications network which connects us." Ultimately, if the global communications network is now to be considered "a single communal organism," then his goal in writing *Dialtones* was to "transform the way we hear and understand [this] multicellular being." By enclosing each participant inside the grid of the ringing instrument, the surrounding music "makes the ether of cellular space viscerally perceptible." By further pointing out that in *Dialtones* it is the phones themselves, and not their owners, that speak to one another, Levin says his participants are invited "to perceive an order in what is otherwise disorganized public noise, and ratify it as a chorus of organized social sound." This "determined Play" (as Levin refers to it) is a way to counteract "the overdetermination of the world of Work," transforming, and causing us to rethink "the noise of business, of untimely interruptions, [and] of humans enslaved to technology."

Sound Maps of Krakow

In April 2002, Matthew Mirapaul of the *New York Times* characterized the Global Positioning System (GPS) and the Internet as "invisible networks of digital information." He continued that GPS "is not strictly considered part of the Internet, but it is a close cousin. Both are invisible networks of digital information."[14] Mirapaul was specifically discussing Jeremy Wood and Hugh Pryor's car drawings. Wood and Pryor are two Englishmen who, since November 2000, have been plotting out gigantic drawings—animals, faces, other figures—over a map of the roads and towns of England.[14] They meticulously trace these routes with their car, tracking their progress as they go with portable GPS equipment that measures and records their movements to within a few yards. Their journeys are then reproduced on the Internet in a scale small enough and fast enough for the figure they traced earlier to become visible.

Wood and Pryor are able to create these virtual drawings thanks to the Global Positioning System, a network of twenty-four satellites—twelve of which are always above the horizon any place on earth—whose triangulated timing signals can be used to calculate one's latitude and longitude and—with the help of signals from a fourth satellite—altitude, too. Operated by the Defense Department—which lifted the restrictions on the sale of portable consumer models in 2000—GPS devices are now used by everyone from hikers, to truckers, to people who make art, art that runs the gamut from the doodlings of Wood and Prior, to the Sound Maps of Krakow (or GPS-Art) being made in Poland by Marek Choloniewski.

Marek Choloniewski (b. 1953)[15] studied organ and composition at the Krakow Academy of Music, where he now teaches and, since 2000, also directs the Electroacoustic Music Studio. Along the way, he cofounded the multimedia jazz/rock band Freight Train, started the Krakow Society of Contemporary Music, and became known as a virtuoso "live computer music" performer. Since December 2000, Choloniewski has been creating interactive sound maps of his hometown of Krakow. With a small group of assistants, he has been driving a car through the streets, tracking his progress, phoning sounds in to the studio from various locations, and allowing the car's route to trigger prerecorded city sounds along the way. Beginning with the second GPS-Art performance in 2001, Choloniewski and his team applied a similar process to film, photographs, and graphic material, which they regard as companion components of the audio, and which takes the "form of puzzles completing the whole map of the city." Because all of these disparate elements are being triggered simultaneously, the composite is webcast live on the Internet, along with a map to track the car's progress in real time, and periodic verbal commentary describing where they are and what is taking place. Choloniewski calls the result "a combination of slide-show, multimedia tourist-guide and city collage."[16]

Choloniewksi's GPS-Art is a new field of artistic activity based on the idea of motion on a large, outdoor scale such as occurs in a city or other open space. Choloniewski says that the portable GPS device is the centerpiece—or "global interactive instrument" as he refers to it—of the entire endeavor, because it is used for both the "creation and processing of the audio and video material." He uses the capability of GPS to interactively measure a number of different topographic parameters as the starting point for all of his work with GPS-Art "as basic information for the live control of the audio-visual composition."

The first GPS-Art project took place on December 16–17, 2000. Sponsored by PTK Centertel and called *GPS-Trans 1,* it took the form of a twelve-hour Internet composition, webcast in four three-hour blocks of time over the two-day period. During the webcast, sounds from various neighborhoods of Krakow and the surrounding area were transmitted over sixteen cell phones to the studio, where they were mixed and transformed. The resulting composite sound was then sent through the Internet, received back some seconds, or even minutes, later (a latency factor inherent in the Net), and then looped and sent out again, creating, as Choloniewski characterizes it, a rising wave of sound. These Internet Loop and Internet Delay systems formed the basis of the sound processing for *GPS-Trans 1*. Choloniewski notes that this two-day webcast was the first noncommercial Internet broadcast activity to take place in Krakow.

GPS-Trans 2, the second part of Choloniewski's "city sound and visual exploration," was a sixty-minute performance on the evening of August 9, 2001. A map of Krakow functioned as a graphic score of this audio-visual composition. The position and speed of the car as it moved triggered and controlled a variety of prerecorded city sounds that were then mixed with the live sounds from the car and transformed in the studio. Simultaneously, a similar mixing and transforming process was applied to the visual materials (film, photographs, etc.), and the composite was broadcast live on the Web. *GPS-Trans 3* was a similar work, occurring for two hours on the afternoon of December 2, 2001, and was webcast live as a part of *Cathedral's* forty-eight-hour webcast of thirty-four concerts streamed live from five continents. In addition to a similar interactive, audio, and visual "map" of Krakow, complete with Internet looping and delay, it included a public performance and monitoring space at the Bunkier Sztuki (or Bunker of Arts), a stronghold of the avant-garde directly across from the Palace of Arts at Szczepanski Square.

For *GPS-InterTrans 4*, a ninety-minute presentation on the evening of June 30, 2003, Choloniewski established what he called a live Internet sound and data bridge between Chicago and Krakow. Chicago was chosen, partly to highlight and explore the connection between the Polish immigrant background of that city and the historical elements of Krakow, and partly because Ryan Ingebritsen, who lives in Chicago, had worked with Choloniewski in Krakow on *GPS-Trans 3*. In *GPS-InterTrans 4*, Choloniewski combined live, interactive videos and animations from Krakow with sounds from both Krakow and Chicago; both Choloniewski and Ingebritsen were able to manipulate and alter these sounds live. Additionally, a car moving through Krakow was used to determine and trigger the sequence and character of events.

Ingebritsen was able to connect his computer with the main GPS receiver in Krakow and, from Chicago, translate the car's coordinates into

MIDI information, which he then used to control various parameters of a sequencer and other processing equipment, "creating rhythms that would become more frantic as the car accelerated and would vary sonically as the car traveled around." There were a number of different levels of interaction possible, because the movement of the car could also affect the performance in Chicago in real time. In past GPS-Art performances, the latency of the Web had meant that Ingebritsen and Choloniewski had been able to communicate only through audio streams that were delayed "sometimes by an interval of up to 1.5 minutes." Now, however, the latency was a mere fifteen-second roundtrip delay (from Chicago to Krakow and back), and the "reaction time from movement of the car to sequencer to the server in Krakow was only about 7 seconds." This made for a far more cohesive performance between the two sites, and Ingebritsen and Choloniewski were able to "synchronize the performance and still maintain the use of Internet delay that [they] explored during *GPS-Trans 3*." They created "long washes of sound" by passing the sound stream back and forth, changing it and adding to it as they saw fit, "until it was something different from what we had started with and the perspective had changed."[17]

Marek Choloniewski sees his various GPS-Art projects as "an artistic transformation of the city," combining wireless cell phone data transmission with Internet transmission. The moving car becomes a "kind of playing finger," and the city "a giant resonating instrument"; an instrument that, thanks to the Web, he can play for the whole world. Choloniewski understands the global implications of his work, and is ready to extend the boundaries of GPS-Art beyond Krakow, "to be realized on land, air, [and] underwater, as well as in outer space."

Scanner

The line between voyeurism and art, if not between what's legal and what's not, is often uncertain in the work of Robin Rimbaud. Using the name Scanner—which he took from the police radio receiver he plays live in performance—Rimbaud samples people's private cell phone conversations, weaving their disembodied, but still personal, narratives into both his recorded music and his ambient-techno stage performances; unsuspecting voices become raw material for his sometimes dark and mysterious sonic collages. Called everything from a telephone terrorist to a techno-data pirate to an audio voyeur, Scanner says that he is merely working with the "sonic debris" that exists "within an indiscriminate ocean of signals flying overhead, but just beyond our reach."[18] As technology gets more sophisticated, you would think it would become more secure; however, Scanner points out that today, more than ever before, privacy is an illusion. Rather than invading privacy, his work has become "an illustration of the end of privacy."[19]

Scanner is also quick to point out that, at least in his recorded music, he uses these found voices carefully and respectfully, changing their pitch and removing any personal references such as phone numbers or full names. As he describes it, "I use the relationships between people, not the people themselves."[20] In a live performance, however, caller anonymity is more difficult to control. Scanner has sampled and played live everything from drug deals to dinner arrangements to illicit affairs; on another night it was phone sex, grocery lists, and a family feud. In a live Scanner performance, any cell phone call within a one-mile radius of the stage is accessible and fair game. Once, he even sampled someone making funeral arrangements, but quickly moved on when he realized what he'd done. It is this feeling of dangerous uncertainty surrounding what may be said next that makes a live Scanner performance not only shocking and disturbing but also quite often spellbinding. But what most intrigues Scanner about using cell phone voices is the impermanence of the sounds, and the magical quality they conger up, adding, "It's almost like ... hearing ghosts."[21]

Born in 1964 in Wandworth, South London, Robin Rimbaud says his love of sound dates back to age eleven and a memorable experience at school, when his teacher played for the class a recording of the prepared piano music of John Cage. Even at age eleven, he felt that Cage's music was "extraordinary ... another world."[22] Two years later, when another teacher gave him a reel-to-reel tape recorder, Rimbaud used it to make tape loops—recording family dinner conversations, sounds from inside the piano (much to the consternation of his mother who played the piano quite well in a more traditional way), and sounds he picked up by hanging the microphone out of the window—listening to these loops incessantly because he thought they were so beautiful. (Incidentally, Rimbaud has all his early tapes, table talk included, neatly filed away, claiming he has saved every recording he has ever made. Considering the fact that he also bought an early record-enabled Walkman and began to keep a sonic diary, the number of cataloged tapes, as can be imagined, is quite substantial now.)

A student of literature rather than a trained musician, Rimbaud says that of all the influences on his work, John Cage "has been a consistent figure." Since hearing the prepared piano in 1975, Rimbaud has attended concerts, read all of his writings, and even met Cage. He told Jose Miguel G. Cortes that it was Cage's "influence that led me to zoom in on these spaces in-between—between language and understanding," summing up the distinction as "taking the ordinary and attempting to make it extraordinary." It was from Cage that he learned "that sound is ever present," and Cage started him on his quest to erase the distinction between public and private space.[23] In 2002 Rimbaud told Tamara Palmer that "chance is a key factor in all that we create," and he embraces "this Cagean approach to be creative."[24]

In early 1993, Rimbaud and his friend Mike Harding started a record label—Ash International—to release records originally made in illegal places, such as prisons, Air Force Bases, and even a runaway train. Rimbaud characterizes the label's early releases—the first two of which were his own—as "work based on sampling that played with copyright laws and with issues of public space and private space."[25] Ash 1.1, for instance, simply titled *Scanner,* includes tracks with names such as "Connection," "A Crossed Line," and "Sometimes a Call is More Than You Bargained For." *Scanner2* (Ash 1.2) soon followed, as did more. These "completely analogue" early Scanner releases were made using only a four-track Tascam recorder and a Digitech Time Machine, which was basically a sampler with "a 7.6-second time delay, [and] an echo."[26] Scanner's sixth album, *Delivery,* a more melodic and therefore accessible album to some, was the first to be released in the United States. By the mid-1990s, Scanner was popular not only with the techno crowd but also with Karlheinz Stockhausen— a pioneer in electronic music—who told Rimbaud, "you're using a sphere of sound that others don't use."[27]

Andy Battaglia notes that it is in some ways fitting that an artist as fascinated by sound as is Rimbaud "would make music explicitly about the act of listening." Battaglia adds, "as a former student of literature [Scanner uses] these disconnected voices, caught literally and figuratively in between stations ... as a blank narrative construct to which we almost always instinctively attach a narrative arc."[28] Transcending their identities, the unsuspecting callers, caught up in their own dramas, become the invisible actors of plays inside our minds, feeding us dialogue, and opening up a secret window onto a world Scanner designs in real time. When he first began to use found conversations, Scanner played them off against environmental sounds, but that after a while he "began to dissolve the voices," making of them a texture that "barely emerges from a sonic ambience that is viral, meshed, conspiratorial, dark, introverted, and organic." In all of his work, he explores "the hidden resonance's and meaning within the memory ... the 'ghosts' within sound."[29] For Scanner, using phone conversations in his work has had the effect of "bringing the human voice back into electronic music," and "giving faceless music a human side."[30]

The Mob Scene

If Scanner's use of private cell phone conversations in performance and Marek Choloniewski's GPS-Art projects are serious endeavors focusing on the artistic implications of the cell phone, GPS technology, and the Web, then the various "mob scenes" that have recently begun appearing in various parts of the world represent a new form of social statement, fueled by similar technology, but reflecting on group action as created by a bunch of strangers, with a sense of humor, incorporating the element of surprise. Actually, there is a lot that is still unknown at this writing about the brief history of the mob scene, or flash mobs, as they are sometimes called. For starters, it isn't known for sure *whose* idea they were in the first place, although somebody named "Bill" in New York usually gets the credit. Although "Bill" has allowed himself to be interviewed, he won't let anyone photograph or identify him, saying only that he is presently "working in the culture industry."[31] In early June 2003, "Bill" started e-mailing his friends, who forwarded his message to their friends, *ad infinitum* (as one can only imagine), considering how quickly mob scenes began to spring up simultaneously in so many different parts of the world. Essentially, "Bill's" message tells his friends a time and place for all of them to meet. Once there, this mob is given directions to the real scene of the action, plus a "mini-script" for them to follow. "Bill" says the reason they have a staging area now is that their first mob action, at a place called Claire's Accessories, didn't include one, and somebody alerted the store.

Little is know about this first mob action at Claire's Accessories. All "Bill" said is that "the store sort of freaked out" because they knew ahead of time. But the second mob scene appeared at Macy's Department Store in Herald Square on June 17, 2003, and it was subsequently documented in both the *New York Times* and the *New York Post*. "Bill" says the premise of all his mob action efforts "is to create an inexplicable mob, somewhere in New York, for 10 minutes or less." In the case of Macy's, more than one hundred people suddenly showed up in the rug department, all claiming to live together in a warehouse commune on Long Island, and to be there looking for "a love rug" big enough to cover their floor. Then, as suddenly as they had come, the mob was gone, leaving no trace that they were ever there. Almost immediately occurring at the rate of one every two weeks or so, the mob scene then struck at the Grand Hyatt Hotel near Grand Central, where, on July 2, 2003, they suddenly began applauding spontaneously from the lobby mezzanine before disappearing into the crowd. The mob then showed up at the upscale Otto Tootsi Plohound shoe store in SoHo, where their pretend bus trip from Maryland supposedly descended, while they stood around making cell phone calls to their friends describing their trip; later, a scene developed at the American Embassy in Berlin, where the mob "wore silly hats, waved flags and popped champagne," drinking a toast to "Natasha ... before vanishing."[32]

It is important to understand—not just with mob scenes, but with cell phones and GPS-Art in general—that the technology that is employed in these actions not only shrinks the actual world into a handheld portable one but also reduces the time factor involved in getting ideas and information from point A to point B. Within a few short months, the mob scene scenario emerged not only in New York but also in San Francisco, Austin, Minneapolis, Dortmund, Rome, Vienna, Zurich, and Australia. But what, if anything, do these Dada-inspired mob scenes add up to? "Bill" says, "people take different messages" from the mobs, some seeing them as social, others as more of a political statement, a kind of "reclaiming the streets you live in." For "Bill," it's just "visually stunning" when the mob "comes together from out of nowhere," but he acknowledges that although the mob is "incredibly friendly, [it] does send a message."

Unfortunately, the message the street demonstrators sent at the first antiglobalization WTO protests and riots in Seattle in 1999 was anything but friendly, and it caught the authorities unprepared for the new level of communication sophistication the protesters now possessed. This early smart mob, as it has come to be called, functioned more like an army, with battlefield "commanders" communicating by cell phone, directing both peaceful protesters and rioters where to deploy and what places to avoid. Howard Rheingold—whose book, *Smart Mobs: The Next Social Revolution,* is one of the first serious works to explore the deeper meaning and significance of political mob actions—notes that smart mobs are quickly becoming a major outlet of political activism. This amplified human talent for cooperation—brought together by the new communication and Internet technologies—can be both beneficial and destructive. Pointing to everything from the radio chips designed to replace barcodes, to sales on eBay, to the wireless Internet nodes now installed in many parks, coffee shops, and hotels, as "products with invisible intercommunicating smartifacts," Rheingold says that the pieces of the smart mob technology puzzle "are all around us now, but haven't joined together yet." Even so, Rheingold says, individual members of smart mobs cooperate with each other in ways never before possible, because each person in the mob carries handheld devices "that possess both communication and computing capabilities." Already, these mobile devices, when "they connect the tangible objects and places of our daily lives with the Internet," begin to mutate, becoming "remote control devices for the physical world." [33]

The Next Big Thing

Computers and experimental music have shared the stage in America since 1957, when Lejaren Hiller and Leonard Isaacson wrote the *Illiac Suite* (a string quartet they composed with the help of a computer), and Bell Labs electrical engineer Max V. Mathews, assisted by John Pierce and Newman Guttman, made the first computer-generated sounds. Since then, a constant parade of new innovations in technology have continually reshaped music in all kinds of exciting but unexpected ways. It is little more than guesswork predicting what the future uses and associations of the computer (and now the Internet) with experimental music may be someday. But there are certain trends and attitudes developing now that bear watching in the future.

The most innovative of the new generation of digital sound artists are the ones working in the laptop-techno scene. Playing in clubs, bars, and coffee houses, alternately jamming and taking solo turns, often sitting around tables with their computers plugged into the club's sound system, these musicians are not so much looking for a following as following the technology into the future. Thanks to such innovative computer programs as Max/MSP, a graphical programming environment for music and multimedia (an extension of the Max program developed in the mid-1980s by Miller Puckette at IRCAM in Paris, and named for Max Matthews), laptop-techno composers are able both to synthesize and process their sounds by creating data-flow networks linking a series of different processing modules together. These composers can design all their own sounds and create their own instruments, virtually, inside their computers. George Cicci, a laptop musician from West Virginia now playing in New York, says that this high level of control is the most interesting to him. The process is simple: "We just take a basic wave form and build on it and build on it and build on it until it's our own."[34] Some laptop artists, not content with the similarity of sounds obtained from the "off-the-shelf" solutions, have begun to develop their own software. GDAM is one of these new programs, created in part by New York laptop-techno artist Geoff Matters, aka geoffGDAM. Standing for Geoff and Dave's Audio Mixer, GDAM is "an open source DJ rig ... that cuts and mixes MP3s like a vinyl DJ gone cyborg."[35]

In addition to the love of technology that all laptop-techno musicians have, there is also an attitude, not so much about the pros and cons of sampling, as about *becoming* the instrument, and finding new ways to interact more deeply with the machine. This attitude of convergence can easily be observed when laptop musicians get together to talk about their computers, a conversation that sounds remarkably similar to the love and respect classical musicians have always bestowed on their violins and clarinets. The important question for the future is whether this developing symbiotic relationship—from computer geek and laptop computer, to man and machine, to musician and musical instrument—is ready to take another step? The answer is: Maybe.

Or maybe it has already begun. Consider, for example, Shawn Hatfield, a leading California laptop-techno artist who works under the name of Twerk. What interests him about working with these new kinds of interactive music programs is how it makes it possible for him to tell the computer exactly what he wants it to do, saying that it feels like "building human replicators to copy the way I would make music." Confessing that he already feels musically incomplete without his computer, he says, "I think at some point, when technology is ready, I will become the machine I'm using."[36]

7

ART AND ETHICS ONLINE

Predicting the future is risky even under the best of circumstances, but patently impossible when it comes to the future of technology, particularly when those predictions must take into account not only the rapid growth of the Internet but also the exponential increases in computing power and speed. And when all the new paraphernalia that will be affected by these ever increasing advances in chip design also is taken into account—wireless personal computers, Web sites, interactive cell phones, smart clothing, global positioning satellites, virtual reality, and online games galore—and then multiplied by some unimaginable nanotechnology-driven growth in capacity and speed all its own, the future of the Web, and of music on the Web, appears to be unlimited, and certainly not to be comprehended, imagined, or accurately predicted very many years in advance.

At the same time, as we approach this fundamental shift in aesthetic self-consciousness and artistic self-awareness (as the current music-mind-body realignment will surely come to be regarded someday), there are persistent artistic dilemmas and nagging ethical questions for which, at the moment at least, no easy answers appear. To further complicate this problem, how artists and listeners, as well as courts and legislatures, may respond to some of these issues over the next decade will almost certainly determine, in some fundamental way, the future course of music on the Web.

One of the main musical challenges Web musicians face today is the continuing search for an artistic level of acceptable sound quality, so that the sheer beauty of sound—what music is all about—comes through and is not forgotten and lost online. Another challenge is the need to find creative new ways to both overcome and, at the same time, musically incorporate the latency factor inherent in the transmission of Internet sound. Latency, the amount of time that it can take for a sound to get from point A to point B on the Web, is greatly influenced by both the distance involved and the amount of Internet traffic occurring at that particular moment. It is this latency factor, heard as a delay inherent in both audio and MIDI file transmissions, that makes a rhythmically synchronized, multisite performance online all but impossible to attain.

The most sensitive unresolved ethical issues concern the legal and moral debate surrounding free and unrestricted copying and file sharing versus copyright and ownership, as well as the question of continued open source development versus restrictive proprietary software, and whether the Web will remain a free environment or become less open and more destined to serve politics and commerce. Ultimately, the key aesthetic question is what long term, lasting effects these issues, and their eventual resolutions, will have on nurturing or diminishing future Internet creativity, and on the more subtle shaping and sustaining of the online artistic content of tomorrow. Although that question cannot be answered today—as none of the other issues raised here can, for that matter—it is not too soon to consider them and reflect on the changes that may eventually ensue.

As with any newly emerging technology, the key artistic questions have always been *"What are we gaining?"* and *"What are we giving up?"* As advanced or innovative as any new technological improvement may at first appear, it almost always presents the potential user with an enigmatic—sometimes either/or—artistic tradeoff. Consider the digital revolution in recorded sound of the 1980s, a time when music consumers switched their buying habits from the analog sounds of LPs and cassettes to the digital sounds of CDs. By almost all accounts, this change was both a major technological breakthrough and a positive aesthetic experience. Nevertheless, there are a significant group of people, among them many professional musicians and recording engineers, who still prefer the "feel" of analog sound, and argue that digital sound—because it only draws samples of waveforms (44.1 kHz/16-bit stereo, in the case of most CDs)—is too cold, dry, and brittle when compared with the warmer analog sounds of LPs, which offer a more accurate tracking of the waveform itself.

Calling the shift to digital technology in the early 1980s a "fundamental change in the history of Western music," Timothy D. Taylor, in his book, *Strange Sounds: Music, Technology & Culture,* labeled it the most important change "since the invention of music notation in the ninth century." Pointing further to the invention of movable type in the early sixteenth century as another historic change that allowed music to "escape its former boundaries" and composers to take a step up "the ladder of social respectability," he noted that a new musical "public" suddenly appeared as a result of this newfound ability to print and distribute multiple copies of musical scores. Taylor concluded that "with each historical technological breakthrough, each technological shift, there are changes in social organization."[1]

For us today, at the beginning of our own "fundamental change," one of the more far-reaching shifts in our own social reorganization, and perhaps a benchmark on which to measure progress, is likely to be that the mass media, and in particular television, will soon be offering a level of participation comparable with the computer and the cell phone. When this potential for interactive access becomes a real-time possibility on such a grand scale—when everybody with a television set can literally get into the act—it is not very difficult to imagine the resulting aesthetic reorientation that might occur, and the new "musical public" this shift could easily engender.

Web Sound

The Web, which started in stillness and silence, began to open up to sounds and moving images in the early 1990s as new multimedia-capable software such as Macromedia Director appeared. Director began as Video Works for the original Apple Macintosh, but spun off into its present incarnation around 1987. A Windows version appeared in the early 1990s, and by the late 1990s the Flash Web media delivery system had been created from basic Director technology. The importance of Flash was that it was the first program to create animations and other interactive

Web page functions using vector-based imaging, allowing for much smaller source files and faster download times. Plus, Flash was designed for use by people who didn't know how to code, so that Web designers could work with it without first needing to acquire programming skills.

A key advantage of this new multimedia software was that it could accept and incorporate any number of different file formats and allow them all to be integrated into one multimedia program without the need for a separate and time-consuming recoding of each individual file. At first, there were three main types of audio files that programs such as Director had to accommodate: AU and WAV files for PCs running Windows, and AIFF files for the Macintosh. Also available, of course, was Standard MIDI, which first appeared in 1983. MIDI files could be successfully handled by almost any computer, because they were small and compact compared with audio files, which were (and still are) huge and packed with data. In the mid-1990s, audio files were at the uppermost end of the maximum file size that could be transmitted online with the bandwidth that was available. A minute of CD-quality audio, for example, sent at 56 kbps could take twenty-five minutes to download.

By the turn of the century, a number of different Web audio formats existed. Of these, the most successful were RealAudio, Windows Media Audio, QuickTime, and MP3. All four supported both the streaming and downloading of music files. Essentially, downloading involves moving an entire audio file to one's own hard drive—where it then permanently resides—before it can be listened to and, perhaps, copied and traded. Streaming, by contrast, allows the user to hear the music when the file is still arriving at the home computer, much like a radio broadcast, but the file disappears when it has played and cannot be saved. Highly compressed, the streamed file was, at first, of poorer playback quality, particularly so in the case of video files that often seemed to jerk from image to image. Another problem with streaming audio and video in the mid-1990s was that the relatively slow delivery speed of 56 kbps, or even lower, meant that the average home computer would regularly "outrun" the incoming data and need to pause for a moment while more arrived. When *Cathedral* first went online in 1997, for example, we could only count on streaming about fifty-eight seconds of audio without a stutter in the music as the buffer in some home computers paused to reload.

Phil Kline with boom box in Washington Square Park, New York City.
Photo: Tom Jarmusch

Tod Machover in the Sensor Chair of the *Brain Opera*.
Photo: Johannes Kroemer

The Mind Forest of the *Brain Opera*.
Photo: Johannes Kroemer

A child explores The Melody Easel of the *Brain Opera*.
Photo: Johannes Kroemer

William Barton, didgeridoo, joins William Duckworth, PitchWeb, as the oldest instrument in the world meets the newest.
Photo: Nora Farrell

The Cathedral Band in performance at the Brisbane Powerhouse in 2002.
Photo: Nora Farrell

GPS-Trans 3 director Marek Choloniewski (with inserts of the GPS-equipped car) during *Cathedral's* forty-eight-hour Web festival of 2001.

Grey Album cover by Søren 'Kaos' Karstensen (www.worldofkaos.com), designed for his own use, but now the de facto cover for everyone with a copy of the album.

Although most audio formats could offer both the streaming and downloading of music files, in the market certain companies gained more attention for one format than for the other. RealNetwork's RealAudio soon became the acknowledged leader in multimedia streaming, and by 2001 RealNetwork claimed an install base for its free downloadable RealAudio player of two hundred million users. Created as a Web media architecture, RealAudio had the ability to stream both audio and video files to home computers over the then existing dial up connections of 14.4, 28.8, and 56 kbps, thanks in large part to the RealAudio and RealVideo codecs, or digital data compression schemes, that RealNetwork developed and employed. A codec is a formula that removes extraneous data from an audio file, thus reducing it significantly in size and making it easier to download or stream. In most instances, this extraneous data is considered redundant in some way and the frequencies that are removed as unessential to the quality of the sound. Perhaps the codec formula takes out the quiet sounds covered over by louder ones, or whole bands of sound beyond the normal range of hearing, or even the noises between the sounds. But no matter what the specific formula under which a codec operates, the disadvantage of a codec is that the finished product is sound that has been "compressed," and the resulting sound is new in ways that can be heard. The advantage of a codec, on the other hand, is that a four-minute song that began as a forty-five megabyte file can be reduced, with MP3 compression, to a file 4 megabytes in size that most home computers can manage in a reasonable amount of time, and that still sounds relatively good.

Microsoft's Windows Media Audio, RealAudio's main competition during the 1990s, gained widespread attention and support because it was included in the Windows operating package, becoming, as it did, an integral part of Windows XP. QuickTime, by contrast, began as a media architecture developed by Apple. Strictly speaking, QuickTime is not a codec but, rather, a container architecture that supports and integrates a large number of other audio and video compression formulas, including its own Qdesign Music codec. During the 1990s, QuickTime offered a relatively high compression rate, and, beginning with QuickTime 5, also accepted MP3 formatted files. In 2002, *MacAddict* reported that over half a million video sites on the Web contained QuickTime content.[2]

By the end of the twentieth century, however, the music codec most people preferred to use was MP3, shorthand for "MPEG 1 or 2, Audio Layer 3." MPEG stands for the Motion Picture Experts Group, an organization that continually determines international standards for compressing and encoding audio and video. With good sound quality developed through a codec offering relatively high compression rates, plus the added advantage of portability with the appearance of the Diamond Rio MP3 player in 1998 (which held an hour of music), MP3 quickly became the audio format of choice for playing downloadable files. For example, by 1997, Macromedia said its Shockwave plug-in, which handled MP3 files, had been downloaded and installed in an estimated fifteen million homes and offices.

As music continued to play a larger role in Web site development and design during the late 1990s, and as record companies and their artists began developing sites of their own, the fact that no audio format offered copy protection—meaning that proprietary music files, once downloaded by anyone, could be copied and freely traded—became an increasing point of concern for these copyright holders. To overcome this free-trade flaw in the software, some companies began to experiment with encrypting the audio files, and embedding secret security safeguards within them. Companies such as Liquid Audio and a2b Music (a joint venture between Bell Labs and AT&T) created "watermarked" codes that remained with a file even through its most distant copies—complete with some form of identifying information such as the original downloader's credit card number—that could trace any unauthorized distribution back to its source. Whereas in a climate both expectant and distrustful, programmers and designers were often asked, especially by their corporate clients, to create multiple versions of the same audio and video for their Web sites, a conglomeration described in 1999 by *Wired* writer Ted Greenwald as "a streaming format (such as RealMedia), a downloadable format (usually MP3), and a secure downloadable format (such as Liquid Audio or a2b)."[3] Different data rates also had to be accommodated, from the super slow 28.8 kpbs to the lightning fast T1, which moved information at 1500 kbps, but which few individual users could afford.

By 2003, cell phone songs and ringtones were becoming the new benchmark for measuring both the latest uses of, and levels of quality for, downloadable digital sound. New models of cell phones played music, and could receive hundreds of songs and play them in a multichannel audio format. Although the American ringtone market was still several years behind Europe and Japan, the buying and selling of ringtones had become a viable business for U.S. record labels and mobile phone networks, with some $80–$100 million worth of sounds commercially downloaded in the United States every year. According to the *New York Times,* cell phone users worldwide bought $2.5–3.5 billion worth of custom ringtones in 2003.[4] If Thomas Dolby Robertson had not quite yet reached his goal of providing cell phone and other handheld-device users with a "rich, personalized, immersive audio experience," both Beatnik, and their competitors, were certainly drawing closer.

Why continue to worry about the quality of online sound? Hasn't it improved dramatically? Isn't it continuing to improve? Even in the case of those annoying cell phone rings that occur today in the most inconvenient of places, isn't the tradeoff, if there is one, that, at least, they all sound better now? The answer, of course, is yes; online sound has improved, dramatically so, and music, in all its many manifestations, has secured a place online. Streamed files no longer stutter, buffers load quietly behind the scenes, and data files, large enough to crash the server several years ago, now flow freely and quickly through the virtual pipelines of cable modems, T1 lines, and DSLs.

But one fundamental problem with online sound has not changed. It is a dual problem inherent in the compression of the sound, which involves the digital redrawing of complex analog waveforms with less accuracy, coupled with MP3 compression that then analyzes this "lesser" signal and discards whole bands of "redundant" information. Through these processes, the original sound, the actual music, has been degraded twice. Unless we, as listeners, are all careful, this lesser quality of sound will remain the online norm. Our responsibility is to remain aware that this difference in quality exists, not allow online sound to stray too far away from the source of good sound, and continue the search until new richer "virtual" ways of capturing and preserving sound are eventually found. John Krogh, a writer for *Electronic Musician,* characterizes these turn-of-the-century audio formats, including MP3, as "just interim technology, the wax cylinders of the digital age."[5] Craig Anderton, writing in

Keyboard magazine, put the problem more bluntly; "data compression" he said "is not about subtlety."[6]

Latency

In digital music, time is measured in milliseconds (ms): a single second is divided into a thousand parts. Although one one-thousandth of a second may not seem to take much time, it can be heard as a click on a CD if a millisecond of silence is left somewhere in the middle of a song. When music is performed live, there is a little more latitude for delay before the music sounds "out-of-sync." But, with a 10 ms to 15 ms difference, the ear can easily hear a delay, one reason why transatlantic phone calls sent by satellite seem surrounded by echoes—their delays are hundreds of milliseconds long.

On the Web, unfortunately, the problem of latency is both noticeable and unavoidable. As Phil Burk was developing WebDrum in the late 1990s, he once measured the roundtrip online latencies from his office in San Francisco to various locations around the world, including his ISP in California (13–140 ms delay), Japan (220–350 ms delay), STEIM in Amsterdam (220–400 ms delay), and Queensland, Australia (330–500 ms delay). Burk concluded that "because a latency of 100 to 300 milliseconds is very typical [online], it is not practical to engage in a traditional real-time 'jam' where musicians play 'in time' with each other."[7] John Maxwell Hobbs agreed, calling a synchronized online jam "next to impossible," and, more importantly, saying he thought "a form of performance that uses the delay as an intrinsic element needs to be developed" for the Web.[8]

The concept of latency, in the form of echo and delay, is not new to experimental musicians; some have used it creatively for years. I've already described two early efforts. Max Neuhaus allowed delayed feedback to amass in his *Public Supply* radio/call-in pieces of the 1960s because he thought it "made a nice texture to the work."[9] John Maxwell Hobbs sent the voice of David Hykes and his Harmonic Choir through a 70-ms phone transmission delay between The Kitchen in New York and the Thoronet Abbey in France in 1995, in an effort to experience the acoustics from one place, live in the space of the other.

But Neuhaus and Hobbs were hardly alone. You also could make the argument that Terry Riley's *In C*, the all-night minimalist anthem of the 1960s, uses a certain kind of self-imposed latency, accepting multiple loops that sound the same, but that begin at different points in time and last for different lengths of time, thus building up great pulsing masses of sound. Certainly Steve Reich's early tape-loop pieces, *Come Out* and *It's Gonna Rain,* are both based on the echo inherent in one tape machine's propensity to run slightly ahead or behind any other. In the late 1960s, Alvin Lucier equipped his performers with hand-held echolocation devices—which measure the minute amounts of time (and space) between a signal and its return—to artistically locate themselves, and their clicking sounds, in space. Called *Vespers,* and named for a species of North American bat (itself an expert at echolocation), Lucier's blindfolded performers had to orient themselves within the latency inherent in echo, and then, by moving as "migrators," "gatherers," or "ceremonial dancers," create music with each other in and around the space by changing the angle of reflection of their echo clicks.

Perhaps the most ambitious experiments with latency have been undertaken by Pauline Oliveros, who has sent the sound of her accordion to the Moon and back several times. The first roundtrip was in 1987 in a piece called *Echoes from the Moon.* With the technical help of former Hub composer Scot Gresham-Lancaster in Haywood, California, and Mark Gummer, a ham radio operator in Syracuse, New York, Oliveros used Gummer's forty-eight-foot backyard dish antenna to receive signals sent on a phone line from Haywood to Syracuse, and then send them through the dish from Syracuse to the Moon, a round trip that added some 2,500 ms, or 2.5 seconds, delay to the signal. More recently, in 1998, Oliveros used some of the large Yagi antenna arrays, as well as the Moon and Mars mapping radio telescope at Stanford University, to bounce sound off the surface of the Moon. Beginning as an audio signal sent by phone line to the telescope, Oliveros's music was converted to radio waves, bounced off the Moon, converted to audio, and played back. Even at light speed, according to "Blue" Gene Tyranny writing in *NewMusicBox,* "the sound delay was about 1.8 seconds, 900 milliseconds each way." Tyranny noted that "a slight Doppler shift on the echo [could be observed] because of the motion of both Earth and Moon."[10]

For Burk and Hobbs, as well as many other musicians working on the Web in the 1990s, the most practical solution to the latency issue seemed to lie in discovering ways to use the phenomenon creatively, or as Burk said, to let "the interaction between musicians ... take place 'out of time' where the arrival time of a message is not critical." The examples he gave included "editing a looping data structure such as in a 'drum box,' or modifying parameters that control an algorithmic sequence generator," pointing out that with a looping data structure it isn't necessary for the individual computers to be synchronized with each other, because "one person may be hearing the beginning of the loop when the other is hearing the middle."[11] ResRocket developed this basic looping structure for its own internal (non-clock-time) editing, a structure based on synchronized MIDI loops; that's why it felt spontaneous. The looping pattern avoided the problem of network latency by giving each home user access to a central loop and the illusion of working in "real time," no matter where on the loop their nonsynchronized computer happened to locate itself during log-on.

Although it may, at first, appear that only music written "out of time" will work online, two groups with experience exploring the creative uses of Internet latency—the alternative rock bands Therefore in San Diego, and Aspects of Physics in New York—have challenged that belief. Working together over a period of several months—and employing various types of communications from chat rooms, e-mail, and Web-based voice mail, through cell phones, pay telephones, and streaming MP3s, to FTP, http, TCP/IP, and text-to-speech synthesis engines—these two groups created an hour-long Internet performance based on Web latency, and premiered it as part of *Cathedral's* forty-eight-hour webcast in 2001. Called *Mail Patterns*, the multisectional work used latency to explore the basic flow and transfer of information and the breakdown of meaning.

Physically, the performance took place in three locations, with Wayne Feldman sending and posting files from North Carolina, Michael Kaufmann and Jason Soares creating live sounds and controlling the main mixing of the sound in San Diego, and F.Math Lorenz adding extra interactive scenarios live from Galapagos (a nightclub in Brooklyn). The primary responsibility for the shaping of the work remained in San Diego with Kaufmann, of Therefore, and Soares, from Aspects of Physics. They would sometimes feed back from the Internet into their mixers the composite sound they had just webcast, thereby creating a megadelay that both groups then used to continue making the piece. For over half of the sixty-minute performance, they worked with beats created in six-minute segments that they mixed, matched, manipulated live, and segued into an artistic whole, all the while adding live instrumentation overtop. As a performance, *Mail Patterns* seemed to fade in and out of rhythmic focus as beats meshed perfectly for a while and then moved apart, or segued into ambient sound. Sometimes, the band responded live "with atrophic and mutating repetition," creating overlaying sounds and gestures characterized by Kaufmann as "a sort of whisper down the line."[12]

Michael Kaufmann has experimented further by using preexisting sounds on the Web to create *Fossil/Residue* in 2002. The score consists of a list of various URLs, some 121 in all, which bookmark active sonic sites, and serve as the "instruments" for Therefore's real-time performance of the piece. Kaufmann said the idea occurred to him when he realized how "high and thick" latent sound on the Internet is being "piled," and wondered whimsically if it was possible for sound to fossilize. He decided he wanted to make a piece in the form of an excavation project, much the way "a DJ excavates histories of music from vinyl." Employing "collage methods, reductive tactics, and erasure" (Kaufmann said he was thinking about Rauschenberg erasing De Kooning), these online sounds are "collected (excavated), edited and compiled, and manipulated live," on stage by the band. Kaufmann says it's not about retrieving, but about receiving, calling it "a tuning in of the Internet and re-transmitting that information as a bibliographic."[13]

How can we handle the basic problem of online latency and its hindrance of rhythmic synchronicity? John Cage often told the story about telling his first teacher, Arnold Schoenberg, that he had no feeling for musical harmony, and Schoenberg replying to him that, because of this, he would always encounter a wall through which he could never pass. Cage replied that in that case he would devote his life to beating his head against that wall. Applying that philosophy to the problems of latency on the Web, if we can't fix it—and that possibility is not yet on the horizon— then we must learn to work with it by focusing our attention somewhere else, as Cage might say. Certainly, experimental music has a history that includes the successful and effective uses of echo and delay, and there is surely more that can be done online. By turning our attention to the creative side of latency, we may find new sounds, new concepts, a new means of expression. On the one hand, the problem of latency must be dealt with, and eventually overcome. Already its effects on rhythmic timing and synchronicity have been diminished with non-time-based systems. With further technological innovations, there is always the hope that new, unexpected ways to overcome this problem will appear.

Copyright and File Sharing

The one issue most polarizing art and the Internet today is the widespread copying and file sharing of music that other people consider their legal property. The practice has become so pervasive that Mladen Milicevic of Loyola Marymount University in Los Angeles placed the online sharing of MP3 files just below the distribution of pirated software and Internet porn as the three types of memes that traveled most frequently between computers in cyberspace in 2001. Meme is a term coined in the 1970s by biologist Richard Dawkins in his book *The Selfish Gene.* The online version of a meme—the cyberspace meme—is any good idea, new phrase, or catchy tune that becomes a societal riff and propagates itself by jumping from computer to computer as if alive, in much the same way that genes and viruses propagate by leaping between bodies. According to Milicevic, "the important rule for memes, as for genes, is that they must constantly replicate."[14] Fortunately or unfortunately, depending on your point of view, the one thing that people on all sides of the downloading-copyright debate agree about is that MP3 files are replicating freely and on a grand scale worldwide, despite everything the Recording Industry Association of America (RIAA) and others have tried to do to stop them.

You could say the file-sharing controversy got its start in 1987 when the method for compressing and broadcasting digital audio was first developed in Germany; or perhaps it was 1992, when the basic technology for MP3 encoding was approved by the Motion Picture Experts Group. But of all the components of the downloading puzzle, the one that caused the most disturbance was the appearance of the file-sharing program Napster in 1999 and its ability to locate and make available for download any requested song residing anywhere on a connected computer, no matter how obscure the song, or how far away the computer. According to Michael Behar writing in *Wired* magazine, the sharing of MP3 files really "didn't begin wreaking havoc on the recording industry ... until 56K modems became standard PC hardware and the Pentium [microprocessing chip] broke the 300-MHz barrier." Musically, of course, the good news was that it no longer took twenty-five minutes to download a song; it could now be done in three or four. The bad news for the record companies was that this combination of a high-speed Internet connection with a simple file-sharing program made the trading of music files all too easy; anybody with a computer and an Internet connection could download the Napster software and do it for free, and in no time at all. Behar concludes, "it was college students, ripping songs from CDs, compressing them, and posting the files on the Web, who proved that MP3 might transform the [recording] industry."[15] This was about the time when digital music files became both a cyberspace meme and a copyright infringement problem that could no longer be ignored.

Napster was the brainchild of nineteen-year-old Northeastern University computer science student Shawn Fanning. Before Napster, file sharing took place on FTP drop sites and UseNet sites, where individual arrangements had to be made and nothing resembling an international registry of songs existed. What Fanning did was to create a piece of software—released on the Internet in May 1999—that made it possible to locate and download a specific song stored on another person's computer. In return, these traders made their own collections of songs available for others to copy. In essence, Fanning's software program established a centralized server that, instead of storing the actual songs on Napster's own computers, simply matched the request for a song from one user with the location of the file in another user's own personal collection, and then connected the two traders to each other in a peer-to-peer environment. The result, to use John Schwartz's terms, created a "collaborative jukebox" drawing on a "massive, collective memory bank" of sounds.[16]

Napster was the first music-sharing software made available online, and its arrival signaled a major transformation in the way music was bought, sold, and shared worldwide—the "grand upset that music is now experiencing," to use Kevin Kelly's description from the *New York Times Magazine* in 2002. The "grand upset" was not only the recently discovered ease of online trading but also the more fundamental shift from analog copies to digital copies. As Kelly described it, "The industrial age was driven by analog copies; analog copies are perfect and cheap. The information age is driven by digital copies; digital copies are perfect, fluid, and free." Describing digitized music as "a liquid that can be morphed and migrated and flexed and linked," he continues that although "free is hard to ignore," the liquidity was what really drew people to online music.[17]

By December 1999, the RIAA, convinced that the recording industry was losing billions of dollars in revenue to this new form of "electronic shoplifting," sued Napster, which it called "a haven for piracy." In addition, a number of individual artists, including Metallica and Dr. Dre, joined in, complaining about their loss of royalties. Napster's legal defense was that it was only giving away software, not engaging in file sharing or copyright infringement, but a lower court ruled against them and the 9th U.S. Circuit Court of Appeals upheld the ruling. By May 2001, Napster was forced offline. At the time, the fifty-million-plus people who used Napster were trading more than a billion song files each month. This number, high as it seems, was down significantly from the peak file-sharing month—February 2000—when close to 2.8 billion songs were downloaded. Abraham Genauer described the demise of Napster as "the dissolution of the largest centralized music community in history."[18]

Unfortunately for the RIAA, by that point Napster was not the only file-sharing service available online. With names such as KaZaA, Gnutella, Morpheus, LimeWire, BearShare, and Grokster, these new services—which grew to over sixty by 2002—more than filled the vacuum left by the closing of Napster.[19] The most popular of these song swapping sites, and the acknowledged successor to Napster, was KaZaA, whose software, by the summer of 2003, had been downloaded over 270 million times. By that time, the *New York Times* said that more than forty-three million Americans—or about half of all Americans connected to the Web in 2003—had used file-sharing software within the past thirty days.[20]

Even though Napster did not physically store MP3 files on its own computers, the fact that it maintained a central index server through which all file requests passed made it legally vulnerable and led directly to the court rulings against it. As a result, these new second-generation file-sharing programs did not have a central server. Instead, they allowed song requests to pass along from machine to machine within the network of file traders, thereby eliminating the center of the network and making it more difficult to legally determine who was responsible in cases of copyright violations. In addition, some of the file-sharing services began encrypting their files, making it even more difficult for the industry to track down individual users. As expected, lawsuits were filed in the Netherlands against KaZaA and in the United States against Grokster and StreamCast Networks, but they were rejected, the courts finding in both cases that the file-trading services were not responsible for how individuals might use free software.

As the number of online file-sharing sites continued to increase, the recording industry began pointing to steadily declining sales figures, claiming cause-and-effect. Although some critics suggested that the problem might have more to do with the quality of music being released than with online file sharing, it grew increasingly difficult to ignore the numbers. By 2002, for example, sales of blank CDs were said to outnumber those of recorded CDs, which were reportedly down some 26 percent from their 1999 highs. In April 2003, the RIAA, responding with what some characterized as a siege mentality, filed lawsuits against four college students for trading MP3 files online, asking for enormous sums of money in damages, and eventually reaching settlements in the thousands of dollars. The *New York Times* facetiously called the move "a business model with a future: sue your customers."[21] Although the suit did little to slow down overall online trading, it did result in many colleges and universities blocking the campus portals used for file sharing, limiting the bandwidth available to each student, and disciplining those who continued to share files. Although this certainly made it more difficult for student traders to operate, it did not stop them, and it had no effect whatever on students who lived off campus, were connected to a different network, and were always willing to share files with their on-campus friends.

In September 2003, some five months after the first four lawsuits were filed, the RIAA brought a second round of lawsuits against online traders, this time a much larger group of 261 people, including a retired grandfather and a twelve-year-old girl. Acknowledging that the RIAA was "intentionally 'playing the heavy,'" a *New York Times* editorial said that "music companies are right to aggressively pursue people, even minors, who steal their products," but also warned that the record industry needed to "improve its technology" and "adapt to the times."[22] Others pointed out the dichotomy between the recording industry and the RIAA's efforts to educate the public to the legal ramifications of copyright infringement (and thus begin to stem the tide of downloaded music), whereas, by contrast, the technology companies were continually building more and better CD burners and increasing the storage capacity of MP3 players. Sometimes this duality occurred between divisions of the same company, as Neil Strauss pointed out in the case of Sony; its music division was making something in the neighborhood of $4.6 billion in music sales, a large part of it from CDs, but its electronics division was making $40 billion, a good part of which came from CD burners and MP3 players.[23] By this time, Microsoft's Windows software shipped with built-in folders to make it easier to share MP3 files online.

During the mid-1990s, the music industry developed several subscription services to sell music online. However, the restrictions on downloading and copying, limited playlists, and confusing fee structures doomed these to failure. But by late 2003, and with the full cooperation of the recording industry by this point, dozens of companies had created legal online stores. Of these, the leading contenders were Apple Computer's iTunes Music Store and Real Networks' Rhapsody. Apple's iTunes—which opened in April 2003—offered a simple pricing policy of 99¢ a song (or an entire album for $10), plus its popular iPod MP3 player, and was the first fee-based online music service to catch the imagination of the downloading crowd. Within the first thirty days, iTunes sold over three million songs, and after four months the number was up to ten million. By March 2004, iTunes had sold fifty million tunes, and hundreds of thousands of iPods had been sold, particularly around the holidays. iTunes also was the first online music store that did not charge its customers a monthly fee, or restrict personal uses of the files, once purchased. Pointing out that iTunes was the first service to make it less expensive to download an album than to buy the CD from a store, David Pogue of the *New York Times* also credits iTunes with being "the first music service that doesn't view every customer as a criminal-in-waiting."[24]

Although the iTunes Music Store, and others like it, may be an important step forward for the recording industry, it is worth remembering that the file-sharing problem has not disappeared; a recent *New York Times* article reported "KaZaA alone has three million to four million users at any given time."[25] As the downloading controversy continues to unfold, a potential outcome may be that even if the recording companies succeed in regaining control, and are able to curtail, the swapping of files, the current attitudes among college students and others—about who owns the music on the Web—is not likely to disappear; after all, this is the generation that grew up believing that music is free. In the final analysis, this issue may not just be about copyright infringement and file-sharing on Napster, but also a first indication—an early warning sign, if you will—of a broader sea change yet to come, brought on, like it or not, by the Web. Because the Internet, in ways both obvious and subtle, is causing us all not only to rethink where music comes from, and whose it is, but also to reimagine and redesign our basic relationship with it, complete with the opportunity to create new customized soundtracks to accompany us through our daily lives.

Open Source

If the file sharing-copyright infringement problem is the most controversial dilemma confronting the online population today, then the open source-proprietary software issue is probably the biggest topic for debate among the programming and corporate communities. At its heart is a defense of the concept of ownership of intellectual property against the idea of free and open work for the common good. Ultimately, the question becomes which of these diametrically opposed approaches is a better model, both technically and socially, for the Web. At first glance, this may seem to be a somewhat esoteric topic for most of us; however, stop for a moment to consider that the Google search engine runs on open source software, as does Apache (the most used server on the Web), as well as large parts of Merrill Lynch and Amazon.com, not to mention an active interest by the governments of Germany and China, and the issue draws closer to all of us than, perhaps, we had first thought it would.

Open source software is any program whose source code (i.e., the basic programming code that enables the software to do whatever it does) is open and available for anyone to use, improve on, and redistribute, if they wish, free of charge. It is the opposite of proprietary software, such as

Microsoft's Windows or Apple Computer's OS X, which is developed and owned by a company and licensed or sold to users for a fee. Open source software cannot be owned; the credit for its care and continued development is shared by a large community of committed programmers working from all parts of the world. Proponents say a major advantage, beyond the fact that it's free, is that software development occurs faster in open source, and tends to be more reliable (as well as more transparent), due to the collaborative nature of open source work and the widespread peer review process it brings into being. Open source programmers, for example, pride themselves on writing good clean code; it's a badge of honor, a calling card of their work for all to see. This by-and-for-the-community attitude inherent in the creation of all open source software is its main strength; open source development is a community-driven undertaking that, in return, has served the online community well. Detractors of open source, by contrast, point to the fact that not all programs will run on Linux (the popular open source operating system), plus, there are no open source solutions available for some problems, and, in case of trouble, there is no direct support to provide quick help. The more fanatical of the detractors—and there are certainly determined personalities on both sides—say open source is socialistic, a threat to intellectual property rights, and antibusiness to an extreme.

Originally called "free software," the open source movement dates its existence from 1984, when the idea was championed by a computer scientist from MIT's Artificial Intelligence Lab named Richard Stallman. From Stallman's work came the GNU General Public License (GPL), a set of rules by which all open source developers agree to abide, the most important of which is that they will share the source code for whatever software they create, thus allowing others to improve on their work and customize it further, and all to use it without charge.

When Linus Torvalds, then a twenty-one-year-old student in Helsinki, posted his source code for Linux on the Web in September 1991, he offered it as an open source development project under GPL rules; by the early twenty-first century, it had become the most popular and well-known of all open source software. Linux is an operating system in competition, first with Unix, and now with Microsoft's Windows. But, unlike the Microsoft Corporation, which has historically—until a recent court ruling—reluctantly revealed its Windows source code only to its best clients and only then in a tightly controlled environment, the Linux source code is on the Web, available for anyone, not only to look at but also to improve on if they can.

Since its first posting, Linux has been continually growing, strengthening, and improving as first one and then another programmer adds a new piece of code. By 1997, some three million home and office computers worldwide ran the Linux operating system. By 2003, it was in use on more than eighteen million computers, leading Gary Rivlin of *Wired* to label Linux "the single largest collaborative project in the planet's history." Rivlin continues that the advantage of constant feedback and worldwide peer review in open source development has created in Linux an operating system "robust enough to run the world's most powerful supercomputers yet sleek and versatile enough to run inside consumer toys," of which he mentions TiVo, television set-top boxes, and cell phones, as examples.[26]

Although some software and technology companies, such as Microsoft, are considered enemies of the open source movement, others, such as Oracle, IBM, and Intel, were among the first corporations to show support. In December 2000, IBM pledged $1 billion to support continued Linux development, whereas earlier that year a consortium of companies, including Intel and Hewlett-Packard, created and funded the Open Source Development Lab to foster and encourage continued Linux growth.

Although Linux and Linus Torvalds—now a Fellow of the Open Source Development Lab—are both poster-child success stories for the entire open source movement, they are not the only example of open source success. The Apache Web Server, for example, now runs some two-thirds of the servers that comprise the Web. It began when a group of open source programmers founded the Apache Group, and set out to modify the most popular Web server of the day: the National Center for Supercomputing Applications' httpd. The Apache Group made a trial version of the Apache server available to beta testers in August 1995, and released a public version in December of that same year. By the end of 1996, the Apache Web Server was more popular than httpd, and by early 2001 it was thought to power almost 60 percent of the Web. The Microsoft server, by comparison, accounted for about 20 percent in 2001, while others fell below that.[27] If any doubt remains concerning the maturity of the open source model, consider Mozilla, a Web browser in competition with Microsoft's Internet Explorer, or Perl, the open source programming language used by Web developers in such numbers that Rivlin says some refer to it as "the duct tape of the Internet."[28]

Perhaps the open source debate would have continued to take place largely behind the scenes had not a small company in Utah—the SCO Group, owners of the rights to the Unix operating system—filed a lawsuit against IBM, claiming that Linux had thousands of lines of proprietary Unix code embedded in it. The suit, which was filed in March 2003, raised issues of Linux ownership, questioned the legality of the open source model, and asked for $1 billion in damages. In August 2003, perhaps to up the ante, the SCO Group began trying to collect onetime fees of $699 from Linux users in the business community, threatening to double them if they were not paid by a certain date. Reminiscent of the RIAA's lawsuits against illegal downloaders, the SCO Group's chief executive, Darl McBride, was quoted as saying, "If we have to sue end users to give us relief for our damages, we will."[29] IBM, by contrast, has filed a countersuit accusing SCO of patent infringement and breach of the Linux GPL. Although some, including Linus Torvalds, think the SCO claim is without merit, everyone has an interest in what the courts will have to say.

Whatever the eventual outcome of the SCO-IBM trial, the fundamental ideas behind open source development are already deeply imbedded, not only in the Web in general but in the online music community as well. From Craig Latta's call for music on NetJam to be public domain in the early 1990s—and even earlier when The Hub sponsored their networked computer performances of the late 1980s—collaborating musicians, particularly those online, have repeatedly been confronted with the question of how best to maintain and distribute intellectual property rights. During the 1990s, the question arose in some form every time a musician participated in the shared development of a piece online, whether through a collaborative compositional process, as on Rocket Network and Beatnik, or a collective jam on the ResRocket or WebDrum sites—all musical examples of an open source development process at work making art.

In the same way that the Internet has freed us from the limitations of geography, and supplied musicians with a new set of Web-based tools, so the open source model has encouraged a community of musical developers to work collectively and artistically on new music. No musician refers to the process in quite those terms, of course; many consider online collaboration an extension of the improvising traditions of jazz, rock, and the avant-garde.

Today, as an ever increasing number of arts-related activities are flourishing online—from individual blogs to group-oriented mob scenes, all voluntary and undertaken more for aesthetic pleasure than financial reward—it seems reasonable to assume that interactive musical collaboration online will only increase in the years to come. Answering the questions surrounding the rights of the artists—particularly in situations where everyone can be considered an artist—and the rights of the creative users—particularly those whose medium is the manipulation of the intellectual property of others—will have an even greater urgency than it does today.

Copy Left

If the question of who owns what, and what's free and what's not, online appears baffling, take comfort in the knowledge that you are not alone. At this point, no one really has an answer, or even sees an end to the dilemma we currently face. To make matters worse, two pieces of legislation enacted at the end of the last century are creating a furor in some circles and causing other people deep concern: the Digital Millennium Copyright Act and the Copyright Term Extension Act, both enacted in 1998. Of the two, probably the one of most significance to file traders and online musicians is the Digital Millennium Copyright Act, and its provision—written in the name of copyright protection—that allows Internet service providers to be held responsible in court for anything unlawful their customers post online, a situation that makes ISPs hesitate to host anything controversial. Robert S. Boynton described this law as "an extraordinary burden that providers of phone service, by contrast, do not share," adding that the new law "gives private parties veto power over much of the information published online." The Copyright Term Extension Act, by contrast, allows intellectual property to remain under copyright an additional twenty years before passing into public domain (under previous law, the term of copyright lasted seventy-five years), a windfall for the record companies, some say, and a piece of legislation Boynton characterizes as "an intellectual land grab, presided over by legislators and lawyers for the media industries."[30]

Intent on improving a copyright system that seems to be falling into the hands of special interests, a nationwide group of reformers, led by Lawrence Lessig of Stanford Law School and Jonathan Zittrain of Harvard Law, have joined with others in a coalition attempting to pull back the restrictive new rules. Known as the Free Culture Movement at Stanford, but referred to at Harvard as Copy Left (a sly reference to the fact that open source code normally has fewer restrictions attached to it), the reformers argue that society benefits far too profoundly from the ability to draw quickly on earlier ideas *not* to insist that copyrighted material pass into public domain in a reasonable amount of time. As Zittrain said, the idea that copyright should never expire is both "fanatical" and "unconstitutional," a reference to "a limited time" clause concerning the granting of copyrights contained in the Constitution. In *Eldred v. Ashcroft*—a suit brought to the Supreme Court in October 2002 challenging the Copyright Term Extension Act—Professor Lessing argued for the plaintiffs that continually extending copyright protection for any intellectual property was not in the country's best interests, and violated the Constitution's call for copyright protection to last for "a limited time." However, the court ruled 7 to 2 that no matter how unwise it might prove, Congress had the power to make the decision. Boynton characterized this ruling, which was handed down in January 2003, as a "major setback" for Copy Left reforms.[31]

The debate over intellectual property, who owns it, and how long it should remain exclusively theirs has become so heated that even the Committee for Economic Development—a business-oriented policy group in Washington that normally deals with larger national and international concerns—issued a somewhat critical report in March 2004, saying that the aggressive RIAA lawsuits against file sharers were bad for both business and the economy. Concluding that the situation surrounding digital intellectual property was too volatile for Congress to have much of a chance, if acting hastily, to make a "good" decision, the group called for a two-year moratorium on any further changes to the existing copyright laws, including copyright extensions. An author of the report, Susan Crawford of Cardoza Law School, suggested to Boynton that "equating intellectual property with physical property" might not be the best thing for continued innovation.[32]

Although the 2003 Supreme Court decision was a setback, the debate over copyright control is far from complete. The Copy Left advocates have been regrouping while continuing to stress, as Boynton says, that "borrowing and collaboration are essential components of all creation," emphasizing the obvious benefits of innovators having the ability to draw freely from a world of unencumbered and unimpeded ideas.[33] As Lessing notes, "when works enter the public domain, the consequence is extraordinary variety and lower cost." Responding to a frequently asked question about how any company could compete in the marketplace against "free" material in public domain, Lessig offers the obvious answer: "Think Perrier or Poland Spring"—companies that have no problem competing with water, a freely available commodity.[34]

8

THE GREY ALBUM:
A CASE STUDY IN
CRITICAL MASS

It's considered common practice in the hip-hop community to borrow and sample each other's work; it's not thought of as stealing but, rather, as a sign of respect. A few years ago some rappers even began making available a cappella versions of one or two of their raps when they released a new album in order to make it easier for others to use their material. So when the rapper Jay-Z's *Black Album* appeared in November 2003, it wasn't so unusual that he would also release some of the unaccompanied solo raps; what was unexpected, however, was that he would make them *all* available, all fourteen tracks. It was almost as if he was challenging DJs to remix his entire album—which he said would be his last—and to show what they could do.

As could be expected, a number of DJs and producers rose to the challenge. Bazooka Joe created *The Silver Album*, Kev Brown produced *The Brown Album*, and Illmind developed *The Black & Tan Album*, while Cheap Cologne made *The Double Black Album*, 9th Wonder made *Black is Back*, and DJ Lt. Dan created *The Black Remixes*, to name but a few. In all, more than a dozen different versions appeared, matching Jay-Z's voice with everybody from Metallica to Bjork to Curtis Mayfield, and everything from "techno blips to string quartets."[1] One of the more interesting concepts was *The Black Album Unplugged*, remixed by DJ Noodles and

Nic Balz, that combined the raps of Jay-Z with the music of the Seattle grunge band Nirvana. But the remix that caused all the commotion was DJ Danger Mouse's mashup of Jay-Z's raps from *The Black Album* with the beats, rhythms, and chords from the Beatles' classic, *The White Album*. Danger Mouse called it *The Grey Album*.

Black, White, and Grey

Working out of Los Angeles, twenty-six-year-old producer, DJ, and New York-area native Brian Burton (a.k.a. Danger Mouse) lists Radiohead, Portishead, and OutKast among his influences. Before making *The Grey Album*, he had already released four CD mixes and one twelve-inch recording, sampling artists from Portishead to Blondie. On stage, he had opened for Dan the Automator, OutKast, and Biz Markie. Danger Mouse told *Rolling Stone* that he had been listening to both Jay-Z and the Beatles on the same day when the idea for *The Grey Album* "just hit me like a wave." He also knew that he would never be able to release the album commercially, but that he made it anyway because of his love for the Beatles and Jay-Z.[2] Calling it a deconstruction-reconstruction "art project/experiment" that took about two weeks to complete, he said that "every kick, snare, and chord" could be traced back to the musical content of *The White Album* via sampling.[3] When the tracks were completed—he used twelve of Jay-Z's original fourteen—Danger Mouse made three thousand copies of the album and gave them away, mostly as promotional material, or to friends. He said that as he mixed the album he "wasn't thinking if what I was doing was legal or not," and that he certainly "wasn't trying to challenge copyright laws," explaining that his motivation was solely creative.[4]

Once released, however, *The Grey Album*—which most people heard as a particularly clever and elegant artistic bridging and combining of contemporary rap with classic rock (*The White Album*, officially called *The Beatles*, came out in 1968)—began to take on a life of its own, first by word-of-mouth and postings on Web sites and blogs, and then because of several highly favorable reviews. *Rolling Stone*, for example, called it "the ultimate remix," as well as "an ingenious hip-hop record that sounds oddly ahead of its time."[5] The *Boston Globe* said it was "the most intriguing hip-hop album in recent memory," and "creatively captivating." [6] By this point, all of the tracks were posted as MP3 files on various Web sites and listeners were beginning to trade them freely over the file sharing networks. The result was that the album began to spread to a far wider audience than anyone, including Danger Mouse, had ever imagined possible.

As *The Grey Album* continued to attract new fans, copies of it began showing up in alternative record stores and on eBay, where they sold for as high as $80 each. By this point, Danger Mouse knew it would only be a matter of time before he "received some kind of legal letter in the mail."[7] As he expected, within a month of the album's release, EMI, which owns the rights to the Beatles' sound recordings, had heard about the project, knew that Danger Mouse had not cleared any of his samples with them, and sent not only him but some of the record stores and eBay sites as well cease-and-desist letters. Danger Mouse complied immediately, presumably destroying any of the albums still in his possession; but, in a textbook example of the birth and growth of a cyberspace meme, the file traders would not comply and dissemination of *The Grey Album* continued to gain momentum.

As can be imagined, the intellectual property rights of a group as popular as the Beatles are controlled and protected in every way possible. In the case of *The White Album,* EMI, a London-based label, owns the rights to the sound recordings (the masters), but Sony Music/ATV Publishing, through a joint venture between Michael Jackson and Sony, own the rights to the actual songs (the publishing). To complicate things even further, it's unclear at the moment who may now own the rights to George Harrison's songs on *The White Album.*[8] Given the fact that record companies often ask for large fees to license samples of their most popular artists, it isn't certain that, even had he contacted EMI, Danger Mouse would have been able to obtain or afford the proper legal clearances.

As EMI continued to press its case by sending letters threatening legal action, the issue began, for fans and activists alike, to take on the nature of a cause célèbre. Although Danger Mouse abided by the cease-and-desist order, others continued to distribute the album freely online, chief among them, the Stay Free!/Illegal Art Web site. In response to what was quickly coming to be seen as an act of censorship, Downhill Battle—a combination watchdog group and music activism project working to bring positive changes to the music industry—decided to organize a protest. As their

February 18, 2004, press release put it, the protest was to be "an act of civil disobedience against a copyright regime that routinely suppresses musical innovation." Downhill Battle cofounder Holmes Wilson declared that "the major record labels have turned copyright law into a weapon," and Rebecca Laurie of Downhill Battle was quoted as saying "EMI isn't looking for compensation, they're trying to ban a work of art." Nicholas Reville, cofounder of Downhill Battle, named the protest Grey Tuesday, commenting that "the framers of the constitution created copyright to promote innovation and creativity," but that "a handful of corporations have radically perverted that purpose for their own narrow self interest, and now the public is fighting back." He concluded: "Remixes and pastiche are a defining aesthetic of our era. How will artists continue to work if corporations can outlaw what they do?"[9]

Grey Tuesday

The first act of coordinated civil disobedience in cyberspace took place on February 24, 2004. Known as Grey Tuesday, it consisted of a coalition of Web sites, brought together by Downhill Battle, all agreeing to post *The Grey Album* and make it available for free download for one twenty-four-hour period. Sites that were supportive of the protest but uncomfortable with the controversy surrounding the hosting of an "illegal" record were asked to turn their Web sites gray for the day. In all, some 400 sites and blogs participated, with 170 or more making the album simultaneously available for download. So many Web sites linked to greytuesday.org that, for the week before the protest, the site "reached the top rankings on Blogdex and Popdex" (Web sites that track which sites are the most popular links with blogs at any given time).[10] When the historic online protest was over, more than one million songs had been downloaded, the equivalent of one hundred thousand albums in a single day. After surveying the protesting sites and analyzing the file-sharing activity, Downhill Battle could "confidently report that *The Grey Album* was the number one album in the U.S. on February 24, [and] by a large margin."[11]

But civil disobedience, as historic as it may be, is not undertaken without some degree of risk. The Monday before the protest was scheduled, lawyers for Capitol Records (an EMI unit) e-mailed preemptive cease-and-desist letters to all the participating Web sites, demanding that they "cease any plans or efforts to distribute or publicly perform this unlawful recording ... identify the names and addresses of any third-parties who have supplied you with physical or digital copies of *The Grey Album*, [and] provide Capitol with an accounting of all units of *The Grey Album* that have been distributed via your website," this last for proper "payment to Capitol in an amount to be discussed." The letter ended, "We demand that you contact us immediately."[12]

Downhill Battle's Reville and Wilson responded the same day, calling EMI's actions a "censorship campaign," claiming a fair-use right to post the music, and saying "we will not be intimidated into backing down." They also said that their actions were "a political act with no commercial interest," and that they would "consider any attempt to stifle this protest to be an abuse under Section 512F of the Digital Millennium Copyright Act."[13] Owners of the other host sites, however, had a range of reactions to the EMI e-mail. On one side was John McHale of teamgoodguys.com, who said he was "hosting *The Grey Album* because it's a work of art," and that he had "nothing to gain from posting it other than feeling proud about standing up for something I believe in."[14]

Waxy.org's daily log presented a wide variety of reactions from individuals participating in the protest. "Margaret" reported on February 23: "I got a preemptive C&D email today. Can they legally require us to give them a full accounting ... when we haven't actually put any of the MP3s on our website, just stated our intent to do so in the future? I'm 14, and this is scaring me kind of a lot."[15] Earlier in the week, on February 20, "Carsten" innocently asked: "How can you steal something that is not even being sold?" And on March 12, "Elec" gave voice to what many disgruntled fans were thinking, and record companies fearing: "I'll make sure from now on that I never BUY anything from EMI, I'll copy it, download it, anything but BUY it."[16]

It was only a matter of time before Sony/ATV Publishing joined the fray. On March 1, 2004, it sent the Internet service provider for the Stay Free!/Illegal Art Web site a Digital Millennium Copyright Act "takedown" notice, demanding that they remove or disable "access to our copyrighted material," and reminding the ISP of their responsibility as "the authorized agent for service of this notice in accord with The Digital Millennium Copyright Act of 1998, 17 U.S.C. 512 et seq."[17] Stay Free!/

Illegal Art's response was to seek legal council and move their Web site to Online Policy Group, a nonprofit ISP devoted to free speech.

Critical Mass in Cyberspace

For the record companies, the legal issues surrounding *The Grey Album* presented an open-and-shut case from the very beginning: the DJ didn't clear the samples and had no right to use them. The day of protest, as widespread as it was, didn't change the fact that the album was completely unauthorized. Legally, the recording industry was on solid ground; as far as international copyright is concerned, the Grey Tuesday protest broke the law. As EMI North America spokeswoman Jeanne Mayer told *Wired*, "There are proper channels to go through, ... [and] they've just been completely ignored.... We authorize samples [and] remixes all the time." Speaking on the day of the protest, Mayer added that the coalition of hosting sites would not be forgiven or forgotten, saying, "EMI plans to take action ... as a matter of course."[18] Perhaps this was a reasonable response when viewed from the perspective of the recording industry, whose lawyers clearly would view this act of civil disobedience as "24 hours of mass copyright infringement."[19] Under current copyright law, the statutory damages could be as high as $150,000 for each occurrence. But five days after Grey Tuesday, as the full extent of the protest numbers became known, Jeanne Mayer declined to tell Lawrence Van Gelder of the *New York Times* whether EMI still intended to pursue legal action against such a large number of offending Web sites, saying only that the protest numbers were "irrelevant to the fact that we are asking those who have illegally made an unauthorized work available to stop doing it."[20]

For the fans and activists, the issues surrounding *The Grey Album* and the Grey Tuesday protest were anything but clear. Although Jonathan Zittrain of Harvard Law School agreed about the illegality of the action, he also pointed out that current "copyright law was written with a particular form of industry in mind," and that with "the flourishing of information technology ... there's no place to plug such an important cultural sea change into the current legal regime."[21] Zittrain noted that remixing and sampling are in a far different category of copyright control than is creating a new version of an already existing song. Under current law, any band can pay a standard royalty and record their version of any song that had previously been recorded, including Beatle tunes, *without* asking specific permission. However, because there are no set licensing fees for samples, the record companies are free to charge exorbitant fees, or to hold the music off the market indefinitely. That, says Zittrain, as well as others, suggests the use of "copyright as a means of control, rather than a means of profit."[22]

In their original response to EMI's cease-and-desist e-mail of February 23, Reville and Wilson of Downhill Battle pointed out that "the current legal environment allows the five major record labels [EMI, Sony, BMG, Warner, and Universal] to dictate to musicians what kind of music they may and may not create and allows them to prevent the public from hearing music that does not fall within their rules." For Downhill Battle the day of civil disobedience was "the perfect way to explain to non-experts why the copyright system needs reform."[23]

The Electronic Frontier Foundation—who almost immediately issued an opinion paper titled, "Grey Tuesday: A Quick Overview of the Legal Terrain"—notes that EMI may, in fact, have no federal copyright protection for *The White Album*, because it appeared in 1968, and federal copyright protection does not exist for sound recordings made prior to 1972. If federal copyright law does not protect *The White Album*, then statutory damages would not apply, either. However, the Foundation also pointed out that some states have their own laws protecting sound recordings made before 1972, and, therefore, "the rights and remedies are likely to vary from state to state." As for Sony/ATV Publishing, the Electronic Frontier Foundation suggested that they would have "at least two hurdles to overcome in order to prove a federal copyright infringement case." First, they would need to show that Danger Mouse had used enough samples to actually "infringe the rights in the Lennon–McCartney compositions," and, second, they would "have to overcome any fair use defense offered by the Grey Tuesday protesters." Regarding "fair use," the Foundation said that there were several factors at work in favor of the protesters, including the fact that *The Grey Album* was not made available online for the purpose of making money; downloads of the album did not substitute for purchases of *The White Album; The Grey Album* represents "a transformative use of the *White Album,* not a wholesale copy"; the posting of the album "is intended as part of a commentary on the use of copyright law to stymie new kinds of musical creativity"; and "a copyright owner is unlikely to license a work for use in a protest that is critical of the copyright owner itself."[24]

Essentially, *The Grey Album* controversy revolves around competing intentions: those to make money, and those to make art. Even though the sampling of beats and clips from the recorded music of others is an accepted art form today, it's important to remember that sampling and looping did not begin with hip-hop. In fact, the Beatles themselves tried it with what Ben Rayner of the *Toronto Star* called "their acid-fried tape-loop collage 'Revolution 9,'" from *The White Album* itself, leading Rayner to suggest that, as a *quid pro quo* gesture, the surviving Beatles might do well to consider sanctioning Danger Mouse's use of their material in *The Grey Album*—an unlikely prospect, to be sure, although an interesting concept to consider.[25] Glenn Otis Brown, executive director of Creative Commons, an organization working to relax the rules while preserving a reasonable and flexible copyright system, asked what may be the most intriguing question of all when he said, "Why not just sign the guy ... and have everybody make a bunch [of money] off of it?"[26]

Beyond the basic legal and artistic issues surrounding *The Grey Album* is the specter of a new form of protest, and the question of whether this type of activity can really have any lasting effect on the recording industry. For Downhill Battle, the answer is yes. Saying that even though the major labels have both political connections and plenty of money to mount a vigorous defense, they point to two potential problems for the industry that may make them more vulnerable in the immediate future. First, in fighting downloading, the recording industry is fighting technology—and as with previous incarnations of recording and copying technology (the cassette recorder and the video tape recorder, for example)—"when you fight technology you almost always lose." Second, the financial outlook for the recording industry is turning bleaker, thanks to the continued growth of the file sharing services, with sales dropping considerably for the fourth year in a row.[27] As for the nature of the online protest itself, its success was a function of critical mass, and the convergence of the open source tradition with group think, almost as if the mob scene were being put at the service of art. If, as many believe, the recording companies have lost perspective and are out of step with that part of the music community that considers sampling a new form of art, then a result of the online community protest was to begin to highlight a misguided industry policy.

What, if any, are the lessons to be learned from this whole episode? For EMI, the results appear mostly negative: bad press; lost revenue, both from unlicensed samples and the unwillingness to license and sell *The Grey Album;* and becoming the object of a mass action of worldwide civil disobedience directed against them, with some disgruntled fans vowing to boycott future EMI releases. For Danger Mouse, on the other hand, it has meant increased exposure and notoriety, with far more copies of *The Grey Album* in circulation and being heard today than there were before EMI began trying to suppress it. As for the activists and their organizations, who seem to have been handed a galvanizing issue on a silver platter, it represents the opportunity both to make an important statement about the inadequacies of current copyright law, as well as to state their case for reform in simple, clear-cut terms, to a far wider audience than was previously paying attention to their concerns. Although the issue of *The Grey Album* in particular and online file trading in general is far from over, one conclusion cannot be ignored: when we look at music through the prism of money, art and creativity often get pushed aside. As for Danger Mouse, who began it all, he said he wished that *The Grey Album* "could have been a regular, commercial release," but that, at the moment, at least, "every day is unbelievable," and "only time will tell what's next for this record."[28]

9
VIRTUAL MUSIC

As should be readily apparent by now, the term "virtual music" is an all-encompassing, "umbrella" concept that, in its broadest and most general sense, includes everything from personalized ringtones to pirated phone calls, the online swapping and selling of digital audio files, to the creating of, and contributing to, new forms of online interactive art. If "the virtual is anything that does not culminate in mass," as Dutch architect Rem Koolhass says, then virtual music is *everything* of a musical nature that exists online in the digital realm."[1] But this broad expanse of material—much of which shares few common traits or goals—is too unwieldy to consider *en masse*. Instead, I will take a detailed look at interactivity—the core and catalyst of virtual music—attempt to place its appearance and development in perspective, and examine the potential for future developments.

Although in the first decade of the twenty-first century we are still in the earliest stages of the development of interactive online music, it is possible to identify some of its basic characteristics. First, and—more important—for the first time, virtual music is a decentralized, universal art form: anyone with a computer and Internet access can be involved, despite their location in physical space. Also, virtual music is participatory; people can alter it in ways that they, as well as everyone else, can hear. Because virtual music is interactive, it can contribute to its own development, a process easier to characterize with neurological or biological metaphors, rather than with mechanical or mathematical ones.

Equally important is the fact that the content of virtual music is inclusive, not exclusionary. There is no one predominant or acceptable method, sound, style, set of instruments, or performing environment for the World Wide Web—and there probably never will be. In cyberspace, there's room for everything; the possibilities appear endless; the future of the Web is filled with sound.

Virtual music also is listened to differently, because it occurs in individual home environments in a virtual space somewhere between the mind and the machine. This sonic landscape arises from virtual music's use of nonlinear forms, meaning not only that the experience is different for each individual but also that someone returning will not have the same experience twice. The music is as it is, when it is, when you are there. Without a fixed beginning, middle, or end, virtual music is free from the constraints of time, offering a continually evolving, always available environment in which listeners are free to enter at any point, explore in multiple directions, and contribute to the shape.

In this type of participatory environment, creativity is not isolated in one or two individuals but, rather, is distributed uniformly throughout the network. For the first time, we have a universal form of music that has the ability to draw in and engage its listeners in the creative process, and to decentralize the act of creating music in favor of community-driven decisions and actions. In this resonant and interpenetrating process, not only are the form and content of musical experiences free to evolve and merge but also there is also a continuous invitation to listeners to synthe-size and recreate. In this sense, virtual music is a new art form, within a new medium, producing an entirely new type of artistic experience. With this degree of decentralized authority, not only is there a redefinition of musical object and musical space but also a restructuring of the traditional composer, performer, and listener roles. In the face of these fundamental shifts in the process of music-making, it grows increasingly necessary to redefine music, as well.

But how does this actually take place? How does music, or any other art form, for that matter, get redefined? Thomas S. Kuhn, in his ground-breaking book from the early 1960s *The Structure of Scientific Revolu-tions*—written when he was still a graduate student in theoretical physics at Harvard—suggests that, within the sciences, at least, progress is not made by a steady accumulation of knowledge but, rather, by a series of intellectually violent revolutions that punctuate longer periods of general agreement within the scientific community at large about how the world ought to be perceived. He described this process as, "a succession of tradition-bound periods punctuated by non-cumulative breaks."[2] Kuhn makes a distinction between the day-to-day, year-to-year work of "normal science," in which basic principles are commonly understood and tested—resulting in the accumulation of further knowledge—and what he calls "scientific revolutions," by which he means those moments of pure insight in which one concept of the world is replaced by a new and incompatible one; some examples include the acceptance of the ideas of Copernicus concerning the movements of the planets, Newton and the laws of physics, and Einstein and the relationship of space to time. Kuhn called this fundamental conceptual change in worldview a *paradigm shift*, and he is largely responsible for popularizing that term.

For Kuhn, a paradigm is a mutually agreed-on set of beliefs that filters, and in some ways controls the way we see and experience the world. Mindsets such as these determine the kinds of questions that are asked and this, in turn, informs and influences our definition of the world. The result of a paradigm shift, which Kuhn says may sometimes take years to reach general awareness and acceptance, always produces a new perspective within the collective consciousness.

If a paradigm shift in music is underway, then its beginnings can be traced back into the 1960s to the aesthetic rebalancing and redefining of the roles of artist, art work, and audiences by the avant-garde in general, and John Cage in particular. As composer Warren Burt observed, not only did "the music" change in the 1960s but also "the venues music was made in changed, the way audiences listened changed, and the way the music was disseminated changed." Listening and attention became "multi-directional rather than unidirectional," and experiencing a work such as Cage's HPSCHD, for example, required listening "in a global, environmental way, and not [just] 'note-by-note.'"[3] This need for new ways of listening was equally true for most of Cage's music from the 1950s on; for Cage, the successful realization of his music required more than the predetermined "re-creation" of his original idea, but instead was a process whereby new and unexpected sounds coming from performers, and sometimes audience members, were allowed to interact with and inform the initial plan.

More than that of any other composer, it is Cage's music from the 1950s forward that sets both the stage and the tone for this nonhierarchic form of creativity. Rather than defining the composer-performer relationship in increasingly minute detail—as was the custom for the past thousand years—Cage created music that, through the use of chance operations, offered an ever-changing field of possibilities, and insisted that the performer, and often the audience, too, join in the creative act, thus blurring the boundaries not only of the process of composition, but also of the methods of its realization and final perception. For Cage, writing music was not an ego-driven, goal-oriented compositional system designed to create "masterpieces" but, rather, an open-ended process— open source, if you will—that fostered a group awareness and individual responsibility that allows the audience, in Dieter Daniels words, "to essentially self-determine its experiences with the artwork." Daniels notes that Cage's point of departure for this blurring of the boundaries was silence rather than technology, citing his "silent" piece from 1952, *4'33"*, as the "ideal open work" because "in it nothing is fixed, [and] everything depends on the conditions of the respective performance."[4] But if the Internet began in both virtual and Cagean silence, it is certainly not silent now, not when composers such as Michael Kaufmann are able to mine it for samples, and millions of audio files are moving through it every day.

Over the past decade, I suggest that there has begun a fundamental paradigm shift in the arts, as well as in the rest of our lives, from a media culture to a cyberculture, with a global audience and global communications and experiences, and worldwide artistic capabilities. To restate this in more musical terms, we are moving from the ancient world of hearing, through the modern world of listening, to the virtual world of creative interactivity. One of the key components of this post-Cagean online musical genre is the ability to have two-way interactive experiences within a multiplicity of immersive environments, a unique relationship of resources characterized in 1997 by composer Larry Polansky (the coauthor of the Hierarchical Music Specification Language [HMSL], along with David Rosenboom and Phil Burk) as "a co-evolution of technology, art, and collaborative processes."[5]

The New Landscape

As surely as the five-hundred-year tradition of medieval and Renaissance instruments yielded to the classical orchestra (whose own three-hundred-year reign, in turn, is slowly coming to an end), and printed scores, so crucial for success during the common practice period, have today grown less important than sound files, the virtual music of the future will emerge from a new landscape of digital instruments, digital techniques, and digital sound. This landscape is being brought into being by the confluence of four key concepts, which not only inform and define individual expressions of it but characterize the very nature of the genre as well. These concepts are: availability, portability, collectivity, and communication. These are the ingredients—the raw materials, the tenets, the givens—around which, and through which, virtual music will evolve.

Availability

Already, it is possible to see that the tools of virtual music will continue to be readily available to all. Affordable computers; inexpensive, if not free, software; and cheap communication paths—including public wireless networks—offering the ability to remain connected for long periods of time; plus faster speeds and greatly expanded storage capacity, are all becoming available in ways both professional and amateur musicians around the world will be able to access and use.

Neil B. Rolnick, a composer and director of the iEAR Studios at Rensselaer Polytechnic Institute—a school positioned squarely on the fault line between music and machine—believes that "the most important development in music technology (or media technology) is the fact that it's so universally accessible." He added that he wasn't talking about professional access to a high-speed, research-based Internet, or complex interactive Max patches, "but rather Garageband and iTunes and Napster," and all the low-cost, yet powerful "soft synths, digital recorders, virtual instruments, [and] virtual DJs" available for nothing, or next to nothing, online. Half of Rolnick's undergraduate students are "making music with [software like] Acid or Reason without knowing anything about computer music."[6]

Nicolas Collins, Editor-in-Chief of *Leonardo Music Journal*, thinks file sharing is equally important for the future, not only as a "powerful, cheap tool for self-promotion by emerging or fringe artists but also one that "gives the consumer tremendous freedom to expand listening, [and] experiment with unknown music."[7] Rolnick agrees that peer-to-peer file exchange is a key ingredient of the music of the future, but adds, "Where I think things will really change is that as we have more ubiquitous high speed connections we'll see new paradigms for musical participation." He characterizes the change as a "big good-bye to Roger Sessions' idea of 'composer, performer and audience,'" and the introduction of a new environment in which "intellectual property/copyright issues take on a whole new meaning, [particularly] when we can all re-compose or participate in re-performing anything we find on the net."[8]

Even at the local level—if one actually exists anymore in the digital realm—access to the tools of digital art is growing easier, thanks not only to libraries and media arts centers but also to the new computer-based arts communities that are forming, with new attitudes about portable computing, the sharing of programs, and interactive art. In New York, this laptop community centers around a project called Share DJ, which, one day a week, takes over a downtown club called Open Air. Founded in 2001 by Barry Manalog, geoffGDAM, and Newclueless, the intention of Share is to provide "an open forum, in real life, for data exchange and media performance." Each Sunday, starting at 5 P.M., Share hosts an open laptop jam, in which "patrons are encouraged to show and exchange ideas, giving each other feedback, catalyzing development of techniques and philosophies in new media." The club has an open-mixer system for both audio and video that lets players patch their equipment into the multichannel, multiroom sound and multiscreen video systems, through which multiple participants are able to jointly compose both the audio and video outputs. Between 2001 and mid-2004, Share's Sunday night sessions supported over 1248 hours of open jams and 200 hours of featured sets, and Share now maintains some 1000 gigabytes of audio archives. With the addition of a wireless hub and a broadband connection, Share has begun to establish "an interactive online presence," and has collaborated with several festivals, including the 2002 Phono Taktik festival, which began with live concerts in New York, and concluded with a streaming NET.JAM when the festival moved to Vienna a few months later.[9]

Also opening in New York in fall 2001—and speaking more to the combined issues of high-tech gadget availability and a reformed social sensibility—was a nightclub called the Remote Lounge. In a two-floor environment best described as an interactive video bar, one hundred cameras, monitors, plasma screens, and projectors are all controllable by patrons who track other customers, up close and personal, as they move about, flirt, and watch each other spy. Every image the cameras capture is visible on a multitude of channel-flipping monitors inside the club, while, on the Web, fresh still-shots of the in-club activities are posted anew each night. (As you can imagine, guests have to waive their right to privacy just to enter.) Although this voyeur's paradise doesn't offer much of a musical experience—beyond the ambient sounds coming from the bar or the dance floor below—it does provide an early glimpse of what's possible in the highly connected social environment of the future. Because, at its core, virtual music is multimedia, with video, even today, sometimes playing an almost equal role with audio, and we can expect this reconception of video to increase substantially as broadband capabilities become more universally available.

Furthermore, through some application of virtual reality or tele-immersion, virtual music will eventually engage all of our senses, and literally transport us artistically to other worlds. Whereas this capability is still in its infancy, there are some people currently working to make it a reality. Jaron Lanier, the inventor of "virtual reality" and a musician himself, is the lead scientist on the National Tele-Immersion Initiative, a consortium of universities studying next-generation Internet technologies. He can envision a day when tele-immersion will be able to draw in the real world, rather than create a virtual one, and give the illusion that "people in different cities are actually in the same room." That, he said, "would change the nature of the game of on-line music."[10]

Portability

In the virtual world of tomorrow, portability—almost all of it wireless—will be taken for granted, something we're beginning to do today with telephones. The demise of the computer as a box glued to the desktop and connected to the wall has been prophesized for years on end. If complete portability hasn't yet fully come to pass, the possibility is closer than ever now. Laptops, palmtops, Gameboys, iPods—the list of portable devices grows longer every year. Neil Rolnick says that for today's professionals this degree of portability "means that most musicians find ways of integrating digital media into their musical lives." For amateurs, the laptop and palmtop are becoming "the portable music making machine [of the age], kind of like the guitar in the 1960s, or the parlor piano in the early twentieth century."[11]

From a technology prospective alone, we can't exclude the gaming experience from our inventory of the new landscape. The games industry (which uses music, after all) is not only bigger than the music industry but within striking distance of Hollywood movies in terms of sales. But, even more important, there are now extremely powerful physics engines driving these games that could be of enormous use to the virtual arts. Whereas the games of the 1990s had to devote most of their processor time to the graphics, today's games use computers with dual processors: one to handle the 3-D graphics, and the CPU to handle artificial intelligence. If any significant part of this vast computing resource were put to the service of music, it could surely produce as credible an experience of playing an instrument as it does today of driving a race car. If a guitar-player or keyboard-player gamer could be made to feel—really feel—a part of a band with other people from around the world, it would, as Jaron Lanier said, really change the nature of the (musical) game.

Another important development in portable digital media is the ease of recording that is built into the latest equipment, particularly the new MP3 player/recorders. Just as amateurs with digital cameras captured some of the most compelling footage of the recent past—from suspected UFOs, to inappropriate police activities, to tornados coming up the road—music may be in for some new sounds, as well as some new combinations of the familiar sounds surrounding us. The composer Michael Kaufmann told me that what interests him right now is the "healthy field recording subculture" that is springing up, and the sounds this group may eventually produce, particularly if coupled with MP3 blogs and developed into compositions through overdubbing and reposting. This newfound interactive ability—literally, *to grow music*—"is changing the concept of improvisation."[12]

What about the role of the artist in this scenario, in which future musical instruments may well be connected to the newest versions of Xboxes and look like next-generation Gameboys? According to Marshall McLuhan, again from *The Global Village*, the role of the artist, as a cultural mediator, is "to keep the community in conscious relation to the changing and hidden ground."[13] To put this in more practical terms, as artists and as listeners, we must stay open to the possibility that the way we make art, perceive music, and participate as audiences will most likely be changing in the coming years.

Collectivity

A critical component of the emerging landscape of virtual music is the sheer numbers of participants that will be involved, and the power—creative and otherwise—that this connected and technically savvy mass of people will be able to evoke. The organizing power of the smart mobs in Seattle, or the critical mass of the Grey Tuesday protest online, are both early examples of what, politically and socially, may lie ahead. In music, the creation of "massively parallel group composition via the web," to borrow Nicolas Collins's characterization, is already underway.[14]

The largest such undertaking to date began in 1998, when the Catalan theatre group La Fura dels Baus unveiled their production of *F@ust 3.0*, complete with a musical score created by cybercomposers. To accomplish this, the La Fura directors turned to Sergi Jordà at the University of Pompeu Fabra in Barcelona, who, together with Toni Aguilar, developed FMOL, or the Faust Music On Line software synth. One of the early virtual musical instruments for the Web, FMOL began as a freeware program for Windows, through which composers could contribute musical phrases and short compositions—at first, all submissions had to be twenty seconds or less—and with which other users could modify both new and existing music by adding tracks and processing the sounds. First open for musical submissions between January–April 1998—and hoping to receive at least the fifty pieces La Fura needed for the production—FMOL collected more than eleven hundred of these brief co-composed works, cataloging them in a database that kept track of the relationships between the scores. Dante Tanzi says that the success of FMOL is based in part on the design of the score-files database, which handles the various layers and tracks, "not as a simple list, but as a tree ... each time the program accesses this database, it receives and updates the tree structure of the composition, allowing the user to see all the branches, with the detailed information of each node."[15]

Between September and October 2000, FMOL sent out a second Internet call for musical contributions—this time of up to sixty seconds in length—for a new production by La Fura, an opera they called *DQ*. By the end of this second production, and a total of some six months accepting scores for the *F@ust 3.0* and *DQ* productions, a collection of over seventeen hundred compositions existed in the FMOL database. This first version of the FMOL software didn't yet support simultaneous real-time jamming but, rather, as Jordà said, supported a "collaborative approach ... closer to e-mail than to chat."[16] Although the last collective composition project Jordà has organized for FMOL ended with the production of *DQ* in 2000, users continue to access the database, download compositions to modify, and post new ones from time to time. Even though Jordà says today he only spends a few weeks a year on FMOL, a new collective composition project with La Fura Dels Baus will probably be coming soon.

As we take inventory of the new landscape and prepare to venture forth, the decidedly nonparallel world of multiuser gaming offers a hint of what the new musical experience might resemble. Games, after all, have no fixed plots, and develop according to players' previous moves. A key element to keep an eye on in the future is the degree to which the distinction between online art and gaming becomes increasingly blurred. Think of a time, for instance, when the artistic experience has the potential of being as entertaining, interactive, and engaging as the gaming experience, plus as meaningful and thought provoking as all good art. Consider the possibility that virtual music has the potential to become a live musical organism, living in cyberspace, growing and changing course because of the collective actions of its users, and we begin to get a glimpse of where we may be going, and what we may encounter along the way.

If you're still unconvinced, and think more reasons of an artistic nature are needed for musicians to consider embracing gaming, then consider Scanner, who once said that as computers became better at simulating the real world, and as the gaming experience became more of "a super hyper reality," that he could see art as being there "to search between these spaces, to make connections, to seduce and amplify."[17] Or listen to Yair Landou of Sony Pictures, who says that "there are three basic human entertainment experiences that go back to the cave: storytelling, game-playing, and music. People," he continues "are looking for a hybrid of those things."[18] Rob Glaser of RealNetworks added that a fourth experience "is being part of a tribe," saying "the fundamental social desire to have a common context is still there."[19]

Communication

How might these new forms of musical interactivity, including gaming, affect the idea of musical communication, a function largely covered until now by the score, an improv chart, or a commonly understood set of oral instructions coming from tradition? And how might ways develop that will allow amateur and professional musicians, not only to coexist, but to enjoy the shared experience of performance? Although we don't yet know the answers to either of these questions, Warren Burt suggests it will probably be in ways already begun, saying "think of Edgar Varese, carefully sculpting the melodic line of *Density 21.5*, considering [as he did so] each motive, pitch, dynamic, [and] phrasing," and then compare that to a performance by The Hub, "where one person composed/improvised pitch, one improvised/composed durations, another one dynamics," all of which was heard in real time. "Both are good pieces," he said, "but one is the result of a single person crafting a fixed piece, the other is the result of a group working through a process, making something that they couldn't individually make otherwise."[20] In scenarios such as this, the top-down model of the maestro and his orchestra, or the diva and her opera, will need to give way to a more democratic, contribute-what-you-can, creative attitude.

Whereas interactive music, on the scale I have described, is, ultimately, a personal experience between individuals, it also may have possibilities on a grand theoretical, if not cosmic, scale. David Rosenboom believes that interactive music, operating in what he calls "a co-creative model form" could be "fundamental for interactions among unknowable kinds of intelligence."[21] His arguments, existing somewhere between the fields of speculative music theory and extraterrestrial communication, are convincing, too; Rosenboom, after all, is now the Dean of the School of

Music of the California Institute of the Arts, and has a reputation as an experimental composer dating back to his "brain wave music" of the late 1960s. In an unpublished monograph titled *Collapsing Distinctions: Interacting within Fields of Intelligence on Interstellar Scales and Parallel Musical Models,* Rosenboom points out that an advantage of operating within the abstractness of artistic media is that it "may enable us to grapple with scales of information and communication that are uncommon in our daily experience, and ways of regarding space and time that are radically different from our usual, primarily linear concepts." If true, and who can say, then *music,* as Rosenboom sees it, can provide "an abstract space for structuring and exploring time-space experience in profound ways that probe the nature of perception, intelligence, cognition, consciousness, and communication," and *musical constructions,* that is, compositions, "serve as gathering points for co-creative activity and environments for exploration." Noting that "communication in music is, *fundamentally co-creative,"* [his emphasis] Rosenboom says that "co-creation may be the only way intelligent entities not sharing a common language can communicate." Pointing out that co-creative practices are common activities in music making, he notes that "the growth of electronic communications networks has given rise to a new phase of experimentation in this regard."[22]

But regardless of the scale, one thing we can be certain of, even at this early stage: communication, always complicated, will, in the 3-D world of the Web, take place on levels so convoluted that it will surely create consequences, both good and bad, many as yet unforeseen. If, as our experiences with *Cathedral,* and Sergi Jordà's with FMOL suggests that ongoing, online, group compositions tend to take on a mind of their own as the communities around which they develop continue to grow and express themselves, then the varying natures and potentials of these new environments should be viewed as unexplored, new landscapes, and the effects of these new forms of communication and interactivity should be carefully thought through. Ryan Ingberitsen told me that in the GPS-Art projects he participated in in Krakow and Chicago, the composers in both locations created "virtual" environments for the performers, in which they then had to interact. The creation of a new space with building blocks taken from the everyday environment really blurred the composer/performer relationship, "since the composer can simultaneously 'perform' the environment in which the performer must live, and can have an immediate response to what the performer does." Ingberitsen described it as "a look into a collective compositional process that could eventually change the way in which society views itself, and the place of the individual in that society."[23]

Will interactive virtual music change the way society sees itself? Or is it an early indication of the social changes that are to come? Will we someday use virtual musical instruments in as yet unimagined ways to make contact, and perhaps communicate, with another intelligence? I don't know, although I certainly enjoy entertaining the idea. In the meantime, I'll end with a thought from Marcus Novak, who, in 1997, suggested that it is possible to stop seeing music as *singular* and begin to see it as *multiple,* that is, "as landscape, as atmosphere, as an n-dimensional field of opportunities." He said that if music becomes a landscape, it will then be possible "to extract as many types of conventional music as there are trajectories through that landscape." Novak concluded, "The new problem for composition is to create that landscape."[24]

Today, a decade beyond the first sounds on the Web, the landscape Novak and others envisioned is emerging. As in a painting, which unfolds slowly, the background wash is finished, and the first broad brush strokes have appeared. But also like a painting, particularly one full of thought and depth and vision, first strokes often get replaced by later ones as the image grows and matures into its final form. Ultimately, of course, the test, the final proof, of a new landscape—whether on flat canvas or in 3-D virtual space—is to be found, not only in its broad vistas and creative vision but also slowly unveiled over time among the details. The "canvas" of virtual music that I have described is only just begun. It will take centuries to complete. It will change our experience of music forever.

NOTES

Introduction: Making Music in Thin Air

1. William Duckworth, "Perceptual and Structural Implications of 'Virtual' Music on the Web," *Annals of the New York Academy of Sciences,* Vol. 999 (November 2003): 254–262. Parts of this talk, which was sponsored by the Fondazione Pierfranco e Luisa Mariani, appear in slightly altered forms in the Introduction, the case study on *Cathedral,* and the final chapter on "Virtual Music."
2. Tom McNichol, "Finally, a Public Resting Place for History's Motherboards," *New York Times,* Section G, Circuits (June 26, 2003): 5. The Computer History Museum may be found online at http://www.computerhistory.org
3. If you're interested in such facts as when the term "microprocessor" first appeared in print (1973), when Microsoft's yearly sales reached $1 million (1978), or when *Time* magazine selected the computer as its "Man" of the year (1983), The Ongoing History of Microprocessors Web site is the place for you. You can find it at http://www.tcs.uni.wroc.pl/~jja/ASK/HISZ-COMP.HTM. Another interesting site, complete with photos and illustrations, is "The History of Computers During My Lifetime," by Jason Patterson. Organized into three sets of pages covering three decades of development, the site is a good place to explore those gone, but not forgotten, computers. The site is located at http://www.pattosoft.com.au/jason/Articles/HistoryOfComputers/1970s.html
4. John Naughton, *A Brief History of the Future: From Radio Days to Internet Years in a Lifetime* (Woodstock and New York: The Overlook Press, 2001), 27.
5. Rosalind Resnick and Dave Taylor, *The Internet Business Guide,* (Indianapolis: Sams Publishing, 1994), 322.
6. The term "cyberspace" was coined by science fiction writer William Gibson. It was introduced in "Burning Chrome," a short story he first read in public in 1981, and then expanded on in his 1984 novel *Neuromancer.* In Gibson's lexicon, the term means a simulated navigable world inside a network of computers.

Chapter 1: A Brief History of Interactive Music

Erik Satie

1. The Erik Satie home page is located at http://www.af.lu.se/%7Efogwall/ satie.html. It is the most complete Satie resource on the Web, and features articles, pictures, audio clips, and a newsgroup discussion.
2. Quoted on the *Springtime in Paris: Erik Satie* page of the Minnesota Public Radio Web site, found at http://music.mpr.org/features/0003_satie/ satie.shtml. The page also includes sound files of the *Gymnopédies* and *Parade*.
3. Roger Shattuck, *The Banquet Years: The Origins of the Avant-garde in France, 1885 to World War I*, rev. ed. (New York: Vintage Books, 1968), 154.
4. Harold C. Schonberg, *et. al.*, "Music: A Long, Long, Long Night (and Day) at the Piano," *New York Times* (September 11, 1963): 45 (2 pages).
5. Stephen Whittington, "Serious Immobilities: On the Centenary of Erik Satie's Vexations," (1999), found at http://www.af.lu.se/~fogwall/ article3.html
6. Quoted in Jean Stein's biography of Edie Sedgwick, *Edie: An American Original* (Knopf, 1982).
7. Shattuck, *op. cit.*, 184.
8. Shattuck, *op. cit.*, 140.
9. Shattuck, *op. cit.*, 184.
10. Alan M. Gillmor, *Erik Satie* (New York: W. W. Norton & Company, Inc., 1992), 232. Originally from Fernand Léger, "Satie inconnu," *La Revue musicale* 214 (1952): 137.
11. Shattuck, *op. cit.*, 169. Also reprinted in *Empreintes*, (May 1950).
12. *Ibid.*
13. *Ibid.*
14. *Ibid.*
15. Whittington, "Serious Immobilities," *op. cit.*
16. Gillmor, *op. cit.*, 247–248.
17. Shattuck, *op. cit.*, 173.
18. Milhaud is quoted on the SatieMart: *Relâche*, Web site located at http:// hem.passagen.sa/satie/db/relache.htm
19. Gillmor, *op. cit.*, 247.
20. Quoted on the SatieMart: *Relâche*, Web site located at http://hem. passagen.sa/satie/db/relache.htm
21. Shattuck, *op. cit.*, 172.

John Cage

22. The official John Cage home page, established by the Cage Trust, is located at http://www.johncage.org. At this writing, the site is not yet active.
23. John Cage, "The Future of Music: Credo," *Silence* (Middletown, CT: Wesleyan University Press, 1961), 4.

24. Cage, "Four Statements on the Dance," *Silence*, 87.
25. Cage, "Credo," *Silence*, 3.
26. Cage, "45' for a Speaker," *Silence*, 190.
27. Calvin Tomkins, *Ahead of the Game: Four Versions of the Avant-Garde* (Harmondsworth: Penguin, 1968), 97.
28. Cage, "Forward," *Silence*, xi.
29. Richard Kostelanetz, ed., *John Cage* (New York: Praeger Publishers, 1970), 77.
30. Cage, "Lecture On Something," *Silence*, 139.
31. John Cage, "Defense of Satie," *John Cage*, Robert Dunn, comp. (New York: Henmar Press, Inc., 1962), 81.
32. Dieter Daniels, "Media Art Interaction: Strategies of Interactivity" from *Medienkunst Interaktion = Media art interaction* edited Goethe-Institut & ZKM, quotes found at http://www.urbanbedtimestories.com/about/bibliography.html
33. John Cage, "Happy New Ears!," *A Year From Monday* (Middletown, CT: Wesleyan University Press, 1967), 32.
34. Dieter Daniels, *op. cit.*
35. Cage, "Diary: How To Improve The World (You Will Only Make Matters Worse) Continued 1967," *A Year From Monday*, 151.
36. Cage, "How To Pass, Kick, Fall, And Run," *A Year from Monday*, 134–135.
37. Cage, "Experimental Music: Doctrine," *Silence*, 15.
38. Cage, "Diary: How To Improve The World (You Will Only Make Matters Worse) 1965," *A Year From Monday*, 18–19
39. Cage, "Experimental Music," *Silence*, 8.

Brian Eno

40. The Brian Eno home page is located at http://music.hyperreal.org/artists/brian_eno/. An active site that is updated regularly, it contains news, a discography, interviews, lyrics, a photo gallery, an info center, and a way to contact Eno directly, among other features.
41. Lester Bangs, "Eno," *Musician, Player and Listener* 21 (Nov. 1979), found at http://music.hyperreal.org/artists/brian_eno/interviews/musn79.html
42. Brian Eno, "This Article is a Musical Instrument" unattributed publication (ca. 1975), found at http://music.hyperreal.org/artists/brian_eno/interviews/unk-75a.html
43. Anthony Korner, "Aurora Musicalis," *Artforum* (summer 1996), found at http://music.hyperreal.org/artists/brian_eno/interviews/artfor86.html
44. Ian MacDonald, "Before and After Science," *New Musical Express*, (November 26, 1977), found at http://music.hyperreal.org/artists/brian_eno/interviews/nme77a.html
45. Bangs, *op. cit.*
46. Korner, *op. cit.*

47. Brian Eno, "Generative Music," a talk delivered at the Imagination Conference in San Francisco, (June 8, 1996), printed in *In Motion Magazine,* and found at http://www.inmotionmagazine.com/eno1.html

48. Michael Bloom, "Ambient 1: Music For Airports," *Rolling Stone* (July 26, 1979), found at http://music.hyperreal.org/artists/brian_eno/interviews/rs79c.html

49. Bangs, *op. cit.*

50. Eno, "Generative Music," *op. cit.*

51. John Alderman, "Brian Eno," n.d., found at http://hotwired.lycos.com/popfeatures/96/24/eno.transcript.html

52. Brian Eno, "Pro Session—The Studio As Compositional Tool," a talk given in 1979 at New Music New York, the first New Music America Festival. Reprinted in *Downbeat* ca. 1979.

53. Richard Williams, "The Brain of Brian," *The Guardian* (May 10, 1996).

54. Eno, "Generative Music," *op. cit.*

55. SSEYO's Web page, with information about Koan Pro, which they no longer support, is at http://www.sseyo.com/products/koanpro/index.html

56. Eno, "Generative Music," *op. cit.*

57. Eno, *op. cit.*

58. Brian Eno, Untitled contribution to an article on music of the future, *The Independent* (March 1, 1996).

59. Eno, "Generative Music," *op. cit.*

60. Alderman, *op. cit.*

61. Andy Oldfield, "Brian Eno's Generation Game," *The Independent* (July 29, 1996), found at http://music.hyperreal.org/artists/brian_eno/interviews/ind96d.html

62. Garrick Webster, "Before and After Science," *PC Format,* Issue 54 (March 1996).

63. Williams, Richard, *op. cit.*

John Oswald

64. John Oswald's Plunderphonic Web site can be found at http://www.plunderphonics.com/

65. Paul Steenhuisen, "Composer to Composer: Paul Steenhuisen interviews John Oswald," *The WholeNote* (May 2003), found at http://members.shaw.ca/steenhuisen/oswald.htm

66. John Oswald, "Plunderphonics, or Audio Piracy As A Compositional Prerogative," found at http://www.halcyon.com/robinja/mythos/Plunderphonics.html

67. David Gans, "The Man Who Stole Michael Jackson's Face," *Wired* 3.02 (February 1995), found at http://www.autumnleaf.com/oswald.htm

68. Steenhuisen, *op. cit.*

69. Quoted in the ESTWeb Interview with John Oswald, found at http://media.hyperreal.org/zines/est/intervs/oswald.html

70. David Keenan, "Interview with John Oswald," *The Wire* (May 1, 2002).

71. Steenhuisen, *op. cit.*
72. Steenhuisen, *Ibid.*
73. Oswald, *op. cit.*

Moby

74. Moby's home page can be found at http://www.moby-online.com. Containing a journal, news, visuals, a shop, info page, and links to other sites, it is the source of this quote and other unattributed Moby quotes in this section.
75. Gerald Marzorati, "All by Himself," *New York Times Magazine,* Section 6 (March 17, 2002): 69.
76. Marzorati, *Ibid.,* 36.
77. Marzorati, *Ibid.,* 35.
78. Ethan Smith, "Organization Moby," *Wired,* 10.05 (May 2002): 90.
79. Marzorati, *op. cit.,* 34.
80. Greg Rule, "Sampling Nation: Techno," *Keyboard* (May 1994): 47.

Chapter 2: *Unsilent Night*: A Case Study in Motion

1. Phil Kline, "2003 Unsilent Night (the Christmas Piece)," found at http://www.mindspring.com/~boombox/xmas.htm. A recording of *Unsilent Night* is available from Cantaloupe Records (21005), released in 2001.
2. Phil Kline, "Bio," found at http://www.mindspring.com/~boombox/bio.htm
3. *Ibid.*

The Boom Box Orchestra

4. *Ibid.*
5. Phil Kline, "Some Notes On Personal Stereo," an unpublished essay written in 2002 and used as program notes by Present Music, found at http://www.presentmusic.org/2002–2003/notes/philkline.html
6. *Ibid.*
7. *Ibid.*
8. Jon Caramanica, "Electric Word: Sonic Boom," *Wired* 9.12 (Dec. 2001), found at http://www.wired.com/wired/archive/9.12/eword_pr.html
9. *Ibid.*
10. Tom Bickley, "Unsilent Night," BA-NEWMUS:11870 (posted December 23, 2003), found at http://eartha.mills.edu:8000/guest/archives/ba-newmus/log0312/msg00151.html

A Living Sound Sculpture

11. Kline, "Some Notes On Personal Stereo," *op. cit.*
12. Tom Bickley, "SF Gate: Cacophony of city sounds and scores of boom boxes make an 'Unsilent Night,'" BA-NEWMUS:11866 (posted December 20,

2003), found at http://eartha.mills.edu:8000/guest/archives/ba-newmus/log0312/msg00147.html

13. Mary Huhn, "Rock the Halls," *New York Post* (December 13, 2003), found at http://www.nypost.com/living/43892.htm

14. Bickley, "SF Gate," *op. cit.*

15. Bickley, "Unsilent Night," *op. cit.*

16. Eve Beglarian, "Phil Kline's Walking Vigil" (September 24, 2001), found at http://www.evbvd.com/newsnotes/911/010924a.html

Sonic Plasticity

17. Kline, "Some Notes On Personal Stereo," *op. cit.*

18. Cantaloupe Music, CA21005 (2001). The Cantaloupe Web site may be found at http://cantaloupemusic.com/unsilentnight/

19. Kline, "Some Notes On Personal Stereo," *op. cit.*

Chapter 3: The *Brain Opera*: A Case Study in Space

1. Frank J. Oteri, "In the 1st Person: Tod Machover," *NewMusicBox* Web Magazine, Vol. 1, No. 6 (October 1999), found at http://www.newmusicbox.org/page.nmbx?id=06fp01

2. *Ibid.*

3. n.a., "Brain Opera Mind Forest," n.d., found at http://brainop.media.mit.edu/onsite/main.html

4. Tod Machover, "The Brain Opera and Active Music," n.d. (circa 1996), found at http://brainop.media.mit.edu/Archive/ars-Electronica.html

The Mind Forest

5. *Ibid.*

6. May Lee, " 'Brain Opera' takes music to new dimensions," *CNN Interactive* (November 29, 1996), found at http://www-cgi.cnn.com/SHOWBIZ/9611/29/brain.opera/

The Brain Opera *Performance*

7. Machover, "The Brain Opera and Active Music," *op. cit.*

8. *Ibid.*

9. *Ibid.*

10. n.a., "Brain Opera Libretto," n.d., found at http://brainop.media.mit.edu/libretto/libretto.html

11. Machover, "The Brain Opera and Active Music," *op. cit.*

Net Music

12. n.a., "The Palette," n.d., found at http://brainop.media.mit.edu/online/netmusic/BOPerf/pinball.html

13. Richard Dyer, "Playing the Future: Tod Machover Brainstorms a Make-Your-Own Opera, Complete With Web Site." *Boston Globe* (July 14, 1996), found at http://brainop.media.mit.edu/~tod/press/media/globe7_96.html

14. Machover, "The Brain Opera and Active Music," *op. cit.*

15. Oteri, "In the 1st Person: Tod Machover," *op. cit.*

The House of Music

16. Dyer, "Playing the Future," *op. cit.*

17. Marcy Mason, "Adventures In Music Classics Meet Techno-Modern Future In Vienna's New Museum," *Chicago Tribune* (October 22, 2000), found at http://brainop.media.mit.edu/~tod/press/media/tribune10_00.html

18. n.a., "Tod Machover's Brain Opera," n.d., found at http://brainop.media.mit.edu/

19. n.a., "Future Music Blender, A New Finale for the Brain Opera," n.d., found at http://brainop.media.mit.edu/hyperins/bovienna/fmb.html

20. Oteri, "In the 1st Person: Tod Machover," *op. cit.*

Interactive Space

21. Machover, "The Brain Opera and Active Music," *op. cit.*

Chapter 4: Music on the Web in the Twentieth Century

1. Chris Brown and John Bischoff, "Indigenous to the Net," a Web-based article that documents the history of computer Network Music in the San Francisco Bay Area, found at www.sfmoma.org/crossfade/. All undocumented quotes in this section come from this article.

The League of Automatic Music Composers

2. Information of the KIM-1 and other early microcomputers can be found at http://members.cox.net/obsoletetechnology/kim1.html

3. An EP recording of The League of Automatic Music Composers was released on Lovely Music Ltd. (NY), on Lovely Little Records, LP 101–6, in 1980. The Lovely Music Web site can be found at http://www.lovely.com

The Hub

4. Nicolas Collins, "Zwischen 'data' und 'date': Erfahrungen mit Proto-Web Musik von The Hub" ("The Fly in the Ointment: Proto-Web Music by the Hub."), *Positionen* 31 (May 1997): 20–22.

5. Kyle Gann, "The Hub: Musica Telephonica," *Village Voice* (June 23, 1987), found at http://www.o-art.org/history/Computer/Hub/HubTel.html

6. The Hub, CD, *Wreckin' Ball*, Artifact 1008 (1994); CD, *The Hub*, Artifact 1002 (1989). The *Wreckin' Ball* CD is still available and may be found at http://www.artifact.com/wreckball.html
7. Brown and Bischoff, *op. cit.*

NetJam

8. John Naughton, *op. cit.*, 180, 313.
9. An expanded list of early discussion groups, plus early FTP sites and Web sites of particular interest to musicians can be found in Scot Gresham-Lancaster's "Magical Musical Tours: A Comprehensive Guide to Musical Resources on the Internet," *Electronic Musician*, Vol. 10, No. 10 (October 1994): 46–62.
10. Craig Latta, "A New Musical Medium: NetJam," *Computer Music Journal*, Vol. 15, No. 3 (fall 1991), found at http://www.o-art.org/history/Computer/MIDI/NetJam.html. Latta also contributed "Notes on the Net-Jam Project" to the *Leonardo Music Journal*, Vol. 1, No. 1 (winter 1991).
11. Craig Latta, "Electronic and Computer Music Frequently-Asked Questions (FAQ)," posted to several newsgroups on March 16, 1995, and currently found at http://www.faqs.org/faqs/music/netjam-faq/
12. E-mail from Craig Latta to the author (December 3, 2003).
13. Craig Latta, *Computer Music Journal, op. cit.*

Rocket Network

14. Andy Reinhardt, "Player Without a Band? Log On, Dude," *Business Week* (September 10, 1998), found at http://www.businessweek.com?1998/38/b3596151.htm
15. Elton John, Sinead O'Connor, and Thomas Dolby participated in a fund-raiser project for Warchild, a British charitable organization, by cutting a record via ResRocket in the spring of 1999. Reported by David Shamah, "User Friendly," *Jerusalem Post Newspaper* (July 28, 1999), found at http://www.jpost.com/com/Archive/28.Jul.1999/Digital/Article-3.html
16. Reported by Colin Berry, "Rocket Launchers," *Wired*, Issue 6.08 (August 1998), found at http://www.wired.com/wired/archive/6.08/newmedia.html?person=paul_allen&topic_set=wiredpeople
17. From http://www.resrocket.com/ (October 19, 2002). The Web site is no longer active; the copyright date of the material on the site is 2001.
18. Tom Kenny, "Willy Henshall, The Rocket Man of the Internet," *Internet Audio* (April 2001): 27, 45.
19. Karsten J. Chikuri, "Riding the Res Rocket: Using a Wind Synth with Res Rocket's DRGN" found at http://www.windsynth.org/studio/riding_the_res_rocket.shtml
20. Kenny, *Internet Audio, op. cit.*

21. The LiveJam Web site may be found at http://www.livejam.com

22. John Alderman, "LiveJam Picks Up the World Beat," *Wired News* (September 10, 1998), found at http://www.wired.com/news/culture/0,1284,14943,00.html

23. From http://www.resrocket.com/ (October 19, 2002). Copyright date of the material, 2001.

24. Peter Drescher, "We Have Liftoff!, Producing a recording session in Rocket Network's online studio.," *Electronic Musician* (April 2000): 116–124.

25. Quoted in Kenny, *Internet Audio, op. cit.*

26. Both Perkins and Froker quoted in John Townley, "On The Trail of The Virtual Recording Studio," *Streaming Media World* (March 17, 2000), found at http://smw.internet.com/audio/reviews/rocket/

27. Gary S. Hall, "Bands Without Borders," *Electronic Musician,* Vol. 18, No. 11 (October 2002): 72–86. The pricing information in this paragraph also comes from this source.

28. Townley, *op. cit.*

29. n.a., "Digidesign purchase file-sharing technology," The Audio Recording Centre (May 8, 2003), found at http://arc.badgerdotcom.co.uk/article-print-151.html

Beatnik

30. Phil Ward, "The Virtual Thomas Dolby," *HYPERinterACTIVE! Magazine* (February 1994), found at http://www.tdolby.com/reading/int_hyper.html

31. J. R. Griffin, "Real Dolby Sound," *Entertainment Weekly* (September 30, 1994), found at http://www.tdolby.com/reading/int_entertainment.html

32. Frank Ahrens, "Thomas Dolby, Deafened by The Silence," *Washington Post* (September 6, 1999), found at http:///www.e-prog.net/bands/dolby.htm

33. Ward, "The Virtual Thomas Dolby," *op. cit.*

34. Katherine Stalter, Interview with *Film & Video Magazine,* n.d., found at http://www.tdolby.com/reading/int_flimvideo.html

35. David Okamoto, Interview with *National Post Online,* n.d. (ca. 1999) found at http://www.tdolby.com/reading/int_nationalpost.html

36. n.a., "Dolby blinds the Net with sonic science," *BBC News Online Network* (May 27, 1998), found at http://news.bbc.co.uk/1/hi/entertainment/97113.stm

37. *Ibid.*

38. All quotes in this paragraph are from the Overview page on the Beatnik Web site, found at http://www.beatnik.com/company/index.html

39. Griffin, "Real Dolby Sound," *op. cit.*

MusicWorld

40. n.a., "Virtual Worlds Platform," Microsoft Research 2001, found at http://research.microsoft.com/scg/vworlds/vworlds.htm

41. *Ibid.*
42. Suzanne Ross, "They're Playing Our Song," Microsoft Research 2000, found at http://research.microsoft.com/seg/music_world.asp#top. Any further undocumented quotes in this section come from this document.
43. John P. Young, "Networked music: bridging real and virtual space," *Organized Sound* 6(2) (2001): 107–110.

IUMA

44. Jon Ippolito, "Cross Talk, Does the art world really 'get' the Internet?," *artbyte*, Vol. 2, No. 6 (March–April 2000): 24–25.
45. n.a., "About IUMA: It All Started at a Time When Companies Weren't Formed in Garages, Bands Were.," n.d., found at http://www.iuma.com/About/
46. n.a., IUMA Press Release: "GoodNoise to Acquire Internet Music Pioneer IUMA" (May 17, 1999), found at http://www.iuma.com/About/pagePressRelease_1.html
47. *Ibid.*
48. n.a., IUMA Press Release: "IUMA Suspends Operations" (February 7, 2001), found at http://www.iuma.com/About/pagePressRelease_16a.html

Cinema Volta

49. E-mail from John Maxwell Hobbs to the author (January 14, 2004).
50. From John Maxwell Hobbs's CV found at http://www.cinemavolta.com/cv.html
51. Kit Galloway and Sherrie Rabinowitz, "The Challenge: We Must Create At The Same Scale As We Can Destroy" (1984), found at http://www.ecafe.com/84manifesto.html
52. n.a., "About the Electronic Cafe International," found at http://www.ecafe.com/about.html
53. John Maxwell Hobbs, 1996 posting on The International Electroacoustic Community Discussion Group, found at http://alcor.concordia.ca/~kaustin/cecdiscuss/1996/1509.html
54. John Maxwell Hobbs, "Turning Cybercasts From Music Promotion to Art Form," *@ New York* (1998), now archived at http://www.cinemavolta.com/organicmechanics/archives/000005.html#more
55. E-mail from John Maxwell Hobbs to the author, *op. cit.*
56. E-mail from John Maxwell Hobbs to the author, *op. cit.*
57. John Maxwell Hobbs, "Web Phases," found at http://www.cinemavolta.com/phases.html
58. John Maxwell Hobbs, "Towards Hypermusic," *Leonardo On-Line* (1998), now archived at http://www.cinemavolta.com/organicmechanics/archives/000003.html#more

59. Kyle Gann, "Freeze, Symphony!," *Village Voice* (February 3, 1998): 131.

60. Hobbs, "Toward Hypermusic," *op. cit.*

WebDrum

61. The WebDrum site may be found at http://www.transjam.com

62. n.a., "Transjam Server FAQ," (1999), found at http://www.transjam.com/docs/faq.html

63. Phil Burk, "WebDrum," found at http://www.transjam.com/jam/drummer.html

64. n.a., "HMSL, the Hierarchical Music Specification Language" (1999), found at http://www.softsynth.com/hmsl/. Further information on HMSL may be found at Phil Burk, Larry Polansky, and David Rosenboom, "HMSL: A Theoretical Overview," *Perspectives of New Music*, Volume 28, No. 2 (summer 1990): 136–178.

65. SoftSynth Jsyn Press Release: "SoftSynth.com Announces Immediate Availability of Jsyn V14.2" (May 8, 2001), found at http://www.softsynth.com/jsyn/press/pressrls_jsynv142.html

66. Philip L. Burk, "Jammin' on the Web—A New Client/Server Architecture for Multi-User Musical Performance," *Proceedings of the ICMC* (2000). Found at http://www.transjam.com/docs/

Chapter 5: *Cathedral:* A Case Study in Time

1. The STEIM Web site is at http://www.steim.org/steim/

The Web Site

2. The *Cathedral* Web site is at http://cathedral.monroestreet.com. All aspects of the *Cathedral* site are accessible from the home page. In addition, extensive documentation about the development of the site, the 48-hour webcast, and the Cathedral Band performances in Australia, Tokyo, and New York are contained in the FACs and Archive pages of the site. The Archives also contains both sound files and photographs of the various performances.

The Virtual Instruments

3. The Sound Pool is temporarily closed for renovations.

4. The PitchWeb is at http://pitchweb.net

The 48-Hour Webcast of 2001

5. Harvestworks Digital Media Center is at http://www.harvestworks.org/

Internet Time

6. Marshall McLuhan and Bruce R. Powers, *The Global Village: Transformations in World Life and Media in the 21st Century* (Oxford: Oxford University Press, 1989), 13.
7. Marcos Novak, "Liquid Architectures in Cyberspace," *Cyberspace: First Steps,* M. Benedikt, ed. (Cambridge: MIT Press, 1992).
8. Dante Tanzi, "Observations about Music and Decentralized Environments," *Leonardo,* Vol. 34, No. 5 (2001): 431.
9. *Ibid.,* 432
10. A. T. Mann, *Sacred Architecture* (Great Britain: Element Books Ltd., 1993), 179.
11. Susanne K. Langer, *Feeling And Form* (New York: Charles Scribner's Sons, 1953), 109.

Chapter 6: Cell Phones and Satellites

Radio Net

1. Max Neuhaus's home page, maintained by the Electronic Music Foundation, can be found at http://www.emf.org/subscribers/neuhaus/index.html
2. From a 1983 interview with the author, published as William Duckworth, "Interview with William Duckworth" *Max Neuhaus, Inscription, Sound Works* (Ostfildern-Stuttgart, Cantz Verlag, 1994), 45.
3. Duckworth, Neuhaus interview (1983): 46.
4. Max Neuhaus, "The Broadcast Works and Audium," n.d., found at http://www.kunstradio.at/ZEITGLEICH/CATALOG/ENGLISH/neuhaus2-e.html
5. Neuhaus, *ibid.*
6. Neuhaus, *ibid.*
7. John Rockwell, *All American Music* (New York: Alfred A. Knopf, 1983), 147.
8. Duckworth, Neuhaus interview, 48.

Dialtones (a Telesymphony)

9. From Golan Levin's home page found at http://www.flong.com/
10. Golan Levin, "Dialtones (A Telesymphony)," n.d., found at http://www.flong.com/telesymphony/
11. David Dayen and Joanna Lux, "Cellphone Symphony," an interview with Golan Levin at TechTV (posted December 19, 2001) and found at http://www.techtv.com/audiofile/print/0,23102,3358391,00.html
12. Levin, "Dialtones," *op. cit.* All remaining quotes attributed to Levin in this section are taken from this Web site.

Sound Maps of Krakow

13. Matthew Mirapaul, "Drawing (and Doodling) With Countryside as Canvas," *New York Times,* Section E (April 1, 2002): 2.
14. Wood and Pryor's car drawings can be found at http://www.gpsdrawing.com
15. Marek Choloniewski's home page can be found at http://www.cyf-kr.edu.pl/~zbcholon/mch/mch.html
16. Marek Choloniewski's GPS-Art can be found at http://www.gps.art.pl/gpsart-e.html. This and all other unidentified quotes are taken from here. The site also contains audio and video documentation of the GPS-Art projects undertaken to date.
17. E-mail from Ryan Ingebritsen to the author (October 22, 2003).

Scanner

18. Jose Miguel G. Cortes, "Catalogue interview with Scanner," Valencia Biennale, Spain, 2001, found at http://www.scannerdot.com/sca_001.html
19. Greg Hilty, "Scanner," *Financial Times* (December 1998), found at http://www.scannerdot.com/sca_001.html
20. n.a., "Scanner," *Stranger Newspaper* (Seattle), (October 1997), found at found at http://www.scannerdot.com/sca_001.html
21. Andy Battaglia, "The Sounds of Science," *Salon.com* (August 5, 1999), found at http://www.salon.com/ent/music/feature/1999/08/05/scanner/
22. n.a., "Scanner in the Works," *Guardian* (September 1999), found at http://www.scannerdot.com/sca_001.html
23. Cortes, *op. cit.*
24. Tamara Palmer, "Interview with Scanner," *Electronic Directory* (July 2002), found at http://www.scannerdot.com/sca_001.html
25. Gil Gershman, "Scanner," *Magnet* #30, n.d., found at http://www.scannerdot.com/sca_001.html
26. n.a., "Scanner & DJ Spooky," *Future Music Magazine* (2000), found at http://www.scannerdot.com/sca_001.html
27. *op. cit.*
28. Battaglia, *op. cit.*
29. Cortes, *op. cit.*
30. n.a., "Scanner," *Stranger Newspaper* (Seattle), (October 1997), found at http://www.scannerdot.com/sca_001.html

The Mob Scene

31. "Bill" as quoted by Sara Stewart, "It's Mob Rule!" *New York Post* (July 21, 2003): 33. All future quotes attributed to "Bill" are from this article.
32. Otto Pohl, "What: Mob Scene. Who: Strangers. Point: None," *New York Times,* Section A (August 4, 2003): 4.
33. Found at http://www.smartmobs.com/book/book_summ.html

The Next Big Thing

34. Johanna Jainchill, "Clash, Then Synthesis: Joys of a Laptop Jam," *New York Times,* Section G (July 10, 2003): 5.
35. Erik Davis, "The Rise of Laptop Techno, Songs in the Key of F12." *Wired,* 10.05 (May 2002): 98.
36. Davis, Erik, *op. cit.,* 101.

Chapter 7: Art and Ethics Online

1. Timothy D. Taylor, *Strange Sounds: Music, Technology & Culture* (New York and London: Routledge, 2001), 3–5.

Web Sound

2. Kris Fong, "Full Steam Ahead," *MacAddict,* Vol. 7, No. 5 (May 2002): 14.
3. Ted Greenwald, "Inside encoding.com," *Wired,* 7.08 (August 1999): 139.
4. Bob Tedeschi, "E-Commerce Report: The ring tone business looks good to record companies—but a do-it-yourself program may cut the profits short," *New York Times,* Section C (February 23, 2004): 5
5. John Krogh, "MP3 for Musicians," *Desktop Music Production Guide 2000* (*Electronic Musician*), 63.
6. Craig Anderton, "Optimize Your Music for the Web," *Keyboard,* Vol. 28, No. 9 (September 2002): 106.

Latency

7. Philip L. Burk, "Jammin' on the Web—A New Client/Server Architecture for Multi-User Musical Performance," *Proceedings of the ICMC* (2000). Found at http://www.transjam.com/docs/
8. John Maxwell Hobbs, "Silicon Alley Views: Perspective: Turning Cybercasts From Music Promotion at Art Form" (July 10, 1998), found at http://atnewyork.com/views/print/0,,8481_251051,00.html
9. From a 1983 interview with the author, published as William Duckworth, "Interview with William Duckworth," *Max Neuhaus, Inscription, Sound Works* (Ostfildern-Stuttgart: Cantz Verlag, 1994), 46.
10. "Blue" Gene Tyranny, "In the 3rd Person: Out To The Stars, Into The Heart: Spatial Movement in Recent and Earlier Music," *NewMusicBox,* American Music Center, Vol. 4, No. 9 (January 2003), found at http://www.newmusicbox.org/page.nmbx?id=45tp00
11. Burk, "Jammin' on the Web," *op. cit.*
12. Michael Kaufmann, "Mail Pattern," found at http://www.theexperiment.org/experiments/experiments.php?experiment_id+6
13. E-mail from Michael Kaufmann to the author (January 12, 2004).

Copyright and File Sharing

14. Mladen Milicevic, "Cyberspace memes," *Organized Sound* 6(2) (2001): 117.
15. Michael Behar, "It's Playback Time!," *Wired*, 7.08 (August 1999): 122.
16. John Schwartz, "For the Ex-Buccaneer, A Pillage-Free Playlist," *New York Times*, Circuits, Section G, (January 1, 2004): 1.
17. Kevin Kelly, "Where Music Will Be Coming From," *New York Times Magazine*, Section 6 (March 17, 2002): 30.
18. Abraham Genauer, "Farewell Napster, and Jewish Tunes To Be Had for a Song," *Forward* (September 27, 2002), found at http://www.forward.com/issues/2002/02.09.27/fast3.html
19. Reported by CNN, July 2002.
20. Amy Harmon, "In Fight Over Online Music, Industry Now Offers a Carrot," *New York Times*, Section A (June 8, 2003): 42.
21. Harry Shearer, "Rx for Music Industry: Seek Out the Old Geezers," *New York Times*, Section 4, Week In Review (April 27, 2003): 7.
22. n.a., "Suing Music Downloaders," *New York Times*, Section A, Editorial Page (September 12, 2003): 30.
23. Neil Strauss, "Behind the Grammys, Revolt in the Industry," *New York Times*, Section WK (February 24, 2002): 3.
24. David Pogue, "The Internet As Jukebox, At a Price," *New York Times*, Section G, Circuits (March 6, 2003): 1.
25. n.a., "Investigators Raid Offices Of Kazaa In Australia," *New York Times*, Section C (February 7, 2004): 2.

Open Source

26. Gary Rivlin, "Leader of the Free World," *Wired*, 11.11 (November 2003): 154.
27. n.a., "OSS: A Success Story," n.d., found at http://cs-people.bu.edu/artdog/project/success_story.htm
28. Rivlin, *op. cit.*, 154.
29. *Ibid.*, 208.

Copy Left

30. Robert S. Boynton, "The Tyranny of Copyright?," *New York Times Magazine* (January 25, 2004): 40–42.
31. *Ibid.*, 42.
32. John Schwartz, "Report Raises Questions About Fighting Online Piracy," *New York Times*, Section C (March 1, 2004): 2.
33. Boynton, *op. cit.*, 42.
34. Anthony Tommasini, "Companies in U.S. Sing Blues As Europe Reprises 50's Hits," *New York Times*, Section A (January 3, 2003): 8.

Chapter 8: *The Grey Album*: A Case Study in Critical Mass

1. Jon Pareles, "Playlist: Silver, Brown, Gray: Jay-Z Every Which Way," *New York Times*, Section 2, Arts & Leisure (March 7, 2004): 27.

Black, White, and Grey

2. Lauren Gitlin, "DJ Makes Jay-Z Meet Beatles," *Rolling Stone* (February 5, 2004), found at http://www.rollingstone.com/news/newsarticle.asp?nid=19292
3. n.a., Danger Mouse Web site, found at http://djdangermouse.com/
4. Michael Paoletta, "Danger Mouse speaks Out On 'Grey Album,'" *Billboard Online* (March 8, 2004), found at http://www.billboard.com/bb/daily/arfticle_display.jsp?vnu_content_id=1000455930
5. Lauren Gitlin, *op. cit.*
6. Renee Graham, "Jay-Z, the Beatles meet in 'Grey' area," *Boston Globe* (February 10, 2004), found at http://www.boston.com/news/globe/living/articles/2004/02/10/jay_z_the_beatles_meet_in_grey_area/
7. Paoletta, *op. cit.*
8. n.a., "Grey Tuesday: A Quick Overview of the Legal Terrain," Electronic Frontier Foundation, n.d., found at http://www.eff.org/IP/grey_tuesday.php
9. n.a., "'Grey Tuesday' Civil Disobedience Planned February 24th Against Copyright Cartel," Downhill Battle Press Release (February 18, 2004), found at http://www.downhillbattle.org/pressreleases/greytuesday_21904.html

Grey Tuesday

10. Bill Werde, "Defiant Downloads Rise From Underground," *New York Times*, Section B (February 23, 2004): 3.
11. n.a., "Grey Tuesday," n.d., found at http://www.greytuesday.org/
12. n.a., "Waxy.Org Daily Log: Danger Mouse's The Grey Album MP3s," found at http://www.waxy.org/archive/2004/02/11/danger_m.shtml
13. Nicholas Reville and Holmes Wilson, "Downhill Battle's response to EMI" (Feburary 23, 2004), found at http://downhillbattle.org/index.php?p=68
14. Katie Dean, "Grey Album Fans Protest Clampdown," *Wired News* (February 24, 2004), found at http://wired.com/news/digiwood/0,1412,62372,00.html?tw=wn_tophead_2
15. n.a., "Waxy.Org Daily Log: Danger Mouse's The Grey Album MP3s," found at http://www.waxy.org/archive/2004/02/11/danger_m.shtml
16. *Ibid.*
17. *Ibid.*

Critical Mass in Cyberspace

18. Katie Dean, *op. cit.*
19. Werde, *op. cit.*

20. Lawrence Van Gelder, "Arts Briefing: 'Grey Album' Downloads," *New York Times,* Section E (February 29, 2004): 2.
21. Werde, *op. cit.*
22. Noah Shachtman, "Copyright Enters a Gray Area," *Wired News* (February 14, 2004), found at http://www.wired.com/news/digiwood/0,1412,62276,00. html?tw=wn_story_top5
23. Reville and Wilson, Downhill Battle's Response to EMI, *op. cit.*
24. n.a., "Grey Tuesday: A Quick Overview of the Legal Terrain," Electronic Frontier Foundation, n.d., found at *op. cit.*
25. Ben Rayner, "Grey Album mixes up trouble," *Toronto Star* (February 29, 2004), found at http://www.thestar.com/NASApp/cs/ContentServer?pagename=thestar/Layout/Article_Type1&c=Article&cid=1077967953161&call_pageid=968867495754&col=969483191630
26. Shachtman, *op. cit.*
27. n.a., "An Introduction to Downhill Battle," n.d., found at http://downhill-battle.org/introduction/index.html
28. Paoletta, *op. cit.*

Chapter 9: Virtual Music

1. Wolf, Gary, "Exploring the Unmaterial World," *Wired,* 8.06 (June 2000): 315.
2. Thomas S. Kuhn, *The Structure of Scientific Revolutions,* Third Edition, (Chicago and London: University of Chicago Press, 1962, 3/1996), 159.
3. E-mail from Warren Burt to the author, (January 19, 2004).
4. Dieter Daniels, *op. cit.*
5. Kenneth Newby, "Letting New Sounds Out of the Bag," *Wired News* (Oct. 30, 1997) at http://www.wired.com/news/culture/0,1284,8128,00.html

The New Landscape

6. Neil Rolnick, e-mail to the author, (June 17, 2004).
7. Nicolas Collins, e-mail to the author, (June 17, 2004).
8. Rolnick, *op. cit.*
9. From the Share DJ Web site found at http://www.share.dj/
10. The interview with Jaron Lanier, in both video and audio formats, may be found in the October 2002 edition of the American Music Center's online magazine *NewMusicBox,* found at http://www.newmusicbox.org. The issue, which the author edited and is devoted to virtual music, is located in the archives.
11. Rolnick, *op. cit.*
12. Michael Kaufmann, e-mail to the author, (June 17, 2004).
13. McLuhan and Powers, *op. cit.,* 26.
14. Collins, 2004, *op. cit.*

15. Dante Tanzi, "Musical Experience and Online Communication," *Crossings: eJournal of Art and Technology*, Volume 3, Issue 1 (2004), found at http://crossings.ted.ie/issues/3.1/Tanzi/
16. n.a., Transmediale Report, n.d., found at http://www.fiftyfifty.org/transmediale/tm_sergi.html. If you would like to experiment with the FMOL software, you can find it at http://www.iua.upf.es/~sergi/FMOL/download.htm
17. Jose Miguel G. Cortes, *op. cit.*
18. Quoted in Chris Anderson and Jennifer Hillner, moderators, "Nextfest, The Shape of Things To Come: Entertainment," *Wired,* Vol. 12, No. 5 (May 2004), 156–160.
19. *Ibid.*
20. Warren Burt, e-mail to the author, (June 19, 2004).
21. David Rosenboom, e-mail to the author, (June 17, 2004).
22. David Rosenbom, *Collapsing Distinctions: Interacting within Fields of Intelligence on Interstellar Scales and Parallel Musical Models,* unpublished monograph, draft version dated January 31, 2004.
23. Ryan Ingberitsen, e-mail to the author, (June 17, 2004).
24. Marcus Novak, "Trans Terra Form: Liquid Architectures and the Loss of Inscription," 1997, found at http://www.t0.or.at/~krcf/nlonline/nonMarcos.html

BIBLIOGRAPHY

Books

Cage, John. *Silence.* Middletown, CT: Wesleyan University Press, 1961.
———. *A Year From Monday.* Middletown, CT: Wesleyan University Press, 1967.
Dunn, Robert, comp. *John Cage.* New York: Henmar Press, Inc., 1962.
Gillmor, Alan M. *Erik Satie.* New York: W. W. Norton & Company, Inc., 1992.
Kostelanetz, Richard, ed. *John Cage.* New York: Praeger Publishers, 1970.
Kuhn, Thomas S. *The Structure of Scientific Revolutions,* Third Edition. Chicago and London: University of Chicago Press, 1962, 3/1996.
Langer, Susanne K. *Feeling And Form.* New York: Charles Scribner's Sons, 1953.
Mann, A. T. *Sacred Architecture.* Great Britain: Element Books Ltd., 1993.
McLuhan, Marshall, and Bruce R. Powers. *The Global Village: Transformations in World Life and Media in the 21st Century.* Oxford: Oxford University Press, 1989.
Naughton, John. *A Brief History of the Future: From Radio Days to Internet Years in a Lifetime.* Woodstock & New York: The Overlook Press, 2001.
Resnick, Rosalind, and Dave Taylor. *The Internet Business Guide.* Indianapolis: Sams Publishing, 1994.
Rheingold, Howard. *Smart Mobs: The Next Social Revolution.* New York: Perseus Publishing, 2002.
Rockwell, John. *All American Music.* New York: Alfred A. Knopf, 1983.
Shattuck, Roger. *The Banquet Years: The Origins of the Avant-garde in France, 1885 to World War I,* rev. ed. New York: Vintage Books, 1968.
Stein, Jean. *Edie: An American Biography.* New York: Alfred A. Knopf, 1982.
Taylor, Timothy D. *Strange Sounds: Music, Technology & Culture.* New York & London: Routledge, 2001.
Tomkins, Calvin. *Ahead of the Game: Four Versions of the Avant-Garde.* Harmondsworth: Penguin, 1968.

Articles

Ahrens, Frank. "Thomas Dolby, Deafened by The Silence." *Washington Post* (September 6, 1999), found at http:///www.e-prog.net/bands/dolby.htm

Alderman, John. "Brian Eno." n.d., found at http://hotwired.lycos.com/popfeatures/96/24/eno.transcript.html

Alderman, John. "LiveJam Picks Up the World Beat." *Wired News* (September 10, 1998), found at http://www.wired.com/news/culture/0,1284,14943,00.html

Anderton, Craig. "Optimize Your Music for the Web," *Keyboard*, Vol. 28, No. 9 (September 2002): 104–106.

Bangs, Lester. "Interview with Brian Eno." *Musician* (1979), found at http://music.hyperreal.org/artists/brian_eno/interviews/musn79.html

Battaglia, Andy. "The Sounds of Science." *Salon.com* (August 5, 1999), found at http://www.salon.com/ent/music/feature/1999/08/05/scanner/

Beglarian, Eve. "Phil Kline's Walking Vigil." (September 24, 2001), found at http://www.evbvd.com/newsnotes/911/010924a.html

Behar, Michael. "It's Playback Time!" *Wired*, 7.08 (August 1999): 122.

Berry, Colin. "Rocket Launchers." *Wired*, Issue 6.08 (August 1998), found at http://www.wired.com/wired/archive/6.08/newmedia.html?person=paul_allen&topic_set=wiredpeople

Bickley, Tom. "SF Gate: Cacophony of city sounds and scores of boom boxes make an 'Unsilent Night.'" BA-NEWMUS:11866 (posted December 20, 2003), found at http://eartha.mills.edu:8000/guest/archives/ba-newmus/log0312/msg00147.html

Bickley, Tom. "Unsilent Night." BA-NEWMUS:11870 (posted December 23, 2003), found at http://eartha.mills.edu:8000/guest/archives/ba-newmus/log0312/msg00151.html

Bloom, Michael. "Ambient 1: Music For Airports." *Rolling Stone* (July 26, 1979), found at http://music.hyperreal.org/artists/brian_eno/interviews/rs79c.html

Boynton, Robert S. "The Tyranny of Copyright?" *New York Times Magazine* (January 25, 2004): 40–45.

Brown, Chris, and John Bischoff. "Indigenous to the Net." A Web-based article that documents the history of computer Network Music in the San Francisco Bay Area, found at www.sfmoma.org/crossfade/

Burk, Phil, Larry Polansky, and David Rosenboom. "HMSL: A Theoretical Overview." *Perspectives of New Music*, Volume 28, No. 2 (summer 1990): 136–178.

Burk, Philip L. "Jammin' on the Web—A New Client/Server Architecture for Multi-User Musical Performance." *Proceedings of the ICMC* (2000). Found at http://www.transjam.com/docs/

Caramanica, Jon. "Electric Word: Sonic Boom." *Wired* 9.12 (Dec. 2001), found at http://www.wired.com/wired/archive/9.12/eword_pr.html

Chikuri, Karsten J. "Riding the Res Rocket: Using a Wind Synth with Res Rocket's DRGN." Found at http://www.windsynth.org/studio/riding_the_res_rocket.shtml

Collins, Nicolas. "Zwischen 'data' und 'date': Erfahrungen mit Proto-Web Musik von The Hub" ("The Fly in the Ointment: Proto-Web Music by the Hub."). *Positionen* 31 (May 1997): 20–22.

Cortes, Jose Miguel G. "Catalogue interview with Scanner." Valencia Biennale, Spain, 2001, found at http://www.scannerdot.com/sca_001.html

Davis, Erik. "The Rise of Laptop Techno, Songs in the Key of F12." *Wired*, 10.05 (May 2002): 98.

Dayen, David, and Joanna Lux. "Cellphone Symphony." An interview with Golan Levin at TechTV (posted December 19, 2001) and found at http://www.techtv.com/audiofile/print/0,23102,3358391,00.html

Dean, Katie. "Grey Album Fans Protest Clampdown." *Wired News* (February 24, 2004), found at http://wired.com/news/digiwood/0,1412,62372,00.html?tw=wn_tophead_2

De Ritis, Anthony. "*Cathedral:* An Interactive Work for the Web." *Proceedings of the International Computer Music Conference*. Beijing, China: ICMA, (1999): 224–227.

Drescher, Peter. "We Have Liftoff!, Producing a recording session in Rocket Network's online studio." *Electronic Musician* (April 2000): 116–124.

Duckworth, William. "Interview with William Duckworth." *Max Neuhaus, Inscription, Sound Works* Ostfildern-Stuttgart, Cantz Verlag, (1994), 45.

Duckworth, William. "Making Music on the Web." *Leornado Music Journal*, Vol. 9, (1999): 13–18.

Duckworth, William. "Perceptual and Structural Implications of 'Virtual' Music on the Web." *Annals of the New York Academy of Sciences*, Vol. 999 (November 2003): 254–262.

Dyer, Richard. "Playing the Future: Tod Machover Brainstorms a Make-Your-Own Opera, Complete With Web Site." *Boston Globe* (July 14, 1996), found at http://brainop.media.mit.edu/~tod/press/media/globe7_96.html

Eno, Brian "This Article is a Musical Instrument." Unattributed publication (ca. 1975), found at http://music.hyperreal.org/artists/brian_eno/interviews/unk-75a.html

Eno, Brian. "Pro Session—The Studio As Compositional Tool." A talk given in 1979 at New Music New York, the first New Music America Festival. Reprinted in *Downbeat* ca. 1979.

Eno, Brian. Untitled contribution to an article on music of the future. *Independent* (March 1, 1996).

Eno, Brian. "Generative Music." A talk delivered at the Imagination Conference in San Francisco (June 8, 1996), printed in *In Motion Magazine*, and found at http://www.inmotionmagazine.com/eno1.html

Fong, Kris. "Full Steam Ahead." *MacAddict*, Vol. 7, No. 5 (May 2002): 14.

Galloway, Kit, and Sherrie Rabinowitz. "The Challenge: We Must Create At The Same Scale As We Can Destroy." (1984), found at http://www.ecafe.com/84manifesto.html

Gann, Kyle. "The Hub: Musica Telephonica." *Village Voice* (June 23, 1987), found at http://www.o-art.org/history/Computer/Hub/HubTel.html

Gann, Kyle. "Freeze, Symphony!" *Village Voice* (February 3, 1998): 131.

Gans, David. "The Man Who Stole Michael Jackson's Face." *Wired* 3.02 (February 1995), found at http://www.autumnleaf.com/oswald.htm

Genauer, Abraham. "Farewell Napster, and Jewish Tunes To Be Had for a Song." *Forward* (September 27, 2002), found at http://www.forward.com/issues/2002/02.09.27/fast3.html

Gershman, Gil. "Scanner." *Magnet* #30, n.d., found at http://www.scanner-dot.com/sca_001.html

Gitlin, Lauren. "DJ Makes Jay-Z Meet Beatles." *Rolling Stone* (February 5, 2004), found at http://www.rollingstone.com/news/newsarticle.asp?nid=19292

Graham, Renee. "Jay-Z, the Beatles meet in 'Grey' area." *Boston Globe* (February 10, 2004), found at http://www.boston.com/news/globe/living/articles/2004/02/10/jay_z_the_beatles_meet_in_grey_area/

Greenwald, Ted. "Inside encoding.com." *Wired,* 7.08 (August 1999): 138–142.

Gresham-Lancaster, Scot. "Magical Musical Tours: A Comprehensive Guide to Musical Resources on the Internet." *Electronic Musician,* Vol. 10, No. 10 (October 1994): 46–62.

Griffin, J. R. "Real Dolby Sound." *Entertainment Weekly* (September 30, 1994), found at http://www.tdolby.com/reading/int_entertainment.html

Hall, Gary S. "Bands Without Borders." *Electronic Musician,* Vol. 18, No. 11 (October 2002): 72–86.

Harmon, Amy. "In Fight Over Online Music, Industry Now Offers a Carrot." *New York Times,* Section A (June 8, 2003): 1, 42.

Hilty, Greg. "Scanner." *Financial Times* (December 1998), found at http://www.scannerdot.com/sca_001.html

Hobbs, John Maxwell. "Turning Cybercasts From Music Promotion to Art Form." *@ New York* (1998), now archived at http://www.cinemavolta.com/organicmechanics/archives/000005.html#more

Hobbs, John Maxwell. "Towards Hypermusic." *Leonardo On-Line* (1998), now archived at http://www.cinemavolta.com/organicmechanics/archives/000003.html#more

Hobbs, John Maxwell. "Silicon Alley Views: Perspective: Turning Cybercasts From Music Promotion at Art Form." (July 10, 1998), found at http://atnewyork.com/views/print/0,,8481_251051,00.html

Huhn, Mary. "Rock the Halls." *New York Post* (December 13, 2003), found at http://www.nypost.com/living/43892.htm

Ippolito, Jon. "Cross Talk, Does the art world really 'get' the Internet?" *artbyte,* Vol. 2, No. 6 (March-April 2000): 24–25.

Jainchill, Johanna. "Clash, Then Synthesis: Joys of a Laptop Jam." *New York Times,* Section G (July 10, 2003): 5.

Keenan, David. "Interview with John Oswald." *Wire* (May 1, 2002).

Kelly, Kevin. "Where Music Will Be Coming From." *New York Times Magazine,* Section 6 (March 17, 2002): 29–31.

Kenny, Tom. "Willy Henshall, The Rocket Man of the Internet." *Internet Audio* (April 2001): 27, 45.

Korner, Anthony. "Aurora Musicalis." *Artforum* (summer 1996), found at http://music.hyperreal.org/artists/brian_eno/interviews/artfor86.html

Krogh, John. "MP3 for Musicians." *Desktop Music Production Guide 2000* (*Electronic Musician*), 58–63.

Latta, Craig. "A New Musical Medium: NetJam." *Computer Music Journal,* Vol. 15, No. 3 (fall 1991), found at http://www.o-art.org/history/Computer/MIDI/NetJam.html.

Latta, Craig. "Notes on the NetJam Project." *Leonardo Music Journal,* Vol. 1, No. 1 (winter 1991).

Lee, May. " 'Brain Opera' takes music to new dimensions." *CNN Interactive* (November 29, 1996), found at http://www-cgi.cnn.com/SHOWBIZ/9611/29/brain.opera/

MacDonald, Ian. "Before and After Science." *New Musical Express* (November 26, 1977), found at http://music.hyperreal.org/artists/brian_eno/interviews/nme77a.html

Machover, Tod. "The Brain Opera and Active Music." (n.d. circa 1996), found at http://brainop.media.mit.edu/Archive/ars-Electronica.html

Marzorati, Gerald. "All by Himself." *New York Times Magazine,* Section 6 (March 17, 2002): 69.

Mason, Marcy. "Adventures In Music Classics Meet Techno-Modern Future In Vienna's New Museum." *Chicago Tribune* (October 22, 2000), found at http://brainop.media.mit.edu/~tod/press/media/tribune10_00.html

McNichol, Tom. "Finally, a Public Resting Place for History's Motherboards." *New York Times,* Section G, Circuits (June 26, 2003): 5.

Milicevic, Mladen. "Cyberspace memes." *Organized Sound* 6(2) (2001): 117–120.

Mirapaul, Matthew. "Drawing (and Doodling) With Countryside as Canvas." *New York Times,* Section E (April 1, 2002): 2.

n.a. "Scanner." *Stranger Newspaper* (Seattle), (October 1997), found at http://www.scannerdot.com/sca_001.html

n.a. "Dolby blinds the Net with sonic science." *BBC News Online Network* (May 27, 1998), found at http://news.bbc.co.uk/1/hi/entertainment/97113.stm

n.a. "HMSL, the Hierarchical Music Specification Language." (1999), found at http://www.softsynth.com/hmsl/.

n.a. "Scanner in the Works." *Guardian* (September 1999), found at http://www.scannerdot.com/sca_001.html

n.a. "Virtual Worlds Platform." Microsoft Research 2001, found at http://research.microsoft.com/scg/vworlds/vworlds.htm

n.a. "Suing Music Downloaders." *New York Times,* Section A, Editorial Page (September 12, 2003): 30.

n.a. "Investigators Raid Offices Of Kazaa In Australia." *New York Times,* Section C (February 7, 2004): 2.

n.a. "OSS: A Success Story." n.d., found at http://cs-people.bu.edu/artdog/project/success_story.htm

n.a. ESTWeb Interview with John Oswald. Found at http://media.hyperreal.org/zines/est/intervs/oswald.html

n.a. "Grey Tuesday: A Quick Overview of the Legal Terrain." Electronic Frontier Foundation, n.d., found a http://www.eff.org/IP/grey_tuesday.php

n.a. Transmediale Report, n.d., found at http://www.fiftyfifty.org/transmediale/tm_sergi.html. If you would like to experiment with the FMOL software, you can find it at http://www.iua.upf.es/~sergi/FMOL/download.htm

Neuhaus, Max. "The Broadcast Works and Audium." n.d., found at http://www.kunstradio.at/ZEITGLEICH/CATALOG/ENGLISH/neuhaus2-e.html

Newby, Kenneth. "Letting New Sounds Out of the Bag." *Wired News* (Oct. 30, 1997) at http://www.wired.com/news/culture/0,1284,8128,00.html

Novak, Marcos. "Liquid Architectures in Cyberspace." *Cyberspace: First Steps,* M. Benedikt, ed. Cambridge: The MIT Press, (1992).

Novak, Marcus. "Trans Terra Form: Liquid Architectures and the Loss of Inscription," 1997, found at http://www.t0.or.at/~krcf/nlonline/nonMarcos.html

Okamoto, David. Interview with *National Post Online.* n.d. (ca. 1999) found at http://www.tdolby.com/reading/int_nationalpost.html

Oldfield, Andy. "Brian Eno's Generation Game." *Independent* (July 29, 1996), Found at http://music.hyperreal.org/artists/brian_eno/interviews/ind96d.html

Oswald, John. "Plunderphonics, or Audio Piracy As A Compositional Prerogative." Found at http://www.halcyon.com/robinja/mythos/Plunderphonics.html

Oteri, Frank J. "In the 1st Person: Tod Machover." *NewMusicBox* Web Magazine, Vol. 1, No. 6 (October 1999), found at http://www.newmusicbox.org/page.nmbx?id=06fp01

Palmer, Tamara. "Interview with Scanner." *Electronic Directory* (July 2002), found at http://www.scannerdot.com/sca_001.html

Paoletta, Michael. "Danger Mouse speaks Out On 'Grey Album.'" *Billboard Online* (March 8, 2004), found at http://www.billboard.com/bb/daily/arfticle_display.jsp?vnu_content_id=1000455930

Pareles, Jon. "Playlist: Silver, Brown, Gray: Jay-Z Every Which Way." *New York Times,* Section 2, Arts & Leisure (March 7, 2004): 27.

Pogue, David. "The Internet As Jukebox, At a Price." *New York Times,* Section G, Circuits (March 6, 2003): 1, 6.

Pohl, Otto. "What: Mob Scene. Who: Strangers. Point: None." *New York Times,* Section A (August 4, 2003): 4.

Rayner, Ben. "Grey Album mixes up trouble." *Toronto Star* (February 29, 2004), found at http://www.thestar.com/NASApp/cs/ContentServer?pagename=thestar/Layout/Article_Type1&c=Article&cid=1077967953161& call_pageid=968867495754&col=969483191630

Reinhardt, Andy. "Player Without a Band? Log On, Dude." *Business Week* (September 10, 1998), found at http://www.businessweek.com?1998/38/b3596151. htm

Rivlin, Gary. "Leader of the Free World." *Wired,* 11.11 (November 2003): 152–157, 206–211.

Ross, Suzanne. "They're Playing Our Song." Microsoft Research 2000, found at http://research.microsoft.com/seg/music_world.asp#top

Rule, Greg. "Sampling Nation: Techno." *Keyboard* (May 1994): 47.

Schonberg, Harold C., *et. al.* "Music: A Long, Long, Long Night (and Day) at the Piano." *New York Times* (September 11, 1963): 45 (2 pages).

Schwartz, John. "For the Ex-Buccaneer, A Pillage-Free Playlist." *New York Times,* Circuits, Section G, (January 1, 2004): 1, 6.

Schwartz, John. "Report Raises Questions About Fighting Online Piracy." *New York Times,* Section C (March 1, 2004): 2.

Shachtman, Noah. "Copyright Enters a Gray Area." *Wired News* (February 14, 2004), found at http://www.wired.com/news/digiwood/0,1412,62276,00. html?tw=wn_story_top5

Shamah, David. "User Friendly." *Jerusalem Post Newspaper* (July 28, 1999), found at http://www.jpost.com/com/Archive/28.Jul.1999/Digital/Article-3.html

Shearer, Harry. "Rx for Music Industry: Seek Out the Old Geezers." *New York Times,* Section 4, Week In Review (April 27, 2003): 7.

Smith, Ethan. "Organization Moby." *Wired,* 10.05 (May 2002): 90.

Stalter, Katherine. Interview with *Film & Video Magazine.* n.d., found at http:// www.tdolby.com/reading/int_flimvideo.html

Steenhuisen, Paul. "Composer to Composer: Paul Steenhuisen interviews John Oswald." *WholeNote* (May 2003), found at http://members.shaw.ca/steenhuisen/oswald.htm

Stewart, Sara. "It's Mob Rule!" *New York Post* (July 21, 2003): 33.

Strauss, Neil. "Behind the Grammys, Revolt in the Industry." *New York Times,* Section WK (February 24, 2002): 3.

Tanzi, Dante. "Musical Experience and Online Communication," *Crossings: eJournal of Art and Technology,* Volume 3, Issue 1 (2004), found at http:// crossings.ted.ie/issues/3.1/Tanzi/

Tanzi, Dante. "Music negotiation: routes in user-based description of music." *Organized Sound* 6(2), (2001): 111–115.

Tanzi, Dante. "Observations about Music and Decentralized Environments." *Leonardo,* Vol. 34, No. 5 (2001): 431–436.

Tedeschi, Bob. "E-Commerce Report: The ring tone business looks good to record companies—but a do-it-yourself program may cut the profits short." *New York Times,* Section C (February 23, 2004): 5.

Tommasini, Anthony. "Companies in U.S. Sing Blues As Europe Reprises 50's Hits." *New York Times,* Section A (January 3, 2003): 1, 8.

Townley, John. "On The Trail of The Virtual Recording Studio." *Streaming Media World* (March 17, 2000), found at http://smw.internet.com/audio/reviews/rocket/

Tyranny, "Blue" Gene. "In the 3rd Person: Out To The Stars, Into The Heart: Spatial Movement in Recent and Earlier Music." *NewMusicBox,* American Music Center, Vol. 4, No. 9 (January 2003), found at http://www.newmusicbox.org/page.nmbx?id=45tp00

Van Gelder, Lawrence. "Arts Briefing: 'Grey Album' Downloads." *New York Times,* Section E (February 29, 2004): 2.

Ward, Phil. "The Virtual Thomas Dolby." *HYPERinterACTIVE! Magazine* (February 1994), found at http://www.tdolby.com/reading/int_hyper.html

Webster, Garrick. "Before and After Science." *PC Format,* Issue 54 (March 1996).

Werde, Bill. "Defiant Downloads Rise From Underground." *New York Times,* Section B (February 23, 2004): 3.

Whittington, Stephen. "Serious Immobilities: On the Centenary of Erik Satie's Vexations." (1999), found at http://www.af.lu.se/~fogwall/article3.html

Williams, Richard. "The Brain of Brian." *Guardian* (May 10, 1996).

Wolf, Gary. "Exploring the Unmaterial World." *Wired,* 8.06 (June 2000): 306–319.

Young, John P. "Networked music: bridging real and virtual space." *Organized Sound* 6(2) (2001): 107–110.

Web Sites

The American Music Center's monthly online magazine, *NewMusicBox:* http://www.newmusicbox.org

The Artifact Web site: http://www.artifact.com/wreckball.html

The Beatnik Web site: http://www.beatnik.com

Phil Burk's WebDrum site: http://www.transjam.com

John Cage home page, established by the Cage Trust: http://www.johncage.org [not yet active].

The Cantaloupe Records Web site: http://cantaloupemusic.com/unsilentnight/

The *Cathedral* Web site: http://cathedral.monroestreet.com

Marek Choloniewski's GPS-Art: http://www.gps.art.pl/gpsart-e.html

Marek Choloniewski's home page: http://www.cyf-kr.edu.pl/~zbcholon/mch/mch.html

The Computer History Museum: http://www.computerhistory.org

Danger Mouse's Web site: http://djdangermouse.com/

The Downhill Battle Web site: http://www.downhillbattle.org

Information on early microcomputers: http://members.cox.net/obsoletetechnology/
    kim1.html
Brian Eno home page: http://music.hyperreal.org/artists/brian_eno/
The History of Computers During My Lifetime Web site by Jason Patterson:
    http://www.pattosoft.com.au/jason/Articles/HistoryOfComputers/
    1970s.html
John Maxwell Hobbs's Cinema Volta Web site: http://www.cinemavolta.com/
    cv.html
Harvestworks Digital Media Center Web site: http://www.harvestworks.org/
The IUMA Web site: http://www.iuma.com
Michael Kaufmann's "Mail Pattern" site: http://www.theexperiment.org/experi-
    ments/experiments.php?experiment_id+6
Phil Kline's *Unsilent Night*: http://www.mindspring.com/~boombox/xmas.htm
Golan Levin's home page: http://www.flong.com/
The LiveJam Web site: http://www.livejam.com
The Lovely Music Web site: http://www.lovely.com
Tod Machover's *Brain Opera* home page: http://brainop.media.mit.edu
Moby's home page: http://www.moby-online.com
Max Neuhaus's home page: http://www.emf.org/subscribers/neuhaus/index.html
The Ongoing History of Microprocessors Web site: http://www.tcs.uni.wroc.pl/
    ~jja/ASK/HISZCOMP.HTM
John Oswald's Plunderphonic Web site: http://www.plunderphonics.com/
Erik Satie home page: http://www.af.lu.se/%7Efogwall/satie.html
The SoftSynth site: http://www.softsynth.com
SSEYO's Web page, with information about Koan Pro: http://www.sseyo.com/
    products/koanpro/index.html
The STEIM Web site: http://www.steim.org/steim/
Wood and Pryor's car drawings: http://www.gpsdrawing.com

Unpublished Material

Kline, Phil. "Some Notes On Personal Stereo." An unpublished essay written in
    2002 and used as program notes by Present Music, found at http://
    www.presentmusic.org/2002–2003/notes/philkline.html
Rosenboom, David. *Collapsing Distinctions: Interacting within Fields of Intelligence
    on Interstellar Scales and Parallel Musical Models*, an unpublished monograph,
    draft version dated January 31, 2004.
E-mail from Warren Burt to the author. January 19, 2004.
E-mail from Warren Burt to the author. June 19, 2004.
E-mail from Nicolas Collins to the author. June 17, 2004.
E-mail from John Maxwell Hobbs to the author. January 14, 2004.
E-mail from Ryan Ingebritsen to the author. October 22, 2003.
E-mail from Ryan Ingberitsen to the author. June 17, 2004.

E-mail from Michael Kaufmann to the author. January 12, 2004.
E-mail from Michael Kaufmann to the author. June 17, 2004.
E-mail from Phil Kline to the author. February 1, 2004.
E-mail from Craig Latta to the author. December 3, 2003.
E-mail from Neil Rolnick to the author. June 17, 2004.
E-mail from David Rosenboom to the author. June 17, 2004.

THE SOUND OF THE WEB
AT THE TURN OF THE
CENTURY

Edited and Produced by Nora Farrell

1. Tod Machover: *Brain Opera*, excerpts   02:41
   The CD opens with a walk through the *Brain Opera*, and four brief excerpts taken from the Mind Forest section. The voice introducing the *Brain Opera* is Marvin Minsky, a pioneer in the field of artificial intelligence, whose ideas on music and the mind were, in part, the inspiration for the work.
   Recording date: 1996
   Credits: Used by permission of Tod Machover. All rights reserved.

2. Scanner: *Phantom Signals*   05:50
   Written and produced by Robin Rimbaud, a.k.a. Scanner.
   Recording date: 2002
   Credits: Used by permission of Robin Rimbaud and Scannerdot Publishing, administered by Bug Music. http://www.scannerdot.com/sca_001.html All rights reserved.

3. The Hub: *Wheelies*   08:03
   The Hub (John Bischoff, Chris Brown, Tim Perkis, Mark Trayle, Phil Stone, Scot Gresham-Lancaster) in concert in Berlin playing Chris Brown's piece "Wheelies." This example comes from the Artifact Recordings CD release *Wreckin' Ball* by The Hub (ART 1008).
   Recording date: May 27, 1993

4. The Cathedral Band: *Alphabet of the Birds* 07:22
   The Cathedral Band recorded live during the first of four webcast concerts at the Mini[ ]Max Festival at the Powerhouse in Brisbane, Australia. Performers include DJ Tamara, records; William Duckworth and Warren Burt, PitchWebs; Nora Farrell, PitchWeb moderator; and Stuart Dempster, trombone, toys, and didgeridoo; with guest performers Simone de Haan, trombone; and William Barton, didgeridoo.
   Recording date: July 27, 2002

5. The League of Automatic Music Composers: *9–6–81*, excerpt 02:55
   A rehearsal of The League of Automatic Music Composers (John Bischoff, Jim Horton, Tim Perkis, Don Day) in Oakland, California.
   Recording date: September 6, 1981

6. Marek Choloniewski: *GPS-Trans 3*, excerpt 03:42
   This Sound Map of Krakow was originally webcast as part of *Cathedral's* forty-eight-hour Web festival in 2001. The performers, including those in a GPS-equipped car moving through Krakow, are Marek Choloniewski, Marcin Wierzbicki, Janek Choloniewski, Mateusz Bien, and Ryan Ingebritsen.
   Recording date: December 2, 2001

7. Sergi Jordà: *F@ust 3.0*, "Tierra Bajo Tierra" 02:54
   "Tierra Bajo Tierra" is a composition made from the FMOL (*F@aust 3.0*) Internet project files. Tierra bajo tierra means earth under ground, or ground under earth, or perhaps, as Jordà suggests, something else. It was composed using seven FMOL short pieces from the *F@ust 3.0* call for music online. The main loop that supports

the entire composition was created by RoLoCo, one of the most active FMOL net-composers.
Recording date: 1998
Credits: Used by permission of Sergi Jordà. All rights reserved.

8. therefore: fossil_residue storeroom exhibition   03:21
   This version of therefore's fossil_residue is a distillation of the live composition, which was first performed at Bucknell University in 2003. Utilizing sounds from the Web—including embedded files, streaming audio, interactive flash programs, and downloadable freeware programs—fossil_residue is a compositional model for the excavating and filtering of online information as a medium for music.
Recording date: Recorded in various phases in 2003 and remixed in September 2004
Credits: Used by permission of therefore, (Michael Kaufmann and Wayne S. Feldman). All rights reserved.

9. *Cathedral*: PitchWeb Jam, excerpt   03:18
   This excerpt is from the first live, beta-test/session of *Cathedral's* multiuser PitchWeb. The performers are Jon Child (the builder of the instrument), Nora Farrell, and William Duckworth. Two days later, the three performers gave the first demonstration of the multiuser PitchWeb at the Harvestworks Digital Arts Media Center summer computer camp for kids in New York City.
Recording date: July 16, 2001
Credits: Used by permission of Monroe Street Music. All rights reserved.

10. Phil Burk: WebDrum Jam   04:50
    The WebDrum tackles the problem of synchronizing musicians playing together over the Web by having them all edit parts of a shared music loop. This recording is one of the first of many online jams between Phil Burk (the inventor of the WebDrum) and Nick Didkovsky. Phil was playing from San Francisco and Nick from New York City. The instrument they are using is the original WebDrum I.
Recording date: October 2000
Credits: Used by permission of Phil Burk. All rights reserved.

11. Golan Levin, Scott Gibbons, and Gregory Shaker:
    Dialtones (a Telesymphony), Section 1   08:23

    Imagine you are sitting in the audience somewhere inside the 20×10 grid of two hundred people, as their mobile phones, preprogrammed with new sounds, begin to ring. This excerpt is taken from the opening section of *Dialtones* and is from the premiere at the Ars Electronica Festival in Linz, Austria. This first movement is performed solely through the choreographed ringing of the audience's own mobile phones, which were dialed via a special software system created by the authors.
    Recording date: September 2001
    Credits: Used by permission of Golan Levin. All rights reserved.

12. John Maxwell Hobbs: Cinema Volta, *June 3rd,* excerpt   06:21

    Hobbs's work, June 3rd, has been on his Cinema Volta Web site since 1993, first as a small, low-fi, 8-bit AU file and now as an AAC recording, from which this excerpt is taken. (Parts of June 3rd, incidentally, also appear as MIDI files in Hobbs's "Web Phase.")
    Recording date: 1993/2004
    Credits: Used by permission of John Maxwell Hobbs. All rights reserved.

13. Phil Kline: *Unsilent Night,* excerpt   03:50

    This performance of *Unsilent Night* took place in San Francisco in 2003, and includes 150 boom boxes, and an audience of over 400. The recording was made by sound artist Greg Weddig.
    Recording date: December 21, 2003
    Credits: Used by permission of Phil Kline. All rights reserved.

14. Marek Choloniewski: *GPS-Trans 3,* excerpt   04:05

    This is the opening section of the Sound Map of Krakow, originally webcast as part of *Cathedral's* forty-eight-hour Web festival in 2001. The speaker introducing the project is Marek Choloniewski.
    Recording date: December 2, 2001
    Credits: Used by permission of Marek Choloniewski and Ryan Ingebritsen. All rights reserved.

    Total Time: 68:11

Index